P9-BJW-791

PANDAS and PANS in School Settings

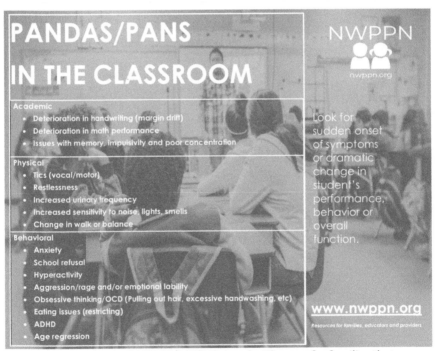

PANDAS/PANS IN THE CLASSROOM

NWPPN
nwppn.org

Academic
- Deterioration in handwriting (margin drift)
- Deterioration in math performance
- Issues with memory, impulsivity and poor concentration

Physical
- Tics (vocal/motor)
- Restlessness
- Increased urinary frequency
- Increased sensitivity to noise, lights, smells
- Change in walk or balance

Behavioral
- Anxiety
- School refusal
- Hyperactivity
- Aggression/rage and/or emotional lability
- Obsessive thinking/OCD (Pulling out hair, excessive handwashing, etc)
- Eating issues (restricting)
- ADHD
- Age regression

Look for sudden onset of symptoms or dramatic change in student's performance, behavior or overall function.

www.nwppn.org
Resources for families, educators and providers

Donated by Northwest PANDAS/PANS Network. Please refer families that suspect PANDAS/PANS to us. We can direct them to a knowledgeable provider and support. Rapid diagnosis and treatment lead to better outcomes.

of related interest

**Understanding Pathological Demand
Avoidance Syndrome in Children**
A Guide for Parents, Teachers and Other Professionals
Phil Christie, Margaret Duncan, Ruth Fidler and Zara Healy
ISBN 978 1 84905 074 6
eISBN 978 0 85700 253 2

**POTS and Other Acquired Dysautonomia
in Children and Adolescents**
Diagnosis, Interventions and Multi-Disciplinary Management
Kelly McCracken Barnhill
ISBN 978 1 84905 719 6
eISBN 978 1 78450 201 0

**Kids in the Syndrome Mix of ADHD, LD, Autism
Spectrum, Tourette's, Anxiety, and More!**
The one-stop guide for parents, teachers, and other professionals
Martin L. Kutscher, MD
With contributions from Tony Attwood, PhD and Robert R. Wolff, MD
ISBN 978 1 84905 967 1
eISBN 978 0 85700 882 4

**The Essential Manual for Asperger Syndrome
(ASD) in the Classroom**
What Every Teacher Needs to Know
Kathy Hoopmann
Illustrated by Rebecca Houkamau
ISBN 978 1 84905 553 6
eISBN 978 0 85700 984 5

NWPPN
nwppn.org

Northwest PANDAS/PANS Network (NWPPN), a 501c3 nonprofit serving Oregon, Washington, and Idaho, is providing **"PANDAS/PANS in the School Setting"** because of a generous donation from the Storm Family Foundation, in hopes of raising awareness about these post-infectious neuroinflammatory disorders that affect 1 in 200 children.

P.A.N.S.-Pediatric Acute Onset Neuropsychiatric Syndrome and
P.A.N.D.A.S.-Pediatric Autoimmune Neuropsychiatric Disorder Associated with Strep.

In both these disorders a normal, happy, healthy child has an acute onset of psychiatric symptoms, disordered eating and/or tics, post infection. Symptoms can include OCD, tics (both motor or vocal), eating restrictions, anxiety, separation anxiety, rage, sleeping issues, urinary frequency (not related to a UTI), daytime and nighttime urinary accidents in previously potty-trained child, ADHD type behaviors, and school regression particularly in math and handwriting.

We ask that you familiarize yourself with these disorders so that any student affected by these disorders can have their symptoms quickly recognized. Please refer any families that suspect PANDAS/PANS to NWPPN.org so we can assist them in finding a knowledgeable provider. You can find more information at our website at www.nwppn.org or email us directly at nwestppn@gmail.com.

If your school or district is interested in a free 30-minute presentation on these disorders, please contact us to schedule.

Together we can help ensure these children don't face a lifetime of misdiagnosis and needless suffering.

Sincerely,
Sarah Signe Lemley and Kym McCormack
Executive Director and Oregon Outreach Coordinator
Northwest PANDAS/PANS Network

NWPPN
PO BOX 19511

NWPPN.ORG

PANDAS and PANS in School Settings

A HANDBOOK FOR EDUCATORS

Edited by Patricia Rice Doran

Foreword by Diana Pohlman

Jessica Kingsley *Publishers*
London and Philadelphia

Figure 8.5 reprinted with kind permission from https://funandfunction.com
Figure 8.6 reprinted with kind permission from https://penagain.net

First published in 2017
by Jessica Kingsley Publishers
73 Collier Street
London N1 9BE, UK
and
400 Market Street, Suite 400
Philadelphia, PA 19106, USA

www.jkp.com

Copyright © Jessica Kingsley Publishers 2017
Foreword copyright © Diana Pohlman 2017

All rights reserved. No part of this publication may be reproduced in any material
form (including photocopying or storing it in any medium by electronic means and
whether or not transiently or incidentally to some other use of this publication)
without the written permission of the copyright owner except in accordance with the
provisions of the Copyright, Designs and Patents Act 1988 or under the terms of a
licence issued by the Copyright Licensing Agency Ltd, Saffron House, 6–10 Kirby
Street, London EC1N 8TS. Applications for the copyright owner's written permission
to reproduce any part of this publication should be addressed to the publisher.

Warning: The doing of an unauthorised act in relation to a copyright work
may result in both a civil claim for damages and criminal prosecution.

Library of Congress Cataloging in Publication Data
Names: Doran, Patricia Rice, editor.
Title: PANDAS and PANS in school settings : a handbook for educators / edited
   by Patricia Rice Doran.
Description: Philadelphia : Jessica Kingsley Publishers, 2017. | Includes
   bibliographical references and index.
Identifiers: LCCN 2016007180 | ISBN 9781849057448 (alk. paper)
Subjects: LCSH: Children with mental disabilities--Education. | Pediatric
   neuropsychiatry. | Streptococcal infections.
Classification: LCC LC4601 .P26 2017 | DDC 371.9--dc23 LC
record available at http://lccn.loc.gov/2016007180

British Library Cataloguing in Publication Data
A CIP catalogue record for this book is available from the British Library

ISBN 978 1 84905 744 8
eISBN 978 1 78450 166 2

Printed and bound in Great Britain

This book is dedicated to all children and families affected by PANDAS/PANS, and to the physicians, educators and other professionals who work with them. We are inspired by your courage and grateful for your perseverance.

Contents

Foreword

For those of us working in the PANDAS/PANS community for the past two decades, this book is a long awaited and groundbreaking guide to understanding the compassionate care of children with PANDAS/PANS, and their families, in the school environment. I have worked for years with children who have PANDAS or PANS and with their families as founder and board chair of the nation's largest parent advocacy organization dedicated to PANDAS and PANS. In this role, I have seen firsthand the tremendous challenges that can face children with these diagnoses as they navigate our school system.

My own family's story is one of hope and healing. In 2007, at the age of seven, my son developed recurrent strep infections, OCD, intense mood swings, tics and movement abnormalities, illegible handwriting, night terrors, intense rages, deep set anxiety, and other neurological symptoms. It is difficult to explain the terror of watching your child disappear. It is painful as that child asks you, "What is happening to me? Make it stop please, Mommy." Eventually, he was healed through antibiotics, tonsil and adenoid surgery to remove underlying infection, and intravenous immunoglobulin (IVIG) therapy. However, our home life was still difficult from time to time, with mild recurrences of symptoms for up to five years post treatment.

The most consistent and crucial relationship in my son's life, other than with us, his parents, was with his school principal. Working with us, the school developed a unique plan where I could visit as needed. Staff made other allowances as well, such as permitting my son to sit quietly if overwhelmed; flexibility in attendance when he needed to stay home on occasion; and altering test taking methods if he was fixating on "perfect" answers. Where some physicians and counselors appeared to be at a loss, the school remained our patient and interested partner throughout the recovery process. I wish that all families could experience this kind of respectful, kind and encouraging environment throughout their recovery. My son is now 16 years old, a confident young man and an excellent student, thanks to the support of the school system as well as aggressive medical treatment.

PANDAS and PANS disproportionately affect children between the ages of 4–13 (although there are outliers on either side of the age range). This puts educators on the frontlines of accommodating students' needs. Indeed, teachers are often among the first adults to see the dramatic effects of this illness on behavior and functioning, and they are uniquely positioned to encourage parents as they seek treatment. The authors of this book have provided an important set of facts, practices and strategies to help educators better assist students with PANDAS/PANS.

My "kitchen table wisdom" gathered from working with this population over the past two decades is this: These children can teach us through their tremendous will to thrive despite setbacks. They triumph in their young adult lives despite physical and emotional trauma both with dignity and intelligence! In this uniquely humbling illness, mental and physical faculties are altered alarmingly and at onset it feels "life-stopping" to all involved. However, having followed over a hundred cases closely for a decade, and hearing anecdotally from many more, I can say that the vast majority (though not all) of these children and families come through this storm, and they go onto college, marriage and careers. We have seen them display amazing strength of character and resilience. They develop into extraordinarily thoughtful human beings. We admire them because they have learned to be patient with themselves and others. Often they go into the helping professions as young adults. Please know, as well, that their healthy outcome is inevitably tied to a very supportive community around them – involving family advocates, therapists and, of course, educators.

As educators, you would do well to encourage families to seek counseling and support. When a child's demeanor changes overnight, often the family becomes estranged from friendships, stops participating in routinely enjoyed activities, and feels isolated and invisible within their former social system. As 504 plans and IEPs for these children are created, please check in with the primary caregiver—encourage them to attend to their own well-being as well as their child's.

There is much hope on the horizon for treating PANDAS/PANS and healing these children. In the meantime, teachers and our schools are the cornerstone of a child's community. Dr. Doran's effort to help you, the educator, better assist children with PANDAS and PANS is an important step forward in comprehensive, appropriate care for children with this complex neuropsychiatric illness. As educators, you are the pioneers of a more humane and compassionate society, where children are educated to accept differences and where stigma regarding mental and physical illness can be eliminated. The more we understand why our children with PANDAS or PANS do what they do, and how best to support them in school settings, the more able and confident learners they will be.

Diana Pohlman, Founder and Chairman
of the Board, PANDAS Network

Acknowledgements

Like all collaborative enterprises, this book reflects the efforts not only of the credited authors, but also of many other individuals. First and foremost, this present discussion of PANDAS and PANS in school settings would not exist without the ground-breaking work of the physicians and scientists who first identified these syndromes, including Susan Swedo, M.D. and numerous others, at the National Institute of Mental Health and at other collaborating institutions throughout the country. The educational community, as well as the medical community, is indebted to the authors of the 2015 diagnostic guidelines, cited extensively throughout this text, and to the authors of other recent studies on PANDAS and PANS, too numerous to mention here, which have expanded understanding of these syndromes and their impact on children and adolescents.

This book would not have come to fruition without Diana Pohlman's tireless encouragement and ideas and, even more important, her dedication to children with PANDAS and PANS and their families. Special education–legally, philosophically and ethically–is built on a foundation of parental involvement and joint decision-making, and we have been grateful to have the support of PANDAS Network, the largest parent advocacy group dedicated to this issue, which Ms. Pohlman founded. In addition to those parents and educators named as chapter contributors, countless others have shaped the ideas and practices presented here. Particular thanks is due to a few of these individuals, namely John Feringa, Kristin Harrison, Paula Gay, Noelle Dunlap, Nicole Metzler, Susan Boyd, and Kelly McGinty, who discussed their experiences, offered innovative suggestions, and shared ideas and resources they had developed. The writing, presentations and advocacy of Jamie Candelaria-Greene, Ph.D., one of the first researchers to address academic challenges and accommodations for students with PANDAS and PANS, have informed many of the recommendations made in this book and continue to provide families with important guidance.

We are grateful to our team at Jessica Kingsley Publishers, including our editor, Rachel Menzies, who first saw potential in the idea of an educator guide focused on PANDAS and PANS. The members of our team at Jessica Kingsley, including Sarah Hamlin, Emma Holak, John Evans and Sophie Soar, have improved this book in countless ways through their professionalism, commitment to the project, and careful and consistent review.

Last but not least, in a book focused on comprehensive and multi-dimensional support for students, we would be remiss if we did not express gratitude to all those, in our own lives, who have provided such support. Some of these individuals are named below; we are grateful to all, whether mentioned here or not, who facilitated completion of this work. These include significant others, spouses and partners; children; extended family and friends; and many colleagues and collaborators within and beyond each of our own institutions.

The Authors

Specific Author Acknowledgements

Such a complex undertaking as *PANDAS and PANS in School Settings: A Handbook for Educators* could not have succeeded without the help of Patricia Rice Doran, the editor on this project and special colleague at Towson University. I am grateful to Dr. Doran for her vision of the book and her grace in seeing it from draft to the final product. I would also like to thank members of my family (Bob, Kelly, and Stacy) for their encouragement and, as always, their support.

Darlene Fewster, Ed.D.

I am thankful for Dr. Patty Rice Doran's leadership, expertise, and patience in facilitating the completion of this book. I'd also like to thank my family, friends, and colleagues who served as great resources and sounding boards throughout the writing process.

Kandace M. Hoppin, Ed.D.

My son Adam's generosity, strength and perseverance has served as an inspiration for me for many years. I am grateful to him for teaching me what courage under pressure, grace and kindness look like.

Amy Mazur, Ed.D.

M. Elizabeth Latimer, M.D., has contributed greatly to my own knowledge of PANDAS, both professionally and personally, and will forever have my gratitude on both counts. Colleagues at Towson University, including Elizabeth O'Hanlon, Ph.D., Elizabeth Neville, Ed.D., and Heather Rasmussen, M.Ed., supported this project through their encouragement, feedback and ideas. Christine Brown, Ph.D., graciously offered to read and critique chapter drafts (in the midst of a blizzard, no less!) and offered invaluable suggestions based on her extensive understanding of neuroscience and brain functioning. Ellen M. Rice, MBA, generously shared her time, her in-depth knowledge of writing and publishing, and her experience in the healthcare field as she reviewed multiple chapter drafts as well and offered encouragement for the project as a whole. Nancy O'Hara, M.D., provided insights about how we view and treat children with PANDAS to inform the final Afterword. Chad Doran, Ph.D., was part of this work from its initial stages through to completion, serving as the first reader of both the prospectus and finished manuscript. While his insights as researcher and parent were valuable, his support and affirmation were even more so; this book would not exist without him. James, Claire, Katie and Julia Doran provided perspective (and frequent entertainment!) over the past year of writing and review and offered numerous constructive suggestions based on their own experiences as school-aged children and teens.

Patricia Rice Doran, Ed.D.

I am thankful for Dr. Patty Doran's generosity of spirit and expertise. I also thank my husband, Matt Stein, for his patience and humor.

Kathleen Stein, Ph.D.

I would like to thank Dr. Patty Rice Doran for inviting me to be a part of this project, along with my family (especially Jo Rogan, Ryan DiPaola, Pam and Finley Trevethan, and Mike, Angela, and Michael Tona), my colleagues in Rehabilitation Science at the University of Buffalo, Margery Henning, MS, OTR, for her assistive technology expertise, and all of the OT students who have joined me in researching PANS.

Jan Tona, Ph.D., OTR

Introduction

This book is designed for school professionals working with students who have PANDAS or PANS (or conditions with similar symptoms). While many of the chapters focus on classroom instruction and may be of great interest to general and special educators, this information is also appropriate for related services professionals, counselors, administrators and other professionals.

Chapter 1 presents a broad overview of PANDAS, PANS and their implications for school professionals. This chapter is intended to provide an orientation to the topic for education professionals new to PANDAS/PANS and a brief summary of the issues for consideration in accommodating students with these syndromes.

Chapter 2 occupies a primary place in the text as a whole because understanding the experiences of parents and family members is essential to identifying and providing appropriate, responsive services—regardless of disability or diagnosis. For children diagnosed with PANDAS and PANS, which place tremendous stress on family members, this principle is even more relevant; appropriately accommodating the needs of these students requires that we understand the full implications of each child's symptom presentation—at home and at school—and also appreciate stressors experienced by parents, children and other family members. In Chapter 2, several parents (some of whom have experience as professionals in school systems) share their children's stories, which vary widely in details such as age of symptom onset, primary symptoms, severity and course of illness. Taken together, these stories are intended to offer some insight into the spectrum of impairment that may result from a PANDAS/PANS diagnosis.

Likewise, in Chapter 3, my co-editor Mary Crombez and I present voices of experience from educators who have worked with students with a diagnosis of PANDAS/PANS. Given the constantly developing state of research regarding these disorders, there are few studies currently which address their impact in the classroom or on student learning and, as a result, much of the available knowledge from the field comes to us in the form of individual teachers' suggestions and recommendations. Chapter 3 includes vignettes from multiple teachers— some of whom are family members of students with PANDAS/PANS, some of whom are not—along with concluding recommendations.

In Chapter 4, Margo Thienemann, M.D., provides essential medical background for educators seeking to know more about PANDAS/PANS. Dr. Theinemann provides an overview of common triggers, including a detailed discussion of streptococcal infection, and describes the process by which brain functioning is impacted. This chapter provides relevant examples from current research, based on Dr. Thienemann's extensive clinical expertise in working with children and adolescents with PANDAS/PANS. The chapter concludes with practical implications for schooling of children with PANDAS/PANS.

Following the medical discussion in Chapter 4, Chapter 5 describes considerations most relevant for the general education classroom, or within Tier 1 of a multi-tiered system of supports (MTSS) paradigm. We believe strongly that educators must be prepared to accommodate PANDAS/PANS symptoms of varying intensity. While much of the second half of this book focuses on adaptations for students with more significant symptoms, Chapter 5, with Dr. Darlene Fewster as the primary author, offers recommendations for creating a brain-friendly learning environment in any classroom, designed in accord with Universal Design for Learning. These ideas, when implemented, have potential to support all learners, especially those with PANDAS/PANS.

Another crucial element in supporting students with PANDAS/PANS is collaborative planning. As PANDAS and PANS are multi-faceted disorders which impact functional performance in a variety of areas, input from multi-disciplinary team members is critical. Chapter 6 addresses important steps in the collaborative planning process, including team membership, considerations for discussion, types of possible plans, and communication with families.

Chapter 7, written by Amy Mazur, Ed.D., presents considerations for selecting and implementing accommodations, modifications or adaptations for students with PANDAS/PANS. Chapter 7 focuses primarily on academic and cognitive functioning, with discussion of reading, writing, and mathematics. As writing and mathematics skills are particularly difficult for students with these diagnoses, these areas bear further discussion. Additional recommendations for homework modification, classroom practices, and the like are included as well.

As the diagnostic criteria for PANDAS and PANS mention motor abnormalities, sometimes including sensory abnormalities, Chapter 8 is important reading for educators, both classroom teachers and related services providers. In this chapter, Janice Tona, Ph.D.,OTR, explores sensory and motor considerations for professionals and describes classroom strategies, accommodations and modifications, and specialized equipment to provide motor or sensory support. Often, such supports will be delivered in the context of a plan created by an occupational therapist, but the strategies are relevant to general and special education and many of Dr. Tona's recommended supports can be implemented within a classroom setting.

Kandace M. Hoppin, Ed.D., explores specific behavioral strategies and interventions for students with PANDAS/PANS in Chapter 9. Behavioral considerations are often paramount for students with PANDAS/PANS and, as this chapter discusses in more detail, teachers may struggle to distinguish between conscious choices, challenging behaviors, and neurological symptoms, as all may have similarly disruptive presentations in the classroom. Dr. Hoppin shares essential strategies for providing positive support to students with challenging behaviors and de-escalating classroom confrontation when possible.

In Chapter 10, Kathleen Stein, Ph.D., presents considerations for transition, both vertical (e.g., from secondary to postsecondary education) and horizontal (from one setting to another within a single school year). PANDAS and PANS are tremendously disruptive illnesses, and ensuring smooth transitions can mitigate the stress students and families are likely to feel as they transition in and out of full-time school; back and forth from homeschool to typical school; from a general education setting to a self-contained one, or vice versa; or from elementary school to middle school, or high school to college. Mandated by federal law in IDEA (the Individuals with Disabilities Education Act) for postsecondary education, transition planning is a best practice at other levels; teams should have early, explicit and focused conversations about what needs a student may demonstrate during transition from one environment to the next.

The Afterword offers concluding thoughts about implications of PANDAS/PANS for our educational system in general and for responsive instruction of students with PANDAS/PANS in particular. Echoing take-aways from the first few chapters, in which parents and educators advocated flexibility and compassion, the Afterword advocates for greater understanding of the unique challenges these students face. At the same time, this final section reflects on some ways in which PANDAS/PANS-friendly teaching may improve outcomes for all, in the best tradition of Universal Design for Learning (UDL).

The idea of UDL, in fact, takes us full circle to the purpose of this book; it is our hope that, in providing recommendations to improve outcomes for students with PANDAS/PANS, we may provide educators with increased knowledge, better skills and more caring approaches to the strengths and challenges that all students bring— particularly this group of students whose symptoms and disorders are often misunderstood.

Chapter 1

What are PANDAS and PANS, and Why Do Educators Need to Know?

PATRICIA RICE DORAN, ED.D.

Joey, a seventh-grader, was diagnosed last year with PANS by a neurologist after a year that brought about puzzling changes in his personality and behavior. Joey's parents reported that he had always been positive, cheerful and helpful at home, going out of his way to do extra chores or comfort family members when they were upset. He was a strong student despite switching schools several times in elementary and middle school due to job-related family moves.

When diagnosed with PANS, Joey was treated with several therapies but still experienced severe flare-ups tied to illness and even seasonal allergies. Joey's teachers identified him as increasingly disruptive and defiant in the classroom during times of symptom exacerbation. In speaking with his parents about their concerns, they pointed out that he would fidget, was easily distracted, and challenged teachers when corrected. At times he would become greatly agitated, particularly if his routine was changed or he felt provoked. On one occasion, he became so disruptive and agitated that the school called his parents to pick him up in the middle of the day for an emergency psychiatric evaluation. Joey failed nearly every subject in the third quarter of seventh grade, with challenges in math, reading comprehension and writing. He struggled to pay attention long enough to follow the teacher's instructions, and completing work was very difficult for him. On one occasion, he reported that it felt as though there were "strobe lights flashing" in his brain. His handwriting was nearly illegible; completing assignments in a timely manner was a constant issue. He missed numerous days of school due to specialist appointments and illness. In school, his teachers found his behavioral challenges increased when the classroom was dusty or when he was outdoors, as his allergies triggered PANS symptoms.

The school, at his parents' request, convened a meeting to begin the evaluation process for special education services. With continued treatment, Joey's neurological and psychological symptoms slowly improved, and brain scans and bloodwork showed that his physical condition had improved as well. After a summer of rest, he returned to school with an individualized education program (IEP) in place to increase his likelihood of success as he continued to heal. Six months later, Joey's mother reported he was passing all his classes, his behavioral difficulties had resolved, and he finally was back to his typical, happy self.

What are PANDAS and PANS?

The physiological context of PANDAS and PANS will be discussed more fully in subsequent chapters. However, the importance of motor skills, learning abilities, and emotional functioning for school success makes it essential for students with PANDAS/PANS to have appropriate support and accommodations throughout the educational process, as Joey's story illustrates. This chapter provides a brief overview of what PANDAS and PANS are, how they impact students' functioning, and why appropriate support and accommodation are essential for students with these diagnoses.

In the late 1990s, a team of researchers at the National Institute of Mental Health (NIMH), led by Dr. Susan Swedo, identified a subset of children with obsessive-compulsive disorder who had elevated levels of anti-streptococcal antibodies (antibodies to the Group A streptococcal bacteria that cause strep throat and other infections). A follow-up study of these children identified additional symptoms common among this group, such as atypical movements (including choreiform movements, which are unusual or jerky movements that sometimes look like piano-playing finger motions), motor and vocal tics, mood swings, restricted eating, obsessive-compulsive behavior, generalized anxiety, and difficulties with school performance (Swedo *et al.* 1998; NIMH n.d.; Swedo, Leckman, and Rose 2012). This syndrome was characterized as Pediatric Autoimmune Neuropsychiatric Disorders Associated with Streptococcal Infections (PANDAS) (Swedo *et al.* 1998), and described more fully in subsequent literature (Swedo *et al.* 2012; Chang *et al.* 2015). (For the PANDAS acronym, "Streptococcal Infections" is abbreviated to "Strep".) In 2012, researchers collaborated to define a related but broader syndrome known as Pediatric Acute-Onset Neuropsychiatric Syndrome (PANS), which presents with similar symptoms but may result from causes other than strep infection (Swedo *et al.* 2012; Chang *et al.* 2015). New studies published in the past two years have clarified diagnostic guidelines (Chang *et al.* 2015), identified presenting features of PANDAS and PANS in clinical settings (Frankovich *et al.* 2015), and described mechanisms of central nervous system involvement (Dileepan *et al.* 2016).

Like some other disorders, PANDAS and PANS cause neurological, cognitive, and psychological symptoms as a result of physical illness. Among others, Lyme disease, post-streptococcal syndromes such as Sydenham chorea (which some researchers see as related to PANDAS), celiac disease, and syphilis can also produce such symptoms as a result of infection or inflammation (Dale *et al.* 2004; Ben-Pazi, Stoner and Cunningham 2013; Washington 2015). Certain types of encephalitis can have neuropsychiatric effects as well, a phenomenon chronicled most recently by Susannah Cahalan in her memoir *Brain on Fire* (Cahalan 2013). For students with PANDAS/PANS, as with other physical illnesses that cause neurological dysfunction, experts believe it is essential to address the immunological, infectious, or physical issues underlying their symptoms (Jenike and Dailey 2012; Insel 2012).

The PANDAS diagnostic criteria formulated by NIMH researchers specified that students' symptoms should be temporally related (i.e., occur generally within a similar time frame) to Group A beta-hemolytic streptococcus (GABHS) infection. GABHS is the agent responsible for what is commonly termed "strep throat," a frequent childhood infection which, when diagnosed, is treated with antibiotics to prevent rheumatic fever and other complications. Over time, some researchers and clinicians questioned whether strep was the true cause of the symptoms described, with a resulting debate in professional literature (Kurlan and Kaplan 2004; Singer *et al.* 2012). A new and expanded category, Pediatric Acute-Onset Neuropsychiatric Syndrome (PANS), was put forward in 2012 and applies to children with sudden onset of neurological or psychiatric symptoms; however, children with PANS need not have had a prior documented strep infection in order to receive a diagnosis as long as they meet the other diagnostic criteria (Swedo *et al.* 2012). Children whose symptoms are caused by illnesses other than strep (such as Lyme disease, flu, or mycoplasma pneumonia) (Jenike and Dailey 2012) also can be categorized as having PANS if they meet the diagnostic criteria, as can children whose symptoms have no identifiable cause (Swedo *et al.* 2012; NIMH n.d.). Among specialists in this area, both diagnostic categories may still be used (see Table 1.1), though PANDAS is considered to be a subset of PANS. There is overlap among symptoms as well as treatments.

Table 1.1 Diagnostic criteria for PANDAS/PANS (Chang *et al.* 2015; Swedo *et al.* 2012; NIMH n.d.; Swedo *et al.* 1998)

PANS Diagnostic criteria	PANDAS Diagnostic criteria
• Abrupt, dramatic onset of obsessive-compulsive disorder or severely restricted food intake (anorexia)	• Presence of obsessive-compulsive disorder and/or a tic disorder
• Concurrent presence of additional neuropsychiatric symptoms, with similarly severe and acute onset, from at least two of the following seven categories:	• Pediatric onset of symptoms (age three years to puberty)
○ Anxiety	• Episodic course of symptom severity
○ Emotional lability and/or depression	• Association with group A beta-hemolytic streptococcal infection (a positive throat culture for strep or history of scarlet fever)
○ Irritability, aggression and/or severely oppositional behaviors	
○ Behavioral (developmental) regression	
○ Deterioration in school performance	• Association with neurological abnormalities (motoric hyperactivity, or adventitious movements, such as choreiform movements) (Swedo *et al.* 1998; NIMH n.d.)
○ Sensory or motor abnormalities	
○ Somatic signs and symptoms, including sleep disturbances, enuresis or urinary frequency	
• Symptoms are not better explained by a known neurologic or medical disorder, such as Sydenham chorea, systemic lupus erythematosus, Tourette syndrome or others (Swedo *et al.* 2012; Chang *et al.* 2015)	

While there are differences between them, both sets of diagnostic criteria describe children experiencing some combination of severe obsessive-compulsive behaviors or other neuropsychiatric difficulties, restricted eating/anorexia, unusual movements, or sensory issues. Students may also experience mood swings, aggression, irritability, sleep issues such as insomnia or excessive fatigue, urinary incontinence or frequent urination, and school difficulties (often manifesting in math and handwriting). Often, healthcare providers may try to determine whether symptom exacerbation occurred soon after a strep or other infection. However, this is not essential for diagnosis (PANDAS Network 2015), as infections may not have had noticeable symptoms and therefore may have been missed at the time by parents or primary care providers. Additional evaluation as part of the diagnostic process may include a neurological examination, clinical history, blood tests, or other procedures (PANDAS Network 2015; Murphy *et al.* 2004). Experts emphasize, and research suggests, that symptoms may present in ways that vary widely among different children or even with subsequent episodes in the same child (Jenike and Dailey 2012; Murphy *et al.* 2012). PANDAS/PANS are considered pediatric conditions: the PANDAS diagnostic criteria require a pre-pubertal onset, and most available research has focused on pediatric patients. There are a few isolated reports of adults exhibiting PANDAS-like symptoms (Nicholson *et al.* 2012), but these have not yet been validated on a larger scale.

While diagnostic criteria have described the symptoms, the precise mechanism that causes PANDAS or PANS is still under discussion by experts (Insel 2012). However, it is thought that PANDAS and PANS involve faulty autoimmune processes, in which the body's immune system reacts erroneously to bacterial exposure by attacking cells in the basal ganglia, an area of the brain related to movement, emotional regulation, and some learning processes (Murphy, Kurlan, and Leckman 2010; Jenike and Dailey 2012). In PANDAS/PANS, the inflammation resulting from this autoimmune process, which is sometimes visible on brain imaging (Insel 2012; Kumar, Williams, and Chugani 2015), can cause difficulties in a range of areas, including motor skills, learning abilities, obsessions and compulsions, and emotional functioning.

The course of PANDAS is often episodic, with symptom flare-ups (often referred to as "flares" or "exacerbations") alternating with periods of remission. These flares may be caused by a new infection (strep, flu, or even the common cold can all induce a flare), exposure to infection (which can create an immune system response even if the child does not contract the illness), or even allergies. Joey, whose story opened this chapter, has intense allergies to grass and has experienced symptom flares from walking across freshly-mowed lawns. Because of the immune system's involvement, children with PANDAS or PANS are frequently considered to be immunocompromised (PANDAS Network 2015) and sometimes require extensive medical treatment, rest, and careful limitation of exposure to other children. This reality underscores the importance of collaborative and positive communication with a student's healthcare team when planning for PANDAS/PANS supports and accommodations.

The episodic nature of PANDAS/PANS can, in fact, be one of the most challenging aspects of the condition for school professionals, as the processes of requesting and receiving accommodations under Section 504 (the federal law prohibiting discrimination on the basis of disability) or requesting an IEP (United States Department of Education 2012; IDEA 2006) often presume a child's status and needs remain stable throughout a school year. However, federal regulations provide that a student can be covered by Section 504 or an IEP even if his or her disability is episodic (United States Department of Education 2012; United States Department of Education 2013); as long as there is data to support the student's eligibility for accommodations or services, a team can create a 504 plan or an IEP which identifies appropriate accommodations and modifications during symptom flares. In such situations, school planning teams should work carefully and respectfully with families and, as appropriate, with the student's healthcare team to determine eligibility for accommodations and services and to discuss how implementation may vary according to symptoms and severity of the exacerbation.

Outcomes, treatment, and family considerations

As PANDAS and PANS were identified relatively recently, with the earliest research published in 1998, there is little long-term data on outcomes for students with either of these diagnoses. However, clinicians with extensive experience indicate that, when identified promptly, PANDAS can be treated and symptoms can be minimized or eliminated (Insel 2012; Jenike and Dailey 2012). While children often are diagnosed well into their school-age years, available evidence suggests many such children may actually have prior episodes which went undiagnosed (PANDAS Network 2015). Anecdotally, parents report positive results when initial exacerbations are caught early and are relatively mild. However, some children whose illness is more complex, or involves multiple infectious and immunological processes, may require longer and more involved treatment.

Traditionally, recommended treatments for PANDAS/PANS involved supportive care and treatment of symptoms, using medication and other appropriate treatments for psychiatric symptoms, such as cognitive-behavioral therapy, eating-disorder treatment, and medication for tics or attention difficulties if indicated (NIMH n.d.). However, there is growing acceptance of treatments which address infectious and autoimmune issues. Current treatments may include antibiotic therapy (used in the short term to address acute infection or in the long term as prophylaxis) (Murphy *et al.* 2010) and immune-based therapies such as steroids, intravenous immunoglobulin (IVIG), and plasma exchange or plasmapheresis, which filter harmful antibodies from the bloodstream (Swedo *et al.* 2012; Murphy *et al.* 2012; Perlmutter *et al.* 1999). Both IVIG and plasmapheresis are more invasive than oral antibiotics or oral steroids, and are typically given over the course of two or more days (PANDAS Network 2015). Some students achieve remission fairly rapidly with one or more of these therapies; some need more involved treatments, with healing taking months or years to achieve (Jenike and Dailey 2012; PANDAS Network 2015). Additionally, new infection or exposure to illness can trigger a new symptom flare by causing another immune-system response (PANDAS Network 2015). Lastly, some families report that they opt for alternative or complementary therapies, focusing on diet (removing gluten and dairy products, for example), nutritional supplements, or natural remedies, practices which have been anecdotally reported to improve children's functioning but which are not considered evidence-based at this time. Families also may continue to use symptomatic treatments, such as medications for tics, ADHD, or psychiatric issues; clinicians may change or monitor medications as needed after a diagnosis of PANDAS/PANS is made. Continued psychological interventions, such as cognitive-behavior therapy for obsessive-compulsive disorder, may be useful as well (Insel 2012; Murphy *et al.* 2010).

In working with students and families experiencing PANDAS/PANS, school professionals may want to keep in mind the substantial burdens that treatment may impose on families. Some PANDAS/PANS specialists do not accept insurance, which means that families typically pay out of their own pocket for diagnosis and treatment and then request reimbursement, if eligible, from their insurance company after the fact. Many insurance companies still consider IVIG and plasmapheresis to be experimental for PANDAS/PANS and therefore will not approve them (PANDAS Network 2015). The cost of IVIG is often thousands of dollars, increasing as children get older and the treatment dose increases. Similarly, plasmapheresis generally is administered in a hospital setting, and bills for this procedure may be five or even six figures, depending on location, services needed, and insurance approval. Even without these more involved therapies, the cost of routine maintenance—prescription drugs, follow-up appointments, additional bloodwork or other necessary testing—can easily overwhelm families.

Why PANDAS and PANS matter to educators

As PANDAS and PANS are relatively new conditions, it is difficult to obtain conclusive data about their prevalence, particularly as awareness has increased dramatically over the past fifteen years. Current figures suggest that over 162,000 children in the U.S. may have PANDAS/PANS, including one-quarter of children diagnosed with obsessive-compulsive disorder (OCD) (PANDAS Network 2015; Westly 2009), and some statistics suggest a prevalence rate for PANDAS/PANS as high as 1 in 200 students (PANDAS Network 2015). Given the size of most schools (even elementary schools), and given the number of students that education professionals encounter in the course of their careers, it is reasonable to assume that most educators will encounter at least one student with PANDAS/PANS, and likely many more, in the course of their careers. Anecdotally, we as authors have worked with numerous teachers who have had students with PANDAS/PANS diagnoses and who struggle to find the resources to support them. The increase in diagnosis since 1998, and the growing awareness of PANDAS/PANS among teachers as well as families, indicates a real need for school personnel to be knowledgeable about the complex issues that can accompany a PANDAS/PANS diagnosis (Fournier 2012; O'Rourke 2003; Tona and Posner 2011).

Familiarity with PANDAS and PANS is also essential for reasons related to assessment and identification. Because PANDAS and PANS are clinical diagnoses and require medical expertise for diagnosis and treatment, school professionals are placed in a difficult position when asked to support a student with PANDAS/PANS. If the student is just beginning the diagnostic process, there is a risk of misinterpreting behaviors as symptomatic of an emotional and behavioral disability, a learning disability, autism spectrum disorder (ASD), or other condition. In fact, students with PANDAS/PANS can be at substantial risk for being erroneously classified as having conditions such as emotional and behavioral disabilities (Candelaria-Greene 2012), even though they are often most appropriately served under the federal category, in the Individuals with Disabilities Education Improvements Act (IDEA), of "other health impairments" (Candelaria-Greene 2012; IDEA 2006).

Given the high potential for inappropriate identification, and the risks of inappropriate service delivery and instruction which may follow, it is essential for school personnel to be aware of PANDAS/PANS, the varied ways in which these disorders may present, and the interventions and supports which, thus far, appear to have had success for students with PANDAS/PANS (Tona and Posner 2011; O'Rourke 2003; Fournier 2012; Rice Doran 2015). Teachers, who are often the first to notice changes in students' behavior or performance, can play an important role in communicating with families and other school professionals about changes in student behaviors that warrant follow-up and evaluation.

While diagnosing PANDAS/PANS is outside the scope of expertise of school IEP teams without medical input, appropriate communication with parents and recommendations for outside consultations as necessary can be valuable elements in the planning process. Classroom teachers, whose presence is mandated on IEP teams, need to know about the symptoms, progression, and prognosis for PANDAS/PANS so that they can make informed contributions to the team and recommend the most appropriate accommodations for each particular student. Given the increase in awareness and PANDAS/PANS diagnoses, it is increasingly likely that every teacher, at some point in his or her career, will be involved in making accommodations and adaptations to support at least one child with PANDAS/PANS.

Teacher awareness is particularly important because of the varied ways that PANDAS/PANS can present. Like children with ASD or multiple disabilities, children with PANDAS/PANS may be affected across a variety of domains and may need support, accommodations, and adapted curriculum in each of those domains. For example, Blair (an eight-year-old third grader with PANDAS) experienced primary symptoms such as irritability, extreme anxiety at home and at school, obsessive-compulsive habits and nightmares, and sudden decline in math skills. But not all students present with symptoms identical to Blair's (consider the example of Joey at the beginning of this chapter). With antibiotic treatment, Blair's anxiety and irritability improved; over time, her math grade rose steadily from a D to a low A. At the same time, Blair's 504 team considered support from a counselor and accommodations for anxiety as well as academic supports and accommodations. This process required judicious balancing at times— Blair's evident need for extended time in math had to be weighed against the fact that being singled out to receive accommodations increased her anxiety level, and the team spent some time discussing ways to provide accommodations within a context that would not increase Blair's discomfort. In considering the value of school counseling sessions for Blair, the team also weighed the counselor's familiarity with PANDAS and expertise in issues such as pediatric obsessive-compulsive disorder in their decision-making process.

How PANDAS/PANS impact school functioning

The process of selecting and implementing accommodations varies according to the particular needs of each student with PANDAS/PANS. Particularly because of these varied needs, teachers should be aware of the different ways that PANDAS/PANS may impact academic and socio-emotional functioning. Subsequent chapters provide more detailed discussion of this topic; the description below is provided as a brief reference.

Attendance

Even before considering the many other issues related to accommodations and modifications within school settings, educators should first and foremost be aware that PANDAS/PANS may have significant impact on a student's attendance. Separation anxiety is a primary symptom of PANDAS (NIMH n.d.), and students with PANDAS or PANS may experience difficulty coming to school, or attending for a full day, during severe symptom exacerbation. During the process of diagnosis and initial treatment, which can itself last several months, students will likely miss school for specialist appointments, which may include visits to psychiatrists, neurologists, behavioral therapists, or immunologists. Parents may also be advised to see additional experts in cardiology or rheumatology if post-infectious complications such as rheumatic fever are suspected. Students who undergo immune-based therapies, such as IVIG or plasmapheresis/plasma exchange (PEX), may miss additional days or weeks of school. Lastly, because students with PANDAS/PANS are considered to be immunocompromised, they may need to be out of school if there is a danger of being exposed to illness, such as during outbreaks of strep or flu.

Planning for possible attendance issues should be an essential element of school discussions, and it is appropriate to address this issue with sensitivity and understanding when speaking with families. Missy, the mother of Hannah (a seven-year-old with PANDAS and other health challenges), recounted with frustration her daughter's IEP meeting, when she perceived the team as reluctant to accept her doctor's letter regarding Hannah's need to be excused from school during FluMist (live vaccine) administration. Missy felt that school officials expressed skepticism because they had limited experience with PANDAS/ PANS or with students who were immunocompromised in general. This type of situation is avoidable with some common sense, prior communication, and respect exercised by all parties. We can imagine a very different meeting if Hannah's teachers had reviewed the letter beforehand, had asked any questions of Missy, and district officials, in advance to ensure the meeting would be productive, and (perhaps most important) had researched PANDAS prior to the meeting so that they could anticipate some of the concerns that Missy might bring to the team.

Obsessive-compulsive and other psychiatric/emotional symptoms

As the diagnostic criteria suggests, PANDAS/PANS is primarily identified with the presence of obsessive-compulsive symptoms, often appearing abruptly or even overnight (Swedo *et al.* 2012). In school-aged children, these may appear to be stereotypical obsessive-compulsive disorder (OCD) symptoms such as repetitive handwashing or concerns about germs. However, OCD may also manifest differently, particularly in younger children (Jenike and Dailey 2012), and students may instead have fixations with repeating activities, preoccupation with specific numbers or objects, reliance on rituals, or even tantrums when a routine or compulsion is disrupted. For example, the parent of one first-grader with PANDAS reported that she could not leave for school each morning unless she had placed a toy in her backpack and double-checked to make sure it was there—which put her at odds with the school's strict prohibition on bringing toys to school. OCD may also manifest as perfectionism, repeated erasures on papers, or the need to have things complete and exactly right before moving on to another task.

In some students, obsessive-compulsive behavior occurs alongside restricted eating, sometimes related to body image issues but often related instead to a feeling of choking on food, characteristic of PANDAS/PANS (NIMH n.d.). Restricted eating behaviors may involve rigid avoidance of (or preoccupation with) certain foods, or a more classic presentation of full-blown anorexia may be present (Calkin and

Carandang 2007; Sokol 2000). Students with PANDAS/PANS may also demonstrate sensory issues, which may at times be confused with compulsions (PANDAS Network 2015; Swedo *et al.* 2012), such as the need to touch or mouth objects, or sensory defensiveness. The parent of one child with PANDAS, in this author's experience, for example, reported that her daughter struggles with attending school assemblies or church during symptom exacerbations because she cannot stand hearing people make loud noises near her. Students may experience rapid mood swings, rage, and even suicidal ideation as a result of neurological involvement (Stewart and Murphy 2014). These symptoms are addressed more fully in the chapters that follow; often, close collaboration among educators, counselors and psychologists, families, and the child's medical team is essential to address emotional or psychological issues appropriately and responsively in and out of school.

Tics and unusual movements

Another primary symptom is the presence of motor or vocal tics and/or unusual movements, particularly those of sudden onset (Swedo *et al.* 2012; Murphy *et al.* 2010). Educators may mistake tics for generalized fidgetiness or attempts at disruptive behavior. Indeed, for any student who engages in repetitive behaviors, teachers should be alert to the possibility that those behaviors may be neurologically based and not voluntary, and should consult families and appropriate school professionals for assistance in appropriate approaches toward such behaviors. At times, students' tics may be so severe or unremitting that they make it difficult for the student to function within the classroom. Here again, teams should work with families and students' healthcare providers as needed to identify appropriate and feasible solutions.

Students may also demonstrate increased challenges with fine and gross motor skills; parents of children with PANDAS or PANS often report abrupt deterioration in their children's handwriting (Swedo *et al.* 2012; Tona and Posner 2011), which may resolve after treatment. All of these issues may present challenges for students and families and for educators, whether they are experienced or inexperienced in dealing with PANDAS.

Academic progress

Neurological impairment can also cause academic difficulty. Research indicates that academic challenges commonly occur in math and executive function (Lewin *et al.* 2011), and students in our experience can struggle with reading and content areas as well. Writing may be an area of challenge, both in terms of organization and in terms of motor skills (Tona and Posner 2011); supports such as skeletal notes, partially filled-in outlines, and keyboard accommodations may be useful (Candelaria-Greene 2012; Tona and Posner 2011). In addition, students' processing and response time may be affected, and extended time may be required across subject areas. Challenges with attention and executive function, common in students with PANDAS/PANS (Lewin *et al.* 2011), may cause students to be misidentified as having ADHD and may cause additional academic difficulties. Accommodations required for academic challenges are discussed more fully in subsequent chapters.

Additional areas of impact

Lastly, PANDAS/PANS may affect various areas that are considered to be non-school-related, but that may nonetheless have a significant impact on student functioning. Some of these areas have been briefly mentioned above; they can include sleep issues (difficulties getting to sleep or staying asleep are common for students with PANDAS/PANS), anorexia or other restricted eating issues (which should be addressed in conjunction with the student's treating medical professionals), anxiety and difficulty in relationships with family members, and urinary issues including bedwetting or urinary frequency. Seven-year-old Jill's family, for example, indicated that they know Jill is on the verge of a PANDAS exacerbation when she has bedwetting episodes, which occur only when she is symptomatic.

Key points to remember

As awareness of PANDAS and PANS continues to grow, students with either disorder are in need of appropriate identification, suitable interventions and supports, and accommodations where necessary

(Tona and Posner 2011). For these reasons, it is important for educators (particularly those who work with students with disabilities) to understand the background, symptoms, and outcomes of both PANDAS and PANS. Key concepts addressed for educators in this chapter included the following:

- PANDAS and PANS are recently-identified neurological disorders in which students exhibit suddenly-appearing neurological and psychological symptoms, potentially caused by an autoimmune response.

- Students with PANDAS and PANS may have tics, obsessive thoughts and compulsions, rage and mood swings, academic difficulties, motor issues, and other physical or psychological symptoms.

- Students with PANDAS and PANS are often served through IEPs or 504 plans, and teams should consider input from the student's healthcare provider as needed, along with input from school personnel in appropriate areas.

Conclusion

Further discussion of these topics is found in the subsequent chapters. Chapters 2 and 3 present family stories and teachers' personal and professional experiences of PANDAS/PANS. Chapter 4 provides an overview of the current medical knowledge regarding PANDAS/PANS. Chapters 5–10 and the Afterword build on those accounts to discuss specific aspects of the educational experience for students with PANDAS/PANS.

References

Ben-Pazi, H., Stoner, J.A., and Cunningham, M.W. (2013) 'Dopamine receptor autoantibodies correlate with symptoms in Sydenham chorea.' *PloS One 8*, 9, e73516.

Cahalan, S. (2013) *Brain on Fire: My Month of Madness.* New York: Simon and Schuster.

Calkin, C.V. and Carandang, C.G. (2007) 'Certain eating disorders may be a neuropsychiatric manifestation of PANDAS: Case report.' *Journal of the Canadian Academy of Child and Adolescent Psychiatry 16*, 3, 132–135.

Candelaria-Greene, J. (2012) *From Crayons to College: PANDAS/PANS in the School Setting.* Presentation at the PANDAS Parents Symposium. Burlingame, CA, 28 April 2012.

Chang, K., Frankovich, J., Cooperstock, M., Cunningham, M.W., *et al.* (2015) 'Clinical evaluation of youth with pediatric acute-onset neuropsychiatric syndrome (PANS): Recommendations from the 2013 PANS Consensus Conference.' *Journal of Child and Adolescent Psychopharmacology 25*, 1, 3–13.

Dale, R.C., Church, A., Surtees, R., Lees, A., *et al.* (2004) 'Encephalitis lethargica syndrome: 20 new cases and evidence of basal ganglia autoimmunity.' *Brain 127*, 21–33.

Dileepan, T., Smith, E., Knowland, D., Hsu, M., *et al.* (2016) 'Group A *Streptococcus* intranasal infection promotes CNS infiltration by streptococcal-specific TH17 cells.' *Journal of Clinical Investigation 126*, 1, 303–317.

Fournier, A. (2012) 'What school psychologists should know about streptococcal infections.' *From Science to Practice (April 2012).* Available at www.apadivisions.org/division-16/publications/newsletters/science/2012/04/streptococcal-infections.aspx, accessed on 2 March 2016.

Frankovich, J., Thienemann, M., Pearlstein, J., Crable, A., *et al.* (2015) 'Multidisciplinary clinic dedicated to treating youth with pediatric acute-onset neuropsychiatric syndrome: presenting characteristics of the first 47 consecutive patients.' *Journal of Child and Adolescent Psychopharmacology 1*, 38–47.

IDEA (2006) *Individuals with Disabilities Education Improvement Act (IDEA), Final Regulations (2006)*, 34 CFR 300 *et seq.* Available at http://idea.ed.gov/download/finalregulations.pdf, accessed on 2 March 2016.

Insel, T. (2012) *Director's Blog: From Paresis to PANDAS and PANS.* National Institute of Mental Health. Available at www.nimh.nih.gov/about/director/2012/from-paresis-to-pandas-and-pans.shtml, accessed on 2 March 2016.

Jenike, M., and Dailey, S. (2012) *Sudden and Severe Onset OCD (PANS/PANDAS) – Practical Advice for Practitioners and Parents.* International OCD (Obsessive Compulsive Disorder) Foundation – PANS/PANDAS. Available at www.ocfoundation.org/PANDAS, accessed on 2 March 2016.

Kumar, A., Williams, M., and Chugani, H. (2015) 'Evaluation of basal ganglia and thalamic inflammation in children with Pediatric Autoimmune Neuropsychiatric Disorders Associated with Streptococcal Infection and Tourette Syndrome: A Positron Emission Tomographic (PET) study using 11C-[R]-PK11195.' *Journal of Child Neurology 30*, 6, 749–756.

Kurlan, R., and Kaplan, E. (2004) 'The pediatric autoimmune neuropsychiatric disorders associated with streptococcal infection (PANDAS) etiology for tics and obsessive-compulsive symptoms: hypothesis or entity? Practical considerations for the clinician.' *Pediatrics 113*, 4, 883–886.

Lewin, A.B., Storch, E.A., Mutch, P.J., and Murphy, T.K. (2011) 'Neurocognitive functioning in youth with pediatric autoimmune neuropsychiatric disorders associated with streptococcus.' *Journal of Neuropsychiatry and Clinical Neurosciences 23*, 4, 391–398.

Murphy, T.K., Sajid, M., Soto, O., Shapira, N., *et al.* (2004) 'Detecting pediatric autoimmune neuropsychiatric disorders associated with streptococcus in children with obsessive-compulsive disorder and tics.' *Biological Psychiatry 55*, 61–68.

Murphy, T.K., Kurlan, R., and Leckman, J. (2010) 'The immunobiology of Tourette's disorder, pediatric autoimmune neuropsychiatric disorders associated with streptococcus, and related disorders: A way forward.' *Journal of Child and Adolescent Psychopharmacology, 20*, 317–331.

Murphy, T., Storch, E., Lewin, A., Edge, P., and Goodman, W. (2012) 'Clinical factors associated with pediatric autoimmune neuropsychiatric disorders associated with streptococcal infections.' *Journal of Pediatrics 160*, 2, 314–319.

National Institute of Mental Health (NIMH) (n.d.) *Information About PANDAS.* Available at www.nimh.nih.gov/labs-at-nimh/research-areas/clinics-and-labs/pdnb/web.shtml, accessed on 2 March 2016.

Nicholson, T.R.J., Ferdinando, S., Krishnaiah, R.B., Anhoury, S., *et al.* (2012) 'Prevalence of anti-basal ganglia antibodies in adult obsessive-compulsive disorder: Cross-sectional study.' *British Journal of Psychiatry 200*, 5, 381–386.

O'Rourke, K. (2003) 'PANDAS syndrome in the school setting.' *School Nurse News, September 2003*, 34–35.

PANDAS Network (2015) *Understanding PANDAS/PANS.* Available at http://pandasnetwork.org/understandingpandaspans, accessed on 2 March 2016.

Perlmutter, S.J., Leitman, S.F., Garvey, M.A., Hamburger, S., *et al.* (1999) 'Therapeutic plasma exchange and intravenous immunoglobulin for obsessive-compulsive disorder and tic disorders in childhood.' *Lancet 354*, 9185, 1153–1158.

Rice Doran, P. (2015) 'Sudden behavioral changes in the classroom: What educators need to know about PANDAS and PANS.' *Beyond Behavior 24*, 1, 31–37. Available at www.academia.edu/15102564/Sudden_Behavioral_Changes_in_the_Classroom_What_Educators_Need_to_Know_about_PANDAS_and_PANS, accessed on 2 March 2016.

Singer, H., Gilbert, D., Wolf, D., Mink, J., and Kurlan, R. (2012) 'Moving from PANDAS to CANS.' *Journal of Pediatrics 160*, 5, 725–731.

Sokol, M.S. (2000) 'Infection-triggered anorexia nervosa in children: Clinical description of four cases.' *Journal of Child and Adolescent Psychopharmacology 10*, 2, 133–145.

Stewart, E., and Murphy, T. (2014) *PANDAS Fact Sheet.* International OCD Foundation. Available at https:iocdf.org/wp-content/uploads/2014/10/PANDAS-Fact-Sheet.pdf

Swedo, S.E., Leonard, H.L., Garvey, M., Mittleman, B., *et al.* (1998) 'Pediatric autoimmune neuropsychiatric disorders associated with streptococcal infections: clinical description of the first 50 cases.' *American Journal of Psychiatry 155*, 2, 264–271.

Swedo, S., Leckman, J., and Rose, N. (2012) 'From research subgroup to clinical syndrome: Modifying the PANDAS criteria to describe PANS (Pediatric Acute-onset Neuropsychiatric Syndrome).' *Pediatrics and Therapeutics 2*, 113, 1–8.

Tona, J., and Posner, T. (2011) 'Pediatric Autoimmune Neuropsychiatric Disorders: A new frontier for occupational therapy intervention.' *OT Practice, November 2011*, 14–22.

United States Department of Education (2012) *Disability Discrimination.* Available at www2.ed.gov/policy/rights/guid/ocr/disability.html, accessed on 2 March 2016.

United States Department of Education (2013) *Protecting Students with Disabilities. Frequently asked questions about Section 504 and the Education of Students with Disabilities.* Available at www2.ed.gov/about/offices/list/ocr/504faq.html, accessed on 2 March 2016.

Washington, H. (2015) *Infectious Madness: The Surprising Science of How We Catch Mental Illness.* New York: Little, Brown.

Westly, E. (2009) 'From throat to mind: Strep today, anxiety later?' *Scientific American*, 5 January 2009. Available at www.scientificamerican.com/article/from-throat-to-mind, accessed on 2 March 2016.

Chapter 2

Parent and Family Voices

Perspectives on PANDAS/PANS

SARAH JANE ALLEMAN, WENDY NAWARA, MSW,
AMY CORSELIUS, AND ANONYMOUS,
EDITED BY PATRICIA RICE DORAN, ED.D.

Because the symptoms of PANDAS and PANS are quite varied and present across numerous domains, with a range of severity, each child's story will be different. For this reason, this chapter presents several stories from families with PANDAS/PANS. The stories shared here represent a diverse set of experiences, with variance in the children's age of onset, symptoms and severity, and subsequent course of treatment. Some of the children described here have remained in school; some have been homeschooled; some have spent time on homebound instruction and then transitioned back to school. However, these accounts all provide insight into the nature of the disorder and, even more, the trauma and disruption of routine that families can experience when their children experience PANDAS/PANS. McClelland *et al.* (2015) provide more insight into these challenges, describing in detail the fear and isolation that families experience when their children are diagnosed with PANDAS/PANS. The impact of these emotions on families' school experiences, and subsequent considerations for educational planning, are discussed further in Chapter 5. The stories below form a sort of prelude to that more academic discussion, providing personal perspectives in the form of parents' first-person narratives of their families' experiences with illness and recovery.

Strep and behavior changes: Jesse's story

Sarah Jane Alleman

"I'm done dealing with him. I'm done...done."

Those were the first words my son Jesse's kindergarten teacher said at yet another meeting about his behavior. It was the beginning of May, and there was still about a month left of school, but his teacher was done dealing with him? There had already been countless meetings and communications in the past few months, but this was by far the most contentious. I thought we were going to be discussing how he could earn back outdoor recess, which had been taken away from him a few days earlier. Let me repeat that...my kindergarten son was no longer allowed to go outside for recess due to his behavior. But now, with his teacher being "done dealing with him," I suddenly had one goal: to keep my son from being suspended from kindergarten.

Jesse began his first year of school with much excitement. But during the second semester, his behavior changed drastically, with outbursts and a poor attitude in the classroom. Art seemed particularly difficult, and there were times I would go to the school to sit in the office while he attended that class. Physical Education was also a challenge for him. There were also various emails from his teacher, many notes in his daily planner, visits with the school counselor, and various sticker charts with rewards that never quite worked. I would also come to the school for any special events and went on field trips. I had looked back over the daily planner his teacher used to report how he had done in school to be sure I was not imagining how uneventful the first semester had been, and he really had done well in school up until February 2010. In fact, his performance during the beginning of the year had qualified him for the Talent Pool, a precursor to the school's gifted program.

Jesse was exhibiting behaviors at school and at home. We'd see OCD (including perfectionism and "just right" tendencies), urinary frequency, fight or flight responses, hallucinations, short-term memory problems, ADHD/impulsivity, oppositional behavior, emotional lability, irritability, rages/tantrums, personality changes, age regression, sensory issues, anxiety (including separation anxiety), sleep disturbances, decline in academic skills, and more. Several times that spring, I was called to pick him up from school. When I arrived, he would be in clear distress and panicked, surrounded by exasperated adults. In hindsight, and knowing now that my son's brain was being affected by PANDAS, it's amazing that we did not see even more issues.

None of us knew exactly what was happening to Jesse as his behavior deteriorated. As his mother, I was doing everything I could do to find help for him. During that second semester, there had been so many school meetings and appointments with doctors and consults with specialists in just a few months. I spoke to his teacher about some possible "bullying" in the classroom. I consulted with the school counselor and gifted teacher for their insights. We saw the eye doctor, and his vision was 20/20. We saw his pediatrician *eight times* from January through May of 2010 to discuss behaviors and to rule out diabetes, anemia, and various other possible issues that could have been causing the behaviors. We met with the doctor who had removed his tonsils and adenoids a few years earlier and discussed allergies. We had an Occupational Therapy (OT) evaluation and attended OT sessions. We saw two psychologists at the time and did screenings for ADHD and Asperger Syndrome...he had neither of those conditions. By the end of the year, we had received an "Anxiety—Not Otherwise Specified" diagnosis for Jesse, and even though it did not seem to fit, we were using it to request a 504 plan for special accommodations.

It was soon after that contentious school meeting that I found PANDAS. It was the middle of the night, and I couldn't sleep due to my worry over my son's school issues. What had happened? What had changed? What caused his strange behaviors? I suddenly remembered a strep infection he had had at the end of December 2009 and how he was different by the end of January. I got up and Googled "strep and behavior changes" and found PANDAS. I sobbed, sitting there in my pajamas as I watched a video of the doctor who helped discover PANDAS, as she described exactly what was happening to my son.

The next morning, I called my pediatrician's office thinking I had found the answer. PANDAS would explain why my son's behaviors had changed so much after a strep infection, and it would explain all of the problems he was having. I explained my findings to a nurse and waited all day for the doctor to call me back, only to be told that it was *not* PANDAS for reasons that I know now were inaccurate. I was given the name of a doctor for a psychiatric referral and encouraged to get a prescription for SSRIs for my six-year-old. I considered making an appointment, but my gut told me that this was more than a mental health issue and something medical had caused my son to change. I had already looked up "brain tumor" on the internet to see if there were bigger issues that nobody could see. I wondered if my son was going to die before anyone was willing to figure out what was wrong with him.

The school issues continued with more and more complaints from the kindergarten teacher. My son never did get outdoor recess back, and he was put in isolation in the classroom with his desk away from all the other children. We ended the year with notes from our doctor allowing us to send Jesse only half-days. By the last day of school, I could hardly look at or talk to the teacher or principal, and I had been a Room Mom when the year began! Years later, I still have trouble driving by our neighborhood elementary school due to the awfulness we experienced during my son's kindergarten year—I often take the back roads instead.

Over the summer, Jesse showed improvement as his anxiety levels lowered and exposure to illnesses decreased. We assumed that school had been a big part of the issue and still do believe there was a lot of stress in that environment. My husband and I decided that we would not be sending my son back to public school for first grade, and we applied to a Montessori school where we were wait-listed. I would homeschool until a spot became available at the private school.

At the end of August, Jesse caught what looked like a cold. In the next weeks (just as I was starting to homeschool), he developed a vocal tic. Then he had a breathing tic. Then he developed a strange fear of his hands after watching a cartoon. Then he had a rage. I took him to the doctor with some PANDAS info in hand and asked for a strep test. Despite the change in behaviors and a positive strep test, the doctor told me again it was not PANDAS, again citing a few reasons that I now know are not valid. She gave me the name of a neurologist I could call on my own if I wanted to pursue PANDAS, and she told me to get him in to see the psychiatrist for SSRIs.

I sought a second opinion with a doctor at a different pediatric office. The new doctor reviewed my son's medical file and the spreadsheets I had prepared showing all of his illnesses and resulting behaviors. After listening to me describe everything that had been happening, she also told me it was not PANDAS and recommended SSRIs. We had demonstrated mental and behavioral changes with infections, but still couldn't get a local doctor to help. Meanwhile, my son's condition was worsening with no relief from his symptoms.

I consulted with a PANDAS specialist in a different state. After reviewing Jesse's records and speaking with us, the PANDAS specialist told us that he was "95–100 percent sure it was PANDAS because it couldn't be anything else." We traveled over eight hours so my son could receive an intravenous immunoglobulin (IVIG) treatment of donor antibodies to help recover his immune system and stop the PANDAS reaction. Jesse was also placed on daily antibiotics to help protect him from more infections. Over the next few years, Jesse continued to react with PANDAS symptoms to any infections/ viruses and any exposures to illnesses. He received another follow-up IVIG treatment in 2012, almost exactly two years after his first procedure, which showed good results again.

In 2013, Jesse enrolled in Montessori school for fourth grade. It was not a perfect year, and neither was fifth grade. The exposure to bacteria and viruses did affect his mood and behavior sometimes. If he did actually get sick, he could miss weeks of school until his PANDAS symptoms subsided enough for him to be able to handle a regular school day. He continues to attend that school now. Being in a smaller, private school environment has been helpful and provides a more understanding community of teachers and administrators. Currently, he is in sixth grade, and the year is going well. Jesse even had a case of strep throat and did not exhibit any major PANDAS symptoms, which we are taking as a positive sign that he is in recovery.

I believe that homeschooling Jesse for three years helped in his PANDAS healing immensely because he was not as exposed to other children's illnesses. When he was able to go back to school, being in a smaller Montessori environment meant fewer illnesses.

His teachers let us know if they notice any odd behaviors, and they notify us when there are bugs going around at school so we can take precautions and monitor our son's health. While we are not out of the woods yet as far as PANDAS symptoms are concerned, it feels strange not to be dealing with the more intense exacerbations we had experienced. We are thankful that he is a good place health-wise for now, though we are also cognizant that symptoms could still occur and so we remain vigilant.

Schools can definitely help on the front line of recognizing that a medical condition is present, since school is where children spend the bulk of their waking hours during the week. With conditions such as PANDAS/PANS, it is important that teachers understand how the symptoms can manifest at onset of the condition, as this can help speed the diagnosis for a child. Knowing how the behaviors can change over time, and wax and wane, can also help teachers provide positive accommodations for the students. It is important for schools to fully support families going through the crisis and extreme stress of PANDAS/PANS. It is devastating, and educators must realize PANDAS/PANS is a medical condition that presents with behavioral and learning issues.

Overall, our son Jesse is a funny, intelligent, spirited 11-year-old. He enjoys acting, telling jokes, writing stories, and drawing, and he hopes to be a movie actor and/or director when he is older. Over the past six years, PANDAS has robbed him of many normal aspects of his childhood. His father and I have been robbed of many normal aspects of parenthood. With PANDAS, it is difficult to even know what "normal" is anymore. Even when you have a "good" day you can't fully enjoy it due to the knowledge that tomorrow might be very bad. Healing your child from PANDAS/PANS can take a long time, and you may never know if he is fully recovered.

Everything you go through during the PANDAS journey makes you want to help other parents that are just finding the condition and seeing wild changes in their child's behavior. I know the desperation parents feel because I have felt it. I write a blog called PANDAS Sucks (pandassucks.com) and founded a PANDAS/PANS support group in my state. I've also given presentations to teachers to help spread awareness about PANDAS/PANS so that fewer students and families have to go through what we went through when the condition hit my son. Jesse's story is full of ups and downs, but it is a positive one. His recovery has taken a lot of time and patience, but there is always the fear that any illness could take him back into a major PANDAS exacerbation.

Three children with PANDAS: Our family's experience
Wendy Nawara, MSW

I am astounded by the strength that my kids, my husband, and I can show when we believe that there is no other choice. We firmly believe our only option is to get better, and that's the way I will see it; that I must see it. There is no giving up.

My oldest child, Michael, began to show PANDAS symptoms at age two. He had been an emergency C-section baby, was frequently sick with respiratory infections, had asthma and allergies, and terrible eczema. He displayed OCD and major sensory defensiveness about foods, and in his toddlerhood we watched him systematically whittle himself down to two consistent edible items: beans and corn chips.

I brought my concerns repeatedly to his pediatrician. He was never overly concerned, as Michael was still growing adequately and meeting developmental milestones appropriately. The doctor appeared to have no worries about his nutrition and how often he was sick. I would try to laugh with the office staff about how often I was in there getting Michael checked out. I thought maybe we should have our own personal exam room, not only because we'd certainly paid them for the privilege, but Michael would get sick with whatever germ was lingering on the surfaces in the room from other children. It never failed—we'd be back the next week. Over and over again. This was our standard operating procedure from October until May every year. When he started school, we tacked on the months of September and June too.

I had to fight for a referral for occupational therapy to address the strange sensory processing issues that had plagued Michael for as long as I could remember. Up until that point it was felt by our doctor that I must not be offering enough foods other than beans and corn chips, but believe me, my husband and I were eating more than just Mexican. The combination of mush and crunch were all that he would tolerate. Michael had begun to vomit when he heard the sounds of wet foods such as pasta and sauce, stew, or oatmeal. He was also highly sensitive to food aromas such as roasted meats or pungent vegetables. It would incite a powerful gag reflex, and, subsequently, a projectile vomit.

I also fought for allergy testing, and we discovered he was allergic to poultry, citrus, wheat, corn, peanuts, eggs, dairy, mustard, kiwi, stone fruits, tree nuts, dust, mold, and grasses. His immune system was clearly hyper-reactive. He spent those early years as one angry little dude on rotational and elimination diets as we tried to get to the sources of his difficulties. If he wasn't literally starving, he was physically sick with viral and bacterial infections. By the time Michael was seven he had had about 20 strep infections; nine alone in that second grade school year. I had noticed head-swinging tics, and rages were now also a part of the picture. I actually documented that he was happiest on ibuprofen; it was almost a miracle drug for me as a mom as it allowed me enough time to address the needs of our two younger kids. When he ultimately had a tonsillectomy/ adenoidectomy, he became a different child within days. He was happy, he was secure, and he no longer grunted and swung his head around in a weird way. What a bonus! But that is also when I found out about PANDAS. A late-night internet search on behavior changes post-tonsillectomy led me to the National Institutes of Health (NIH) website, with its earliest attempts at describing the syndrome. I finally knew what was going on with this child! And I finally thought I could put it all behind us. Lightning never strikes twice, right?

Our second son, Christopher, and our youngest, a daughter, Laura, were the "healthy" ones, or so we thought. They had no history of allergies. Although they were frequently ill as babies, we just thought it was par for the course in our family. I expected, and enjoyed hearing, "It's normal" in the pediatrician's office, even though my instincts were always on high alert, because truth be told...what had happened with Michael was nowhere near normal for the general population, but it was normal for my family.

Christopher's PANDAS experience came out of nowhere while we were on a family vacation. He was having symptoms of urinary frequency and was clearing his throat incessantly, reporting that something was in there and that he must get it out. I knew in my heart immediately what was going on, but tried to swallow my fears and move on with life. He was excited by the thought of starting his fifth grade year, and denied that anything was seriously wrong.

A few weeks into the school year he began to express his fears to me every day as we would drive to school. He would explain that he didn't know why he was afraid to go to school, but that he had an uncontrollable feeling of dread as we would round the last corner closest to the school. Tears would well up in his eyes, and he'd fight to hold them back. Only a few times could he not get out of the car, thankfully. He was trying so hard to conquer what he knew to be an irrational fear, but sometime the floodgates would open. In those moments, I would cry right along with him because it was obvious that he had no idea why he was feeling this way.

It was heart-wrenching to see him struggle so hard with something so simple and expected in his daily life.

By October's parent–teacher conferences, it was apparent that something needed to be done. His teacher reported that his throat-clearing had become a distraction to the other kids in the classroom. At home I began to notice it too. His best friend of many years would say, "Be quiet. Stop doing that!" He'd ask, "Why can't you make it stop?" and would announce he was leaving. Sometimes he wouldn't come back for weeks.

We spent months in and out of the pediatrician's office. I believe they already viewed me as "that crazy parent." But this time I also had the experience, and the hindsight, to recognize my past mistakes, and I knew what was going on. I was positive that this was PANDAS.

During those frightful months we were in the pediatrician's office once every two to three weeks. My son was presenting with a throat-clearing tic, increased urinary frequency, a choreic neck roll, and a weird and very uncharacteristic physical clumsiness that could not be explained. After each visit, I would leave the office hiding my tears because they would not or could not help us. At one point they offered proton pump inhibitors because they felt the throat-clearing tic was related to acid reflux. I said I would try that, but that I wanted him tested for strep. My request was met with clear disdain. I had only asked for strep testing, a simple throat swab, and instead I'd get this in response; "Mrs. Nawara, in order to have strep a child needs to present with a sore throat at a minimum. He does not have a sore throat. He does not have a red throat. He shows no nausea, and no fever. Your child does not have strep throat."

"This is PANDAS!" I would scream. Our doctor's incredulous response was that PANDAS was very rare and couldn't possibly be happening to my child. I was told that I needed to ignore the tics because bringing attention to them would just make them greater. How could I possibly ignore that my son was wetting himself at age 10? He was scared every day. The weird movements and strange noises he was making were causing his friendships to suffer. His self-esteem was in the garbage. His grades clearly reflected the relapse-remit pattern of PANDAS, but his teachers seemed paralyzed in making a formal move towards helping him. They were looking to my lead, but I was getting nowhere with the doctors I had to look to for help.

After the fifth month of regular doctor's visits and clear requests for help, I finally broke into tears in the office. I demanded a throat swab for the final time. I must have looked like a woman possessed. The nurse took pity on me and ran it. A few minutes later, the doctor walked in, smug and gloating. The rapid screen came back negative for strep. I was so confused. I had been sure this was it. Her condescending demeanor made me sick to my stomach. Again she droned on with the same nonsense: "Mrs. Nawara, in order to have strep a child needs to present with a sore throat at a minimum. He does not have a sore throat. He does not have a red throat. He shows no stomach issues, and no fever. Your child does not have strep throat." Ad nauseam.

"Culture it," I meekly responded. Then more strongly, "Culture it for three days. I want answers for why my son is this way. I feel like I am losing my child."

Four days later and right before the December holidays, I got a call from the nurse at the pediatrician's office. It was positive. I asked her for copies of all three of my children's records on the spot, and went in to pick them up a few days later, never to be seen there again. Now I had to get down to the business of finding a new medical provider who would step out of the box and think; someone who could treat this "rare" medical condition.

I spent countless days and nights researching the condition and the doctors who treat it. One day I came upon a website for a doctor who was actually very close to our home. This guy was world-renowned and in my eyes "famous." I was completely intimidated. What if this wasn't it? In my heart, I really did want to deny that any of this was happening, so I did not call him right away.

But late one night, as I continued my research on a laptop in bed, my wonderful husband flipped channels in the background for white noise. In his own distraction, he just happened to stop flipping long enough for my ears to pick up the intro for a Medical Mysteries show just starting. I knew immediately. From the first teaser the show provided about the boy's symptoms, I just knew. I said nonchalantly to my husband, "I'll bet this kid has PANDAS." And I was right. Within moments of the credits rolling, I was on Amazon ordering a book about PANDAS, *Saving Sammy: A Mother's Fight to Cure Her Son's OCD* by Beth Maloney (2009).

The next morning I dug up that local doctor's contact information and emailed him. We were in his office two days later. Christopher had a confirmed case of PANDAS.

During those early diagnostic days, I was very scared. I felt we were dealing with something enormous and life-changing. I felt compelled to follow the advice of this expert, even to the point of denying some of my own mommy gut feelings. I wanted to be able to rely solely on this doctor for all of our medical needs, so he became not only our specialist, but our pediatrician as well. I wanted to sit back and relax and let someone else do the driving. I wanted it fixed and over. I wanted to return to our regularly scheduled programming and just get on with our lives. I didn't like the prospect of waiting for the fix. We followed a traditional route of treatment at that time—steroids and antibiotics—and were pleased with the initial results.

Christopher had nearly five months symptom-free. But at the same time I was unable to stop myself from researching for more answers, because I had already seen the comings and goings of this disorder in my first son. I was not convinced it was not coming back. I did all that I could to understand the mechanisms behind the disease so that I could circumvent the disorder's progress.

Christopher's symptoms came back with a vengeance at the start of the new school year. Re-exposure to a new school and many new friends caused an explosion of new tics and obsessions. In addition to his throat-clearing, he added a violent head-thrusting that on occasion would knock him out of balance, pushing him over. He was rolling his eyes in the back of his head. He had always been a picky eater, but now foods and their textures and smells would make him nauseous. He began eliminating many foods from his diet. His handwriting degraded to illegibility. He was fatigued beyond what I could believe was possible for a boy of his age. He was sleeping over 12 hours per night.

This was not right. At first we wanted the quick fix that the steroids and antibiotics provided. I knew this wasn't a long-term solution though. We needed to find a way to suppress the hyper-reactivity of Christopher's immune system, while also protecting him from picking up every little new germ and keeping the chronic bugs down to a minimum. We needed the bigger guns of IVIG. In brief, IVIG floods the immune system with healthy antibodies. Its efficacy is still questioned in mainstream medicine to some extent, despite studies that show success. Because of this, insurance coverage is difficult to get. We decided to have it done regardless of the cost. We needed to get him better.

Within a few weeks of Christopher's IVIG, his sister Laura came down with a strep infection that she couldn't shake. Nine rounds of antibiotics and six months later, she began showing PANDAS symptoms. She was fretful, obsessive, and had significant chorea. Eight months after that, Michael began exhibiting another exacerbation that finally landed him with a PANDAS diagnosis, 13 years since we saw his first symptoms.

One, two, three, like dominoes they fell. It was devastating and almost completely paralyzing to know that we were staring down a beast of a disorder in not just one, but all three of our children, and quite possibly facing financial ruin if we took the necessary steps to get our children well.

I tell this very long story before I even touch on the role that the schools played because I would love for educators to know what happens first. I want educators to fully understand just how exhausted and frustrated the parent is who comes in for help: the one who fights like a feral animal at IEP/504 meetings, or the one who is completely despondent and appears to not care. I also tell that story because I used to be a school social worker and was apt to make quick judgments with my colleagues as we sat on the other side of the table intimidating the parents (even though we like to think that never happens). I know first-hand how frustrated and helpless both the parent and the professional feel when faced with a problem that is not easily solved.

Three children at three different ages and stages meant three very different experiences. Regardless of my unique background as a school professional, which allowed me to understand both parent and educational perspectives, and my full comprehension of special education laws, I was fully unprepared for what came next. Our experience at the junior high was the most troubling to me and resulted in calls to the U.S. Department of Education's Office of Civil Rights, a few attorneys, and the hiring of a bulldog of an advocate. Christopher was a junior high student at that time. At first it was difficult to prove the illness to the school, because he did his best to act normally all day long. But what his teachers never saw was that he would literally crawl up the stairs and into his bed every day because holding it together at school was grueling. His constant level of fatigue led to an inability to complete his homework, which they insinuated was due to his laziness and my poor parenting skills. I ended up having to surreptitiously videotape my son at his worst so that they could see what life was really like for him. They were shocked, and I felt like I had violated his privacy to prove a point. It was not my finest parenting moment. I shouldn't have had to do that. My word along with the letter from our doctor should have been enough.

When I was able to successfully jump through all of the hoops to get him on a homebound tutor's caseload, the school stopped communicating with me and the tutor. It was as if he wasn't there, so he (and I) were no longer their problem. They refused to alter the curriculum enough so that he could feel successful even if it was just for an hour a day, and also told the tutor it was not her place to do so. It was a fight to get them to understand that he rallied for the tutor and the rest of the day he was sleeping, and therefore he still was not able to complete all of the same work that his peers at school were completing. We needed modifications to the amount, but not necessarily to the content. I wanted to know he had mastery and that required educational creativity and flexible teacher attitudes toward chronically ill children. As his parent, I was terrified he'd be held back.

A few of his teachers were kind. However, I always felt as though, if teachers tried to make life easier for Christopher as he recovered, administrators would tighten up in a manner that seemed strange and unfeeling. From my perspective, it seemed as though the teachers were not supposed to help him, or at least not get caught by the principal. When we tried to reintroduce him back into school, we were met with more administrative resistance. I would have thought that administrators would be glad to have him "in school," but as soon as I asked for help creating the plan to get him back in the door to resume his full education, they refused, stating it was unsafe for him to be there. I felt as though my own words were turned against me in a power play to control my child's access to education. Because yes, in the darkest days of his illness, the exposure to the petri dish of germs at his school was too risky for his health. He needed time for his immune system to relearn how to function and for his brain to heal. In the meantime, our school administrators denied him access to what would have been small steps toward reintegration— participating in extracurricular activities—despite his 504 plan and the rights it afforded him. Their rationale, contrary to what was stated in his 504 plan, was that if he was too ill to attend class, he must be too ill to participate in extracurricular activities.

There are two great things that we try to remember from that rocky time period. One was that one teacher set up a Skyping system so that my son could be "present" in a class as much as he was able.

The students loved taking responsibility for him. Another class made a big get well card for him that we still have almost six years later. Those simple, and seemingly minor, efforts helped him to feel included and remembered.

My experiences in both the elementary building and our high school since then have been much more productive and effective. Maybe because I became well-known amongst the district administration? Maybe because I just refused to give up? Probably a little of both, but most definitely also because I was forced to declare, repeatedly, my own expertise on both PANDAS/PANS and my own children.

I completely understand that both PANDAS and PANS are uncharted territory for the majority of educators (and many healthcare providers too). In this day and age, 54 percent of children are chronically ill, with conditions ranging from asthma to developmental delays to obesity (Bethel *et al.* 2011). This reality places a great burden on teachers who have to support all of those children and their various needs. I believe and know from experience that it is harder to be a teacher or an administrator than any other job. I actually felt sorry that my children did not fit into the box, so that their teachers' jobs would be easier. Initially, I really wanted them to be the experts, and to tell me what was best. But the more I thought about it, the more I realized that I was the only expert on my kids and what they were enduring. It was having educators and administrators value my expertise as the parent that finally turned things around and renewed my trust in them. We pooled our strengths, thus effectively teaming together to work toward the benefit of their students, my children.

I am happy to report that Michael is now in college pursuing a degree in Communications. Christopher is currently investigating colleges and plans to study Classics. Laura is in high school on a part-time schedule after having taken a year away from the public school system to get healthy. PANDAS/PANS has not completely left us, and it is my gut feeling that we will always be faced with some autoimmune and immunological challenges. All three have flares now and then, but they have learned to manage their health needs with grace and perseverance. It is my hope that teachers, administrators, and other education professionals can come to a place of understanding and acceptance of what many of today's children with chronic illness face. By the time these kids are seated in their classrooms, they have already tackled some seemingly insurmountable challenges.

Jake's story: From an autism diagnosis to PANDAS/PANS

Amy Corselius

Through the early years of elementary school, my son Jacob attended a public school like most children his age. He was a cub scout and enjoyed many hobbies including fishing, Lego, riding his bike, Pokémon, collecting rocks, and building forts. Jacob was a precocious child with a well-developed vocabulary and advanced reading skills and his teacher referred him to the gifted and talented program for enrichment activities. He was socially quirky but we did not make much of it considering he seemed so bright in other areas. By mid-year of first grade Jacob's quirks became more obvious, including complaints that his clothes were scratchy, his insistence on following elaborate daily routines, and his preference for playing independently rather than interacting with his peers. Teachers noticed that Jacob seemed to be socially lagging behind his peers and his father and I were concerned enough to have him evaluated by a psychologist who diagnosed him with Asperger Syndrome. Even though I did not feel that he fitted all of the diagnostic criteria for Asperger Syndrome, I was nonetheless relieved to have a reason for the social delay. The diagnosis also helped us find more support, including weekly sessions with a psychologist for social skills development and weekly occupational therapy for sensory issues. Teachers seemed much more understanding of Jacob's quirky behaviors once he had a diagnosis, despite the fact that he did not meet the criteria for special education services at that time.

A few months into third grade Jacob seemed to be socially and emotionally regressing. He developed severe separation anxiety and some days he would lock himself in the bathroom, refusing to leave the house. In the classroom he would become easily frustrated and would climb under his desk and growl at his teachers. Once a child with beautiful handwriting, Jacob now could barely hold a pencil. His writing became illegible, making it very difficult for teachers to grade his work (Figures 2.1 and 2.2).

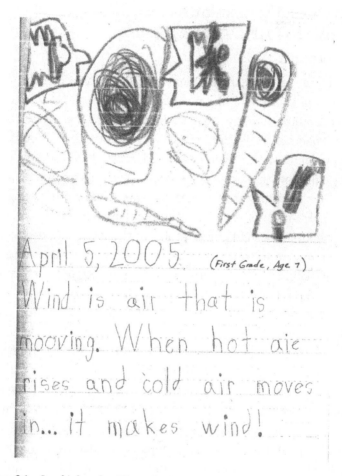

Figure 2.1   Jacob's handwriting prior to symptom onset

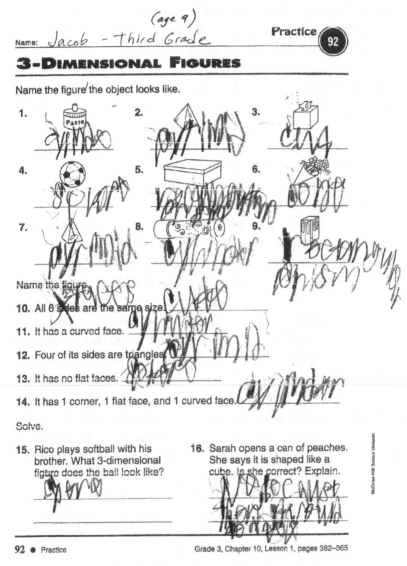

Figure 2.2   *Jacob's handwriting during symptom exacerbation*

He also had trouble comprehending math concepts and retaining his multiplication facts. Each day Jacob developed more confusing and disruptive behaviors. By January he could not walk down the hall without retracing his steps and touching the walls. He refused to do classroom assignments and would yell at teachers when he perceived they were demanding too much of him. He developed flight behaviors and would run through the school with teachers chasing after him. Once they caught up to him, he would kick and spit. I could hear him talking under his breath to himself, his left eye blinked uncontrollably, and he became forgetful. He restricted his eating and lost weight. He obsessively washed his hands and sniffed each bite of food before eating it. When I tried to hug him he would stiffen and pull away. He developed insomnia and dark circles appeared under his eyes. He seemed pale, weak, and fatigued. When I asked him why he repetitively touched walls and retraced his steps he told me that his brain told him he "had to do those things or something bad would happen."

Jacob's concerning behaviors came to a head in the spring when he had suicidal ideation at the age of nine. His pediatrician was quick to prescribe an antidepressant. He also gave us a referral to a psychiatrist who subsequently diagnosed him with obsessive-compulsive disorder (OCD) and prescribed antipsychotic medications to reduce irritability and calm disruptive behaviors. Unfortunately Jacob was so emotionally unstable at that point that he finished his third grade year on home and hospital instruction. At the same time educators re-evaluated his social and academic abilities and determined that he qualified for special education services. The Individualized Education Program (IEP) team scrambled to write an IEP that could be implemented for fourth grade. However, my husband and I decided that Jacob's needs would be better served by a small private school for children with learning disabilities. The staff at the new school were willing to follow the recommendations of the public school IEP, but Jacob continued to have emotional outbursts, disruptive behaviors and compulsions that interfered with his school day. His short time at the private school came to end after he ran out of the building where the school sat on a busy road, and it became obvious that they did not have the resources to keep him safe with such unpredictable behaviors.

After that incident, we immediately re-enrolled Jacob in the public school system and, based on his history of emotional instability and disruptive behaviors, it was determined that he would be more successful at a non-public special education school thirty miles from our home. I was dumbfounded at how quickly Jacob regressed with no explanation for his decline. Less than one year earlier he was attending school with his neuro-typical peers and now he was in a school with children who had severe autism, brain injuries, and learning disabilities. By the time Jacob arrived at the new school in the spring of his fourth grade year, he had so much anxiety about being in a classroom that even simple tasks overwhelmed him. However, I was relieved that he would be safe knowing the staff were professionally trained to handle disruptive behaviors, even if it meant he would be physically restrained at times. He was assigned a one-to-one aide, received daily occupational therapy, and weekly counseling sessions. He had good days and bad days but overall the more supportive and restrictive learning environment seemed to benefit him and he excelled academically. Eventually the IEP team determined that he would benefit from a school that had a more challenging academic program, and he transitioned to a school fifty miles from home for middle school that seemed to better meet his academic needs. He struggled to fit in socially, as many of the students seemed much more "street-smart" and Jacob was fairly immature for his age. Some of the students at the school were identified as having behavioral and conduct disorders and he witnessed angry students throwing chairs around the classroom and using foul language during class and lunch. At the time, Jacob's diagnosis of Asperger's continued to drive his IEP services and, despite his behavioral outbursts in the form of yelling or running out of the classroom when frustrated, he was a fairly mild-mannered, socially naïve middle schooler.

Over the years it seemed strange to me that Jacob's OCD symptoms, sensory issues, anxiety, and disruptive behaviors would wax and wane. When his symptoms waned, he seemed more like a neuro-typical child: he was calm, cooperative, focused, and engaged in his daily activities. When his symptoms waxed he would report that his brain felt "puffy," and that he would feel like he was losing control of it. On these days, he was more anxious and uncooperative, his mood was labile, he could not focus on daily activities including class work, and his OCD symptoms were more intense. None of the physicians or practitioners involved in his care had an explanation for this, nor could I find information on the internet, which is where I often turned to research Asperger's and OCD. Medications only partially relieved Jacob's OCD symptoms and weekly therapy did not seem to be helping at all.

One day a friend of mine who knew that Jacob was struggling with OCD recommended a book to me called *Saving Sammy: A Mother's Fight to Cure Her Son's OCD* by Beth Maloney. It was the first time I had ever heard of Pediatric Autoimmune Neuropsychiatric Disorders Associated with Strep (PANDAS). I combed the internet for more information and found a specialist to evaluate Jacob for PANDAS. For the first time in the nine years since Jacob first showed symptoms, the doctor ordered blood tests to evaluate his immune system function and look for evidence of infections. The thorough doctor gave her final impressions and told us that Jacob was suffering from a severe case of PANDAS with an underlying primary immune deficiency. This treatment would require antibiotics and monthly immune-modulating medication called intravenous immunoglobulin (IVIG) to regulate his faulty immune system. The doctor was not surprised that Jacob had been previously diagnosed with Asperger's but she felt this was incorrect and that his social delay and behavioral regression were better explained by PANDAS. The doctor believed that Jacob had developed the disorder around age four but that his worst exacerbation occurred at age nine, when he deteriorated in third grade. Jacob was thirteen and in seventh grade by the time he was properly diagnosed and his doctor decided that in order to reduce his exposure to new infections, he should no longer attend school and instead receive home and hospital instruction services. Five years later, he continues to receive school instruction at home because of his compromised immune system. Eventually Jacob was diagnosed with PANS because his symptoms seem to be exacerbated by infections other than strep.

It is hard to imagine how educators managed to teach Jacob during the time when his symptoms of PANDAS/PANS were so extreme on some days and on other days they were barely noticeable. Even with an IEP in place, support such as a behavioral intervention plan (BIP) was fairly futile because he did not have predictable patterns of disruptive behaviors. The daily provision of OT wasn't always needed, as his sensory needs varied from day to day. He had a scribe available to him, yet some days his handwriting was completely legible and he demanded independence. He could comprehend a new math concept one day and the next day the same concept was foreign to him, creating much frustration for both teacher and student. If he had been properly diagnosed with PANDAS/PANS and treated for the disorder earlier in elementary school, I often wonder if he would have been easier to teach because, at the very least, educators would have understood why his behaviors and educational needs varied from day to day. Jacob's behaviors such as refusal to do classwork, growling, fleeing, retracing steps, and so on confused everyone. He was viewed as being annoying by peers and a behavioral problem by teachers. Perhaps with a proper diagnosis he would have been able to remain with his neuro-typical peers in a less restrictive school program. Perhaps our school system would not have had to spend so much money for his placement at non-public schools and the costly transportation to get him there each day.

It's important to note, when Jacob displayed abrupt changes in his behaviors and handwriting, it was never suggested to us that he be evaluated by a medical doctor for neurological concerns. We learned many years later that these symptoms were a manifestation of neurological dysfunction.

Today at age eighteen, Jacob is 85 percent recovered from his daily symptoms of PANDAS/PANS. He continues to receive medical treatments to regulate his immune system. While he continues to have exacerbations of his symptoms following illnesses in the form of obsessive thoughts, social anxiety, changes in handwriting, and decline in math skills, these exacerbations are now mild and short-lived. He was weaned from antidepressants and antipsychotic medications three years ago. It was determined that he no longer qualified for special education services, so his IEP was suspended. He is dually enrolled in high school and college, and continues to learn through home and hospital instruction, as well as online college classes. He will graduate from high school this year and plans to continue with college to pursue a degree in biology with a focus on ichthyology. When I asked him how he has been affected by his long history of being misdiagnosed, he told me that his dad and I seem more affected by it than he does. He does not seem to remember the worst of it all.

As one could imagine, Jacob's misdiagnosis, subsequent proper diagnosis and complicated medical treatments have had a profound effect on our family. At the time that Jacob had his worst exacerbation of PANDAS/PANS symptoms, between third and seventh grades, my husband and I started to settle into the idea that we had a special needs child who would never be able live independently and we planned for his future accordingly. Once Jacob was placed in a non-public school for students with disabilities, we were led to disability resources, including a lawyer who advised us on special needs estate planning and a social worker who outlined the social services and government funding that would be available to Jacob as an adult. Imagine our shock to learn many years later that Jacob's issues were actually being caused by a treatable autoimmune disorder. He has been under aggressive medical treatment for five years now, and it took one whole year of treatment before sustained improvement in Jacob's condition was seen.

Our shock at Jacob's initial diagnosis of PANDAS/PANS has evolved into joy as we have watched him heal from the disease. He has made enormous gains socially, as his brain is much less preoccupied with obsessive thoughts, compulsions, and anxiety. He no longer has behavioral outbursts when he is frustrated, his sensory issues are minimal, and his handwriting and math skills have improved. Once we saw lasting improvement after his first year of medical interventions, we were able to shift our focus away from raising a child with special needs and towards helping him reach his goals of earning a college degree, being gainfully employed, and living independently. Jacob has real hope of attaining these goals now and we are very grateful to all of the educators who showed him an enormous amount of patience and understanding during his worst times.

Natasha's story: PANS-induced anorexia
Anonymous

"We have to get her anorexia under control *now*," the doctor said.

Hearing this about my nine-year-old daughter Natasha was the most terrifying moment of my life. After dropping the kids off at home with my husband, I went for a late-night grocery shopping trip to restock our kitchen with foods that might possibly tempt our precious daughter to start eating again. All of our healthy eating habits flew out the window; as I pushed my cart up and down the deserted aisles, the doctor's words echoed in my head: "Just get calories into her. You can't let her body go into starvation mode." Before, I had always shopped with so many priorities in mind: pesticide residue, the food pyramid, cost considerations. This time, I grabbed junk food from the shelf and threw it into the cart with abandon—all of those kid-favorite foods that we bought rarely and tried to balance out with vegetables. Six gallons of ice cream? Check. Whipped cream in a spray can? Check. Packaged pudding, sugar cereals? Pringles and snack mix? Check, check, check, and again check.

That night, my kids thought they had hit the junk food jackpot. Over the next few weeks, we gradually became used to a new routine: high-calorie milkshakes with whipped cream as an after-school snack; pancakes and waffles with cream and fruit topping for breakfast every day; bacon, steaks, and cheeseburgers for dinner.

Gradually, Natasha's increasingly restricted eating patterns relaxed; she began to try first one and then another of the tempting foods that she hadn't touched in months, and she began to put on weight for the first time, literally, in a few years. For this, I had several things to thank: not only our new high-calorie smorgasbord, but more importantly, the course of high-dose antibiotics that our doctor had prescribed. It turned out that her anorexia, along with a host of other symptoms we hadn't seen as connected, was caused by an aberrant response to a typical back-to-school strep throat infection, complicated by concurrent mycoplasma and later flu exposure. The PANS diagnosis also explained the sudden changes in handwriting that both she and her brother Gabe, who turned out to have the same diagnosis, had experienced; the failed math tests, unusual for both; the insomnia and night waking that had become part of our routine; the irritability and irrational fears (Natasha once hid from a pizza delivery driver because she was convinced he wanted to shoot her).

Over time, our children recovered, slowly and sometimes inconsistently, and we returned to a more healthful diet as well as a calmer routine. Natasha, more affected than Gabe, still relapses when exposed to someone with strep or even the common cold. With the help of cognitive behavioral therapy, immunomodulatory drugs and continued antibiotics, she has not only regained her body weight but regained her confidence and resilience. She and her brother are adamant that this disorder does not define them—a notion with which I struggle, still shaken by that first day in the doctor's office and, I suspect, still recovering from those confusing and challenging months.

In the past two years, I have learned a tremendous amount about parenting, about mental and physical health (and their interconnectedness), and critically, about the importance of being nonjudgmental—toward children and their parents both. Some days, I feel as though we nearly fell off a cliff, wandering in the dark. Where would either of our kids be, had we not stumbled upon this obscure illness after weeks of late-night Google searches? Suppose we hadn't had the ability to travel to—and pay for—the out-of-insurance-network physician who eventually diagnosed them? What happens to children who never get that diagnosis, who cycle through years of treatments for the wrong illness?

As I hear more stories, I also realize how lucky my kids and I are. Our school was accommodating from the first moment we shared this diagnosis with them. Our kids were given flexibility in attendance and tardiness—our school administrator was adamant that we put their health first, even if it meant missing first period in order to get a healthy breakfast. The same administrator recommended a 504 plan for Natasha, who still utilizes accommodations (extra time, homework flexibility, graphic organizers for writing, and visuals for math) when she's symptomatic. Our school nurse has been supportive and understanding. Natasha's teachers have agreed to let us know if they notice any changes in eating patterns; and when other students are visibly sick, they have agreed to move Natasha away from them, altering small-group assignments or seating assignments if needed. We approached the school, at the beginning of this year, to explain that we were hesitant about returning to school and considering homeschooling. The administrative team immediately set up a meeting so that we could discuss various options with our assistant principal, the school nurse, the school counselor, and the pupil personnel worker. Together, we went through the different options (concurrent home teaching for students with chronic illness; home and hospital teaching for students with significant health issues; homeschooling for families that wanted to leave the public system entirely). I left with a sense of relief and gratitude that our school staff members were so understanding. Our kids are still in school, but I know that, if that ever needs to change, we have a range of options available, and I am grateful that their teachers and school leaders are on board with doing whatever we need to do to help them succeed. That positive, helpful attitude is one of the main reasons our kids are still in school.

Key points to remember

While each of these stories offers its own take-away, several themes emerge that may be useful for education professionals to keep in mind as they seek to understand the experiences, perspectives, and challenges of families whose children have a PANDAS/PANS diagnosis. As McClelland *et al.* (2015) found in their study of families' experiences, receiving a diagnosis of PANDAS/PANS can be marked by fear, a sense of frustration and a sense that professionals are not really hearing their concerns. These findings are echoed in the stories shared here. Some concrete guidelines for teachers working with families are presented below that draw upon the shared experiences presented in these stories:

- *Bear in mind that families' experiences differ.* Each of these stories is as unique as the people in it. While PANDAS/PANS share some central diagnostic features (Chang *et al.* 2015; Swedo, Leckman, and Rose 2012), the way in which these features affect individual children can vary widely. Supports and accommodations that have worked for one child with PANDAS may not meet the needs of other children with the same disorder, depending on the varying presentation of symptoms (Rice Doran and O'Hanlon 2015).

- *Remember that families find themselves under significant stress.* One study several years ago found that mothers of children with autism spectrum disorders demonstrated stress patterns similar to those seen in soldiers in combat (Seltzer *et al.* 2010). While PANDAS/PANS and autism are different disorders, anecdotal evidence and qualitative research have both found that stress levels for parents dealing with this disorder are also high (McClelland *et al.* 2015; Rice Doran and O'Hanlon 2015). Siblings of children with PANDAS/PANS, whose experiences have not been studied in research, are anecdotally reported to be under stress as well (Rice Doran, unpublished manuscript). As challenging as it can be for a parent to experience a child's sudden and violent behavior changes, it can be anticipated to be even more stressful for a child to experience his or her sibling's sudden descent into rages, compulsions, paranoia, or suicidality.

- *Ensure that plans are flexible to accommodate the changing nature of symptoms and performance.* While a child may initially present with anorexia, as in Natasha's story, that symptom may resolve and be replaced by other ones. Academic performance may vary widely as symptom exacerbations occur and then are treated; even attendance patterns may change based on a student's physical health, as in some of the stories shared here. Understanding and flexibility on the part of teachers, and willingness to adapt plans and add supports as needed, can alleviate some of the challenges that accompany these changing symptoms. Allowing children some flexibility in structuring their return to school, for example, or adapting their schedule both fit into this category and may alleviate some of the challenges inherent in returning to a school setting.

- *Communicate frequently and responsively.* As parents have shared their experiences in this chapter, strong communication between school and home, or the lack thereof, emerges as a theme in several narratives. Poor communication can both injure the lasting relationship between families and school personnel and, more importantly, impede a student's ability to receive the support he or she needs. Finding positive comments to make about students, and building on students' strengths in discussions and planning, can help to improve communication.

Implementing a system for frequent updates can also be valuable, whether that be electronic (daily or weekly emails) or more old-fashioned (a communication notebook that goes back and forth between home and school).

- *Differentiate between voluntary and involuntary/unvoluntary behaviors.* In this chapter, one parent reported hearing her son's kindergarten teacher declare she was "done dealing with" her child. Most teachers would agree such a sentiment is unacceptable on the part of teachers, whether voiced to parents or not. However, that comment does reflect the frustration school personnel—particularly general educators without specialized training—may feel as they encounter students with challenging behaviors. Tantrums, school avoidance, extreme OCD, defiance, and rage may all occur regularly with PANDAS/PANS and yet may fall outside the range of behaviors that general educators feel comfortable addressing. It is important to remember such behaviors are likely not voluntary, but rather neurologically driven as a result of encephalitic processes (Chang *et al.* 2015; Lewin *et al.* 2011). This knowledge, in and of itself, may not make it easier to identify the right supports for students—but it should help school personnel craft appropriate support plans without assigning personal blame or assuming ill will on a student's part.

Conclusion

Like many other disabilities, PANDAS/PANS may also present along a spectrum, leading to unique challenges for parents and family members, teachers and other education professionals, and students themselves. Showing awareness of the different experiences families may have, and understanding some of the challenges PANDAS/PANS may present, can help to alleviate some of the stress families may feel throughout their child's illness and can lead to more positive and productive relationships. Chapter 5 describes simple strategies that can be implemented in the general education classroom for students with a PANDAS/PANS diagnosis, and Chapter 6 provides a more extended discussion of strategies for fostering collaborative and positive relationships while planning for students with PANDAS/ PANS. Before that discussion, though, Chapter 4 presents teacher perspectives, offering experiences and advice from teachers familiar with PANDAS/PANS who share their perspectives on effective planning and supports.

References

Bethel, C., Kogan, M., Strickland, B., Schor, E., *et al.* (2011) 'A national and state profile of leading health problems and health care quality for US children: key insurance disparities and across-state variations.' *Academic Pediatrics 11*, 3 Suppl., S22–S33.

Chang, K., Frankovich, J., Cooperstock, M., Cunningham, M.W., *et al.* (2015) 'Clinical evaluation of youth with pediatric acute-onset neuropsychiatric syndrome (PANS): Recommendations from the 2013 PANS Consensus Conference.' *Journal of Child and Adolescent Psychopharmacology 25*, 1, 3–13.

Lewin, A., Storch, E., Mutch, P., and Murphy, T. (2011) 'Neurocognitive functioning in youth with pediatric autoimmune neuropsychiatric disorders associated with streptococcus.' *Journal of Neuropsychiatry and Clinical Neurosciences 23*, 4, 391–398.

Maloney, B. (2009) *Saving Sammy: A Mother's Fight to Cure Her Son's OCD.* New York: Random House.

McClelland, M., Crombez, M., Crombez, C., and Wenz, M. (2015) 'Implications for advanced practice nurses when Pediatric Autoimmune Neuropsychiatric Disorders Associated With Streptococcal Infections (PANDAS) is suspected: A qualitative study.' *Journal of Pediatric Health Care 29*, 5, 442–452.

Rice Doran, P., and O'Hanlon, E. (2015) *Families' Experiences with PANDAS and Related Disorders.* Poster session at Council for Exceptional Children Convention, San Diego, April 2015.

Seltzer, M.M., Greenberg, J., Hong, J., Smith, L., *et al.* (2010) 'Maternal cortisol levels and behaviour problems in adolescents and adults with ASD.' *Journal of Autism and Developmental Disorders 40*, 4, 457–469.

Swedo, S., Leckman, J., and Rose, N. (2012) 'From research subgroup to clinical syndrome: Modifying the PANDAS criteria to describe PANS (Pediatric Acute-onset Neuropsychiatric Syndrome).' *Pediatrics and Therapeutics 2*, 113, 1–8.

Chapter 3

Education Professionals' Voices

Perspectives on PANDAS/PANS

MEGAN DERITTER, M.ED., MELISSA GIAMPIETRO, M.ED.,
ANONYMOUS, AND LAURA COOK, LSW,
EDITED BY PATRICIA RICE DORAN, ED.D
AND MARY CROMBEZ, M.ED.

Introduction

As PANDAS/PANS are relatively new diagnoses within the medical community, they are likewise new within the framework of school special education and educational programming. Education professionals, who may have had extensive training in areas such as autism spectrum disorders or attention-deficit/hyperactivity disorders, often remain unfamiliar with the concept and impact of PANDAS/PANS until they encounter a student who has one of these diagnoses (Rice Doran and O'Hanlon 2015). The process of providing accommodations, then, may cause professionals to feel they are improvising or constantly retrenching; they often need to continue to revise and modify plans as their awareness of the disorder improves or as symptoms change. Precisely because few teachers have extensive experience with these disorders, the voices and experiences of those who do are particularly relevant. As many educators know, field-tested advice from a colleague is often the best professional resource available.

This chapter presents teacher voices. The educators contributing to this chapter have worked with students who have PANDAS/

PANS diagnoses, or disorders with similar symptoms, in a variety of settings: home or home tutoring, general education classroom, special education classroom, related services, or other capacities. Some, though not all, have dual roles as relatives or family friends of children with PANDAS/PANS in addition to their educational expertise. Here, they present their perspectives, and strategies, offering lessons drawn from experience to enrich other teachers' planning and processes.

Organization and communication: Key to student success

Megan DeRitter, M.Ed., Instructional Guide,
Monarch Academy, Glen Burnie, MD

I have worked with several students who have PANDAS or PANS diagnoses. Both experiences varied greatly. During my first experience, I was contacted by our special education coordinator and informed that a new student who had a PANDAS diagnosis would be in my classroom starting in the fall. I knew very little about the diagnosis. This lack of knowledge was also true for our special education coordinator and some of our administration. Before meeting with the family, we all sat down to do our research and learn more about the possible conditions of our new student. Unfortunately, there was very little to be found. With our bit of knowledge related to the autoimmune disorder, we met with the mother and father of the student hoping to learn more. They walked us through their child's previous experience with school and the changes they saw in their child. This brief but detailed meeting gave us a better picture of the child we would be working with.

In my other experience, I became aware of a student's PANDAS diagnosis about halfway through the year. There were some slight changes in behavior, but nothing alarming. It was not until her parent informed me of this new diagnosis that I was aware of it, as my former experience with PANDAS was very different.

Some challenges that have been exhibited in the classroom include problems with participation in whole-group and small-group settings, communication, time management, organization, transitioning, tardiness, and absence. Externally, these challenges may appear to be a struggle for a typical student of any age; however, the challenge for teachers is learning about what is happening internally for the student. These challenges can have a large impact on social development and appropriateness within the classroom, as the students I worked with were not inclined to interact with others or participate in classroom discussions. One student often preferred to work alone and very rarely agreed to work in a group. Some behaviors observed when this student was asked to work in a group included throwing pencils or pens, scribbling on the group work sheets, and other distractions. These behaviors led to peers questioning, and struggling to trust the student in a group setting. When I spoke with the students one on one, they were often quiet and would rarely respond with more than a grunt or shrug of the shoulders. One student began to communicate with me using a note system or limited verbal communication. Finding a way to communicate with the student, within the boundaries of what they felt comfortable, was difficult but very worthwhile.

Transitioning caused quite a bit of anxiety for one student at our school who needed to be escorted by an adult, at different times of the day from her peers, in order to avoid crowds and the anxiety she felt when standing in lines. As she became more comfortable with the school setting this eventually passed, and she was able to join our lines. In the beginning the child would miss the beginning and end of lessons and would also miss the feeling of class unity, being able to walk down the hall with the class.

Organization and time management should be taught to all students, but for our students with PANDAS, these two skills were extremely difficult. Papers could rarely be found, work was not completed or sometimes not even started in the designated time, and it was always an adventure to look in their desk.

As for tardiness and absences, students would regularly miss key parts of the day, causing difficulties with social interactions with peers and understanding grade level content. We did identify some supports and interventions to address these needs. For one of the students, we also put a plan in place for the child to meet her new teacher, and the school psychologist before the first day of school. To make the transition even smoother, the school psychologist also agreed to meet this student outside and walk her into the building on the morning of this first day. Realizing that a whole school day may be too long to reintroduce the student to school, we organized for her to attend for a small portion of the day at first, adding an hour each day as the week progressed. By the second week the student was expected and able to attend for the full school day. With suggestions from the family during our first meeting, I met with the student to discuss our daily schedule and any modifications, ensured teacher proximity, assisted with organization, and provided extended time on assignments.

Another helpful strategy is checking in with the student each day to get a sense of how they are feeling internally. This could just be a simple "How are you?" or a longer conversation about events happening at home or at school. Keeping a routine and daily schedule can help the student know what to expect throughout the day. I also tried to limit transitions for one of the students and differentiated in the classroom as necessary. One strategy I wish I had implemented more often was copying their completed work at the end of each day, so if they did happen to lose it I had a copy of where they left off rather than having to provide a fresh worksheet with nothing completed. Setting a timer is also a great way to help students begin managing their time—but start small, asking them to work and focus for two minutes, then three, and continue building on this. Some students might need the timer right on the desk and others might want you to keep track for them. As mentioned before, proximity is key. Take time to consider where the student should sit on the floor, at the desk, standing in line, and so on. This may reduce anxiety and support focusing. You can even ask the student what he or she prefers.

My biggest bit of advice that I would give to teachers is to talk with the child's parents. Communicate with them, ask them questions, note your observations and share them with parents. I also suggest regularly talking with the student, keeping track of their participation throughout the day, and celebrating it! It is most likely that you are the most trusted person in that room and the one they hope to count on, while peer relationships have taken a back seat. Take the time to build a relationship with the student and his or her family. And always have extra copies of work!

PANDAS as a parent and educator: Dual perspectives

Melissa Giampietro, M.Ed.

As a teacher and an educator, understanding PANDAS and PANS has made me think a lot more about the students I work with. On a macro level, if you have that change in awareness out there, that is a positive thing. In my own classroom, it also gets me thinking about that change in behavior. I will bring that up to parents if I feel that I can. You have to tread really carefully there.

My son has been in a regular public elementary school from first grade through sixth. In kindergarten I had kept him in a full-day kindergarten. He had signs and symptoms of ADHD and we kept him in kindergarten to minimize transition; then he went to elementary school, and finally we ended up putting him in a Montessori school in seventh and eighth grade. He did have special education services in school. The challenge with PANDAS is that it changes at any given moment—the symptoms wax and wane. For my son, there seems to be a disconnect between how these symptoms manifest themselves in school and how they manifest at home. Sometimes the demands are different; sometimes they're higher at home, sometimes at school. His mental state at any given time changes.

I think it's important to have a teacher who is able to be flexible, think on his or her feet, and make the necessary changes at any given moment. As a parent, I try to be very flexible with teachers. Just because it's written in his IEP one way, that doesn't mean it must be that way all the time. It's challenging, because OCD waxes and wanes. There may be some days that you have to throw every tool up your sleeve at this; there may be other days that they can get by and look like everybody else. There were days my son couldn't get out of the parking lot; what's a teacher going to do with that? There were days when he would be literally stuck in the classroom; he could not move to go to gym class. On my son's IEP, we wrote supports in on an as-needed basis, with qualifying terms that operationally define what that means so that it is clear when supports are needed and when they are not. Short of revamping the IEP form in and of itself, I believe that kind of flexibility is needed in writing those documents, as the form and process do not offer the flexibility needed to support a student with PANDAS and PANS. The whole purpose of an IEP is to provide an individualized education. But as most IEPs are written, teachers and schools have to provide supports all the time or risk being out of compliance.

I've been on both sides of the table, as educator and parent. It's really easy to pass judgment and think the parents aren't doing everything possible. The same goes for parents, who may think the teacher is not doing everything in his or her power. In that case, a therapist or facilitator can be a neutral third party and can help get everybody on the same page, speaking to what is in the best interests of the student. Once I had that person come to the IEP meeting, it gave the IEP team a different perspective.

For a long time we tried to accommodate my son's OCD and anxiety by using distraction. We were in a cognitive behavioral therapy (CBT) program that used exposure and response prevention (ERP), which is a completely different mindset from what happens in school. There needs to be tight communication between the child, the parents, and the school, because if you're trying to use a behaviour management technique that isn't compatible with CBT/ERP it will undermine your CBT/ERP. It's going to be a train wreck, in fact. Asking a therapist to put your plan in writing for the IEP team, even if you have to sacrifice a therapy session to have them do that for you, is important, so everyone is on the same page. Often, the therapist can't go to the IEP team meetings, but I was lucky enough to find one who was willing to do it.

For accommodations, I have adopted the idea of "whatever it takes." With a learning disability, there are certain things that work for almost every student. However, with PANDAS or PANS, you don't know what you're going to get on any given day, and so the severity of a student's symptoms and the accommodations needed at any given moment will vary.

For my own son, a hands-on setting, with a small class, is most conducive to his learning style. He has done very well in a Montessori-style program, where he is learning time management skills and receiving guidance but figuring problems out on his own. His IEP is designed to remediate some learning issues, including his decline in math due to PANDAS. There are not many behavioral supports in his IEP, as his school is already doing many of those things for all students.

Reduced stress has been good for my son. It is important for teachers to reduce stress for all students, in fact. You have to find the right place for the child, to match teaching styles with learning styles. If you are really looking at your students as individuals, whether they have PANDAS or PANS, whether they have an allergy or another health impairment, whether they have special education needs or not, there's no one-size-fits-all for anything in education. This may become more difficult, though, when teachers have, for example, 27 students in one classroom. It can become challenging to see each student as an individual when you have so many.

Being a parent of a child with PANDAS, as well as an educator, has affected me. In a sense I am angry about having to write IEPs all the time because part of me thinks that, if we all just did what it took, we wouldn't need the IEP. I also look more acutely at what my own students need when I work with them. PANDAS and PANS are unique; they include a little bit of everything. You could pick almost any disabling condition out of the ones you could possibly qualify a child with, and it would probably fit in some way. How can you possibly write an IEP for that? Today it may be OCD, and tomorrow it may be something else that creates the biggest challenge for that student.

Teachers also need to be aware that there can be post-traumatic stress for parents. My husband is really helpful in dealing with all this. If my son has a tiny flare, it all comes rushing back. When I'm falling apart, I can go and hide and know that my husband has got this covered.

I also believe it is really important to educate people about PANDAS and about disabilities in general. For a child with tics, for example, consider how scary it would be for the other children to hear this child yelling out obscenities. There is a possible role for self-disclosure there, as the child might become empowered by trying to let their classmates know what is going on and what might help.

Schools emphasize attendance, and so some families send their child to school when they are sick. But people don't realize that while your child may be having a fever that can be controlled with ibuprofen and they're okay in school, my child may end up with anxiety or rage because of that exposure. For that reason, educating schools and principals, so that they make parents aware, is important. When there are communicable diseases in school, parents of children with PANDAS or PANS have to know about it so that they can take precautions. It's a lot of work for a teacher to be thinking all the time about PANDAS and PANS. And it is exhausting for the parents, but people don't realize that it's also exhausting for the kids. I look at my son and think, it's got to be really hard for him.

This issue also calls into question how we conceptualize special education as a whole. Since I've been learning about this with my own son, I think about how many kids are in service under psychiatric diagnoses. How many of them might really have a medical disorder that could be treated with antibiotics? If you make this information widely available in a school district, you might avoid a special education referral and thousands of dollars in costs for each child with PANDAS or PANS whom you can identify.

Knowledge, compassion, and understanding: Keys to successful support
Anonymous

In my career as an early childhood special education provider, I have worked with families whose children have required varying degrees of educational support within the "least restrictive environment." However, in recent years, my role has included finding the appropriate services/accommodations for my own child, who has required a 504 plan for neurological impairment that fluctuates substantially throughout any given calendar year. Additionally, I have spent the past few years being present with other parents as a support person and advocate during the process that leads to a diagnosis of PANDAS/PANS or autoimmune encephalitis (AE) (the two are linked and some see PANDAS/PANS as a form of encephalitis). Although each story varies, the differences are often subtle and the similarities striking. Many parents have reported to me that they are stunned to learn of another child saying or doing exactly the same thing as their own, even thousands of miles apart.

Our daughter experienced her first episode of marked dysfunction at the age of seven and a half. It was an overnight, absolute change in personality and function; everything about her was different. In a heartbeat we had to learn to live with a different person. She had to learn to live as someone else. She will tell you she doesn't have much memory of that experience and for that we are grateful. I like to think that her "amnesia" for this period in her life is her brain's way of coping. It helps me to think that perhaps there's a point when your neural network becomes so overloaded that the brain doesn't have a capacity for memory and therefore my child is spared detailed recollections of that terrifying period in her life.

Being both mom and teacher, I was poised to observe the dramatic changes in our daughter from multiple perspectives. The following were some of the educational features that developed immediately: dysgraphia (an inability to write when formerly proficient); decline in math skills; incapacity to read words on a page, or if able to read the words unable to comprehend their meaning despite exhibiting competence just days before. As a parent and teacher, such changes were frightening to observe. Consider this kind of dysfunction from the child's perspective: to lose skills that once were intact, perhaps even effortless, without understanding the neurological changes involved, must be absolutely terrifying! And, unfortunately, reading, writing, and math are not the only skills a child suffering from an infection-triggered immune event may lose. For our child, fine motor skill dysfunction was not limited to using a writing utensil. Despite playing the piano for several years, she was unable to make her fingers move at the keyboard. Practically overnight, she was no longer able to play an established, well-known tune in her repertoire. The same was true for using her fingers to play her violin and double bass in the orchestra. Her frustration and anger were expressed in extreme outbursts, making it exhausting for her and us as well.

With our list of concerns, concrete examples of the losses we'd witnessed, and deep-seated fear, we visited our pediatrician, who had known our daughter for her entire life and was well aware of her baseline function and behavior. She knew she was an athlete (competitive gymnastics, travel soccer, volleyball), musician (pianist, violinist, and bassist in a children's orchestra), engaging friend and family member, and academically competent. I don't reflect on these attributes to appear a braggart. On the contrary, it was the sudden and absolute loss of these defining characteristics that made her illness so profoundly distressing. At the end of a long and emotionally draining appointment, our pediatrician introduced us to an acronym we would loathe yet eventually embrace and even advance through advocacy and support—PANDAS.

We were at a huge advantage because our physician, our frontline resource, knew about PANDAS. At the time, the only treatment option suggested by the National Institutes of Health (NIH) was to see a psychologist. Since it takes weeks to get an initial appointment with a psychologist, and PANDAS presents with a relapsing and remitting course, our daughter was back to baseline, with no treatment of any kind, by the time she was seen by the psychologist. After two visits the psychologist discharged us from her caseload as she could not substantiate a reason for us being there; little did she know we would return nearly four years later.

During that almost-four-year period our daughter actively engaged in all kinds of school and extracurricular pursuits. However, she chose to forgo attending the daily specials/electives provided by the local public school system. She enriched her curriculum with various other school options but in much smaller, reduced class sizes for short periods throughout any given week rather than seven continuous hours per day in a traditional school setting. In hindsight, these more limited interactions may have allowed her immune system extra recovery time between exposure to infection, allowing her to remain symptom-free.

I am not necessarily advocating for children with PANDAS to remain out of school for years at a time. However, I do believe that some children may require considerable time away from the traditional school model to allow their brain to heal while ensuring their faulty immune system is not exposed to additional stress before it is sufficiently stable. For these students, for whom re-exposure in the traditional school milieu is problematic, homebound services should be provided through the public school system. In the best of all worlds, I would advocate for a "clean room concept"—a classroom environment exclusively for students with immune system dysregulation, accommodating their learning in a unique room, perhaps one designed with HEPA (high-efficiency particulate air) filtration, in a particularly quiet space with low lighting, with a purposely limited number of students. Such a structure would not only accommodate the sensory needs of children who present with PANDAS but also protect their immune functioning as well. In addition to having a "clean" classroom with infection-prevention measures in place, students may need to avoid toxic areas (gymnasium, locker room, etc.).

Whether such a room would have helped our daughter, I do not know. Nearly four years would pass before we would witness the next exacerbation of autoimmune encephalitis, preceded by a booster shot at a sports physical which taxed her already-stressed immune system. This exacerbation included disabling OCD, incapacitating sensory sensitivities, intense fight or flight response, emotional lability (including raging anger), separation anxiety (requiring her to be with me at all times), and urinary frequency (which, combined with OCD, yielded hours of bathroom routines each day). Additionally, she discontinued her participation in all activities, including school. She stopped playing the piano, stopped being in the orchestra, stopped being able to read, exhibited dysgraphia, and developed some physical kicking actions that were later identified by her PANDAS physician as adventitious movement.

Eventually, we secured an appointment with a PANDAS specialist and traveled about four hours away seeking medical care and assistance. Our daughter screamed for the entire drive. Her sensory sensitivities were so heightened that despite the 85 degree temperature we could not put the air conditioning on or roll down the windows because of the pain the blowing air created. The drive was sheer torture for her. I can never say this enough: if living with (or teaching) a child with PANDAS is hard, imagine how much worse it is for the child!

So what was her school experience during this period? From September through January she had variable function relative to school work. Some days she could complete some work, other days she could not. By the end of January she was unable to complete school assignments. Her days were spent completing rituals, despite having twice-weekly CBT appointments. Her sleep was so affected that she would remain awake for 36–72 hours at a time, sleep for 2–4 hours, and then repeat the cycle. The brain cannot function on that kind of sleep schedule, so school took a back-burner to simply meeting our child's day-to-day needs—sleep, nutrition…the basics.

So after ten months of symptoms, three months of high-dose antibiotics, multiple blood draws and various doctor's appointments, our daughter received her first IVIG. The following five weeks were a painful exercise in what the leading PANDAS physicians call "turning back the pages." Symptoms came and went with varying degrees of intensity until, at eight weeks post-IVIG, our daughter was able to attend a summer music camp. While there, a 12-day sleepaway camp, she played the piano and engaged socially with peers and adults. Several years prior she had actually won the "Outstanding Camper of the Year" award at this particular camp. To go from being named "Outstanding Camper," to becoming so OCD that basic function is impossible, wearing clothing is painful, and eating and sleeping occur outside of any typical schedule, to attending a camp setting, functioning beautifully—well, that IVIG was a gift of life for our child! I'll never forget the moment I arrived to pick her up that year. She ran to me and she hugged me. It was the first time in many, many months that she was able to touch me, to be in physical contact with anyone. It didn't mean the OCD was gone, but it was at a level where she could touch me. As our daughter has grown she has reported to us that she still had symptoms but attending camp helped her tremendously.

As her symptoms continued to diminish through that summer, our daughter asked to return to public middle school in the fall. The school was a great source of support. She started the year with some OCD while preparing to get ready in the morning, and some compulsive fidgeting with the zipper on her backpack while at school. It wasn't until much later that she informed us that she was bullied in school for that OCD presentation. The school had written a 504 plan proactively in the event of another exacerbation, and in February I called to set those accommodations into motion, as my daughter began to have trouble writing the letters in her name. By the following morning, my daughter was given a laptop. The school was 100 percent on board with the accommodations in her 504. Unfortunately, by the day after that, our daughter was unable to attend school or even complete assignments from home. On my visits to the school, her teachers had tears in their eyes as they told me how saddened they were by her dramatic decline. I was truly grateful for this empathy and compassion from school personnel. School employees and officials seemed to understand that the dysfunction was not purposeful on our child's part, nor could it be addressed by some "good old-fashioned discipline" (something I have heard far too many times from far too many families whose children are suffering from PANDAS/PANS).

We completed another IVIG treatment, and she attempted to attend school the following year (eighth grade) but left in October, saying the level of illness in the classrooms was just more than she could manage. She attended an arts magnet school for one semester of ninth grade on a reduced schedule. She attended for three hours in the morning, went home for a few hours, and then returned for rehearsals in an effort to balance the time spent in that infectious environment. The teachers were able to ensure her health as a priority, and the school accommodated the schedule without difficulty. She completed her core course work as a homeschooled student and completed electives and required graduation credits (in PE and fine arts) through the school system.

The high school did not re-create a 504 to replace the middle school 504. They simply promised that they would make any accommodations necessary. And, in fact, they did. However, this year we learned that that was an unfortunate mistake when we attempted to secure accommodations for our daughter for college placement exams. The College Board required an active 504 in order to provide accommodations despite her physician's lengthy report. For that reason, she was unable to take her exams with accommodations.

As of now, she is enrolled in community college courses as a dually enrolled homeschool student. She has spent many summers making up the work she has missed during the school year as her symptoms often flare considerably during the winter months. We have experienced many different school programs, all willing to work with us to accommodate our child's medical needs. Over time, further testing led to the discovery that our daughter presents with immune dysfunction beyond just the streptococcal issues of PANDAS. She now presents with an elevated ANA (antinuclear antibodies), a key marker for autoimmune disease. Her most recent MRI indicates hyperintensities and a sleep study with EEG indicated multiple sleep anomalies.

Treating for other infections in addition to the strep has produced considerable benefit.

What is remarkable is that she can be so dysfunctional (she can't read, write, or really do anything) when she is in an exacerbation. Yet, when she is functional, she is a successful student, an engaging and kind friend, and a competent young woman. She does say that her brain works differently than it did before PANDAS. She has explained that her brain just doesn't think the same way anymore. She doesn't have the concentration or the focus required for high-level performance. She says, "I think differently than I used to. Now it's a huge process to think and it doesn't seem logical anymore." When she's well she has a very high level of self-awareness. When she is in an exacerbation, I think she still has that self-awareness but she can't always articulate it.

We're among the lucky ones. We have a wonderful support system and no one in our support system has ever been negative about our experience. They have all accepted our medical odyssey and assisted us in any possible way. This includes our medical team and educators as well as family and friends. There are other families who aren't able to speak to their own family members about PANDAS or its impact on their lives.

Knowledge is power, even for young children. At the age of seven our daughter was screaming on the floor, upset and unable to express her frustration. We couldn't talk to her; nothing would help. Then, a few days later, it happened again. This time, she said to me, "I forgot how to write the letter M. I got the first hump but I couldn't write the second one." She could write some letters though, so she actually did an experiment (completely on her own) and she figured out which letters she could write and which she couldn't, and she did that every day until her ability to write letters was gone. Then I explained to her what dysgraphia was. Understanding that she was not alone, that there was a name for what she was experiencing, was a great relief.

Compassion is key. When we completed the 504 plan at the middle school, the counselor never questioned me. I knew what to do because I had the educational background and knew how to approach it. I had a letter from a medical doctor. But a family shouldn't feel in jeopardy of losing their child, or that they are being considered bad parents, because they haven't gone to school due to an exacerbation of PANDAS.

Understanding the system is important as well. My daughter was successful in part because I knew what kind of accommodations to request. Certainly, the writing device was crucial for the dysgraphia, but other accommodations might not be as obvious. At one point my daughter couldn't go to gym; human perspiration in an unventilated gymnasium created a toxic environment for her. The school never balked at this request. In addition, my child could leave a classroom at any time. If her OCD became too intense, if the room got too noisy—she could just stand up and exit. She had three safe places she could safely go, because if your accommodation is to go to the library but when you arrive there it's full of students, it's not a safe place anymore. Another accommodation was the ability to take tests in a quiet, private environment as well as extra time to take a test. As my child is now old enough to attend community college as a dually enrolled high school student, I am impressed with the masterful work completed by the Office of Students with Disabilities at her college. They have developed an exceptional plan that can be altered at a moment's notice.

I do hope that the public school systems can adapt their philosophies to become supportive and compassionate by learning how the system can best meet the needs of children suffering catastrophic neurologic dysfunction. One of the biggest challenges to developing effective accommodations is that the symptoms of PANDAS/PANS fluctuate. My daughter's symptoms look different during each exacerbation, so the accommodations written three months ago may no longer be appropriate yet others may be required. This kind of variability is hard on everyone. The family is in a constant state of flux. The schools feel their accommodations are not working, or the child is not cooperating with the plan, when in fact the symptoms have morphed and different accommodations are needed. I have also found, from working with parents over the years, that educators are often unsure how to address an outburst by a student with PANDAS/PANS. In the event of an outburst, I have found the following to be helpful:

- Do not approach the child or make eye contact. Eye contact and encroaching on the child's personal space triggers the fight or flight reaction, intensifying the outcome rather than defusing it.

- Keep a safe distance, ensuring the child and others are safe, all the while avoiding a confrontation with the child.

- Become trained in non-escalation techniques, or have a colleague who is trained ready to step in.

One additional recommendation is to bear in mind that educators are not medical professionals; rather than questioning or debating a medical diagnosis (as some parents have reported happening), students are best served when we work with the family and healthcare team to help the student succeed in school. Similarly, be sure you are basing decisions on the most recent research. Older research is misleading and controversial, but many new, valid, and reliable studies have been published in the past few years. As a parent and an educator, it is my hope that schools and families will learn to work together to assist children who suffer from PANDAS/PANS without adding to the already considerable burden placed on the child.

The importance of awareness and advocacy
Laura Cook, LSW

I work as a behavior therapist and mobile specialist for children, and in that role I work with two brothers who both have PANDAS/PANS. Their mother is absolutely wonderful in terms of being an advocate for PANDAS/PANS. She's been through the ups and downs of this illness so many times, and so she is able to help, and educate me, when the flare-ups happen. She has also experienced some frustrations with the system; sometimes doctors would dismiss her and say, "This doesn't exist." I believe this disorder exists and is absolutely legitimate; I see a difference in my students when there are a lot of viruses in the school, particularly in late fall. I see them compulsively apologizing, or saying they want to change their behavior and not being able to.

One of the biggest challenges I face is education; not many people know about PANDAS/PANS. One of my students has had difficulty in school for two reasons. These include, first, being ostracized by peers, and, second, having teachers not respond appropriately. His peers call him Anger Boy, and they often know he will have difficulty in certain situations. He is placed in an emotional support classroom, which he does not really like.

In some respects, his teachers also do not know enough about PANDAS/PANS to be able to respond appropriately. For example, he was provided with a point system for behavior, and that further aggravates him because he knows he will not be successful. Recently, I was with him while he was being disciplined for something rather minimal, and it reinforced his belief that he was being treated unfairly because the behavior was really outside his control. As his therapist, I try to explain to him that we have to focus on what we can change.

This year we are still building rapport. The student feels embarrassed by practicing his coping skills, and he's starting to have outbursts more frequently as we get into winter and cold and flu season. He is very self-aware, which is wonderful. Talking through things with him is very therapeutic. He also deals very well with anything physically active. He is a strong student physically; he likes to climb, he likes to run. We sometimes have talk therapy on a playground.

A student with PANDAS may be a real perfectionist, or may doubt himself or herself. With my students, we are still working on the idea that it's okay not to be the best at everything. Sometimes, a student may struggle with schoolwork in terms of rushing through work too fast, or becoming upset or worried if they finish later than everyone else.

In my experience, there is a great sense of advocacy with parents of students who have PANDAS/PANS. They are willing to take the initiative, which is good because the lack of knowledge about this disorder is really unfortunate. I run a supervision group for my organization, and I tell my colleagues about this. I can say, "One of my students has this, and after plasmapheresis, everything was better. Literally the next day everything was different. No delusional thoughts, no rage, everything was gone." In the past I have talked to schools about replacing a behavior chart, for example, with a paragraph about behavior at the end of the day. A student doesn't always need to see the good, the bad, and the ugly along with all the comments.

One classroom I have seen, where students have challenging behaviors that are not necessarily disability-related, has integrated services where a child can, at the drop of a hat, say, "I need to go to the therapists' room," and they just go—it's that simple. Something that fluid would be wonderful for students with PANDAS/PANS, particularly if the teachers were also knowledgeable enough to recognize when a break was needed.

Key points to remember

Perspectives of other educators are particularly important in the case of PANDAS/PANS, where teachers likely have not had the opportunity to learn about the disorder in school or to gain experience working with other students and families dealing with this disability. The accounts of educators provided here, while representing a range of experiences, highlight a few common themes and worthwhile principles to keep in mind:

- Remain nonjudgmental.

- Advocate and build awareness among colleagues.

- Remember that your paradigm and your understanding may be challenged by the presentation of PANDAS/PANS symptoms; have an open mind.

- Be flexible.

- Emphasize communication, organization, and collaboration with families.

Conclusion

Experienced educators, some speaking in their dual roles as parents of children with PANDAS/PANS, provide glimpses in this chapter of day-to-day instruction, and its ups and downs, for children with PANDAS/PANS. They also provide recommendations for strategies and considerations for professionals in similar roles. Finally, they offer ideas about global changes that would make our school system, as a whole, more responsive to the needs of this population. These ideas, and similar ones, are referenced again in the Afterword. Practical strategies for educators supporting students with PANDAS/PANS will be discussed in later chapters, particularly Chapter 5 (PANDAS/PANS in the General Education Classroom) and Chapter 6 (Collaborative Planning for Students with PANDAS/PANS) along with chapters on subsequent academic, sensory, and behavioral accommodations. First, though, Chapter 4 offers a summary of current medical knowledge regarding the diagnosis and treatment of PANDAS/PANS.

Reference

Rice Doran, P., and O'Hanlon, E. (2015) *Families' Experiences with PANDAS and Related Disorders.* Poster session at Council for Exceptional Children Convention, San Diego, April 2015.

Chapter 4

Medical History and Context of PANDAS and PANS

MARGO THIENEMANN, M.D.

To understand PANDAS and PANS, it is necessary to understand a few fundamental concepts about group A beta-hemolytic strep, other infectious triggers, the brain, and the immune system. The following overview provides this context and relates it to issues that may frequently arise for professionals working in a school setting.

Group A beta-hemolytic strep

Group A hemolytic *Streptococcus pyogenes* (GAS) is a ubiquitous human pathogen whose preferred host is school-age children. Because of the dangerous, possibly lethal, aftermath of GAS infection, whereby rheumatic heart disease may develop, schools frequently send home strep letters to inform families of schoolmates' infection with GAS. This book focuses on another rare but serious aftermath of GAS infection, PANDAS (closely related to PANS). As this chapter focuses on the medical explanations of PANDAS, it begins with an introduction to GAS.

GAS is a nimble bacterium, able to evolve into different strains to evade host defenses, survive, and propagate. Infection with particular strains of GAS and changes in population characteristics (crowding, access to effective treatment, natural selection following fatal childhood illness) results in GAS manifesting as different syndromes.

One, Sydenham chorea, a post-GAS movement and psychiatric disorder, was first described in the Middle Ages and still occurs occasionally now. Another, scarlet fever, has varied in its severity over time. While GAS's scarlet fever in eighteenth century Europe and America was a mild illness, the virulent scarlet fever of the nineteenth century caused epidemics that killed as many as 30 percent of the children affected. Between 1910 and 1940, severe scarlet fever mysteriously disappeared, but a different GAS-related illness, heart disease due to acute rheumatic fever (ARF), became the most common killer of youth aged 5–20 years in the U.S. Because of the advent of penicillin (in 1942) and increased awareness and treatment in the U.S., GAS pharyngitis has rarely led to ARF since the 1960s (except for isolated outbreaks at two military bases and in schools). In underdeveloped countries, complications of ARF (rheumatic heart disease, RHD-related endocarditis, and stroke) and invasive GAS diseases continue to kill half a million people per year, ranking GAS among the top ten most common fatal human infections (World Health Organization 2005). Changing its manifestation in the 1980s, necrotizing fasciitis (a flesh-eating bacterial GAS infection reported in the Civil War) and toxic shock syndrome increased in frequency. Perhaps because of GAS strain mutation, perhaps because of changes in antibiotic use, tonsillectomies, or other human factors, the latest evolution of GAS infection complication is PANDAS.

Of all sore throats (pharyngitis) in children aged 5–15 years, GAS causes about 25 percent, usually termed "strep throat," (viruses cause the remainder). GAS pharyngitis symptoms include sore throat, swollen tonsils and lymph nodes, abdominal pain, nausea, vomiting, stomach ache, fever, and rashes (including perianal or perineal rashes). Alternatively, symptoms of strep throat can often be minimal; infection often goes unidentified and patients recover (or suffer complications) without seeking medical care, increasing the risk of subsequent complications.

GAS infection most often follows exposure to airborne droplets from an infected person. A newly infected person is usually asymptomatic for 2–5 days. If detected, GAS pharyngitis is treated with a course of penicillin or amoxicillin in children and symptoms resolve within several days. If treated with antibiotics, those with GAS pharyngitis remain contagious for up to 24–48 hours. If untreated, GAS pharyngitis symptoms can last 10–12 days, risking transmission to others and complications (such as ARF).

Diagnosis of Group A Streptococcus (GAS)

Diagnosing GAS pharyngitis depends on identifying GAS in the throat. Most frequently, primary care providers perform an in-office rapid throat swab test for a GAS antigen. That test can miss up to 30 percent of infections. Culturing the material gained by swabbing the throat identifies infection definitively. Clinicians may also order lab work to identify "strep" titer levels (anti-GAS antibodies in the blood). These titers collected at different times can detect the *stage* of the immune system's antibody response to GAS infection, but one set of titers does not diagnose GAS (or PANDAS). The diagnosis of GAS pharyngitis may be missed (1) if the throat is not swabbed "aggressively" (on the back of the throat or on the tonsils); (2) if only the in-office rapid-strep test is used; or (3) if one checks only one set of strep titers rather than monitoring for change in titer levels, as most children and adolescents have been exposed to GAS at some time and show "positive" titers, and some children fail to make the antibodies that are checked. The term "strep carrier" describes the 20 percent of adults and children in whom GAS lives but does not cause symptoms or an antibody response. It is not certain that this carrier state is completely benign (Murphy *et al.* 2007). To prevent ARF, GAS infection must be treated. When close contacts of someone who has had post-streptococcal complications are carriers, they should be treated, too.

Human immune response

Our immune systems constantly scan cells and molecules in our bodies, detecting, removing and destroying foreign material such as bacteria, viruses, and cancer cells. The system causes an immediate, non-specific inflammatory reaction (the innate immune system) that you might see as the redness and swelling soon after getting a splinter. The immune system also has a delayed specific response (the adaptive immune system) in which it manufactures proteins (immunoglobulins) that label specific foreign material (molecules called antigens) for destruction. Immunizations rely on this response, exposing us to material so that we produce antibodies, and cells remember how to attack that material if we are exposed later. Nearly a dozen different types of cells, five types of immunoglobulins, and numerous molecules, including cytokines, complement, and cell surface markers, work together to defend against the constant internal and external assault of everything that is not "us."

Amazingly and generally, healthy innate and adaptive immune systems work together and keep us well. However, immune system deficiencies and clever pathogen adaptation can interfere with our abilities to eliminate infections and cancer cells. As well, our immune system can overreact, as is the case in allergic and anaphylactic reactions and in auto-inflammatory and autoimmune disorders. In allergies, the system over-produces the type of immunoglobulin that stimulates itching and hives. In autoimmune disorders, the system's ability to distinguish "self" from "non-self" malfunctions and the immune system attacks its own body.

GAS and the immune system

In those with healthy immune systems, when a pathogen such as GAS enters the body, the body initiates a local inflammation (innate immunity) and signals other parts of the immune system that GAS has invaded. Within days, the adaptive immune system is manufacturing antibodies designed to stick to the GAS, labeling it as bacteria to be destroyed (Cunningham 2012). When certain immune cells "see" enough antibodies attached to a bacterium, the immune system kills it and cleans up the mess. The innate immune system then has learned to recognize GAS and is ready to muster up a response when GAS reappears.

Unfortunately in some people, and likely with some specific strains of GAS, the immune system malfunctions and attacks normal, healthy tissues. In ARF, antibodies attach to proteins and carbohydrates on heart muscle and heart valve tissue that "looks" (to the antibodies) like the proteins and carbohydrates on the surface of GAS. This unlucky mistaken identity is called *molecular mimicry*. Antibodies on heart tissue initiate an autoimmune reaction that harms the heart. Each time the individual has another GAS infection, the immune system kicks into action, leading to further heart damage. In people who have had the post-GAS autoimmune disorder ARF, treating and preventing GAS infections is critical to prevent heart disease, heart failure, and death.

The autoimmune reaction associated with ARF may also cause joint inflammation (rheumatic arthritis) and Sydenham chorea (SC). In SC, antibodies to GAS found in the blood can attach to nerve cells in the brain's basal ganglia, limbic system, and cortex, leading to inflammation which may change nerve function (Brimberg *et al.* 2012; Dale 2005; Dale *et al.* 2012; Kirvan *et al.* 2006; Macri *et al.* 2015). Children with SC experience an array of motor, emotional, and sensory symptoms. Motor symptoms include chorea (uncontrollable, purposeless, non-rhythmic, abrupt, rapid and unsustained writhing movements that occur while awake), ballismus (forceful flying out of limbs), facial grimacing, difficulty with fine motor activities such as writing, low muscular tone and weakness, and dysarthric or explosive speech (Wei and Wang 2013). Children with SC also suffer from obsessive compulsive symptoms (over 70% of patients), extreme moodiness, separation anxiety, psychotic symptoms, inattention, and hyperactivity (Swedo *et al.* 1993; Swedo *et al.* 1997). This syndrome has similarities to PANDAS, described below.

Months elapse between GAS infection and the onset of SC (Swedo 1994). Treatment consists of treating GAS infection and rest. An SC episode typically resolves in less than a year, but symptoms may recur with environmental stress, GAS, or other infections. Diagnosing SC and rheumatic arthritis are important as their presence signals ARF and the necessity of treatment of GAS to prevent heart damage.

Because each additional GAS infection risks activating the autoimmune process and furthering cardiac damage, children who have had ARF must continue to be treated with prophylactic antibiotic treatment for years (Armstrong 2010). Biweekly shots with penicillin are the most protective (and painful) regimen, but faithfully adhering to that regimen is more successful than penicillin twice per day, as missing a single dose increases vulnerability to GAS infection for four days.

In summary, GAS pharyngitis is a common childhood illness that, in vulnerable individuals, may initiate an autoimmune reaction.

Post-GAS autoimmune reactions can affect a variety of organ systems, including the brain.

When the autoimmune reaction involves the heart, long-term antibiotic treatment is necessary to prevent future GAS infections and additional damage. After an episode of ARF, other stressors, including other infections, may reactivate the autoimmune process.

PANDAS

When studying children with childhood-onset OCD or SC, researchers at the NIMH noted that, in each group, in some children obsessive-compulsive symptoms and/or tics started *abruptly*, *dramatically*, and *severely*. In these children symptoms improved and worsened over time in a saw-toothed pattern. They wondered whether, like SC, some early-onset OCD stemmed from an autoimmune process. Therefore, they recruited 50 children whose OCD or tics began suddenly, or worsened suddenly and significantly, within six weeks after a GAS infection. None of the children qualified for the diagnosis of ARF or SC. Many parents could pinpoint the day and time the symptoms started. The average subject was aged seven years, more frequently male, and severely impaired. In addition to tics or OCD, the children suffered from marked moodiness and rages, separation anxiety day and night, age-inappropriate behavior, and night-time difficulties. Surprising symptoms of handwriting deterioration, enuresis (wetting day and night), and encopresis (incontinence of feces) were observed.

The group proposed the name Pediatric Autoimmune Neuropsychiatric Disorders Associated with Streptococcal Infections (PANDAS) to describe this syndrome. PANDAS shared some common elements with SC, such as GAS history, OCD, and neurological changes, but PANDAS symptoms differed from those of SC by starting sooner and more dramatically after infection, exhibiting a different movement disorder and lacking associated ARF symptoms (Swedo et al. 1998). Since its description, PANDAS has been the subject of energetic research and active controversy. Researchers have further characterized the disorder and have developed animal models. Reviewing the evidence, it appears that in some individuals (whose characteristics have not been defined by research) GAS infection (perhaps by certain strains) results in immune system activation such that brain tissue is affected, causing the behavioral and motor symptoms of PANDAS.

PANS

Concern developed that children with OCD and tics *not* due to PANDAS might be misdiagnosed and inappropriately treated with antibiotics or therapies to affect the immune system. Singer and colleagues observed that a variety of infections had been reported to precede PANDAS-like symptoms in children, including *Borrelia burgdorferi*, herpes simplex virus, varicella zoster virus (VZV), human immunodeficiency virus (HIV), *Mycoplasma pneumoniae*, flu, and the common cold. They proposed that the entity PANDAS be dropped and replaced by CANS (Childhood Acute Neuropsychiatric Symptoms), a diagnosis requiring an explosive onset of defined symptoms similar to those described in PANDAS patients but without a specified cause (Singer *et al.* 2012). In attempting to address these concerns, researchers and clinicians (Swedo, Leckman, and Rose 2012) met and defined another new syndrome, Pediatric Acute-Onset Neuropsychiatric Syndrome (PANS).

PANS differs from PANDAS in its definition of cardinal symptoms, which can present as OCD or significantly restricted food intake, not OCD or tics as required in the PANDAS diagnostic criteria. Both definitions require that the illness onset be sudden and severe and require concurrent presence of at least two of the following: anxiety, emotional lability and/or depression, irritability, aggression and/or severely oppositional behaviors, behavioral (developmental) regression, deterioration in school performance (inattention, restlessness, diminution of math or visual-spatial skills, sensory or motor abnormalities), and somatic signs and symptoms, including sleep disturbances, enuresis, or urinary frequency. Sensory issues manifest as intolerance to noise, light, textures, smells, and tastes, and they may significantly interfere with daily life. Food restriction may follow from these sensitivities, from relative difficulty swallowing, from typical eating disorder concerns, or from OCD symptoms, such as fear of outdated food. Diagnostic criteria for PANS are listed in Table 4.1.

Table 4.1 Diagnostic criteria for PANS (adapted from NIMH 2015)

1. Abrupt, dramatic onset of obsessive-compulsive disorder (including severely restricted food intake)

2. Concurrent presence of additional neuropsychiatric symptoms, with similarly severe and acute onset, from at least two of the following seven categories:

- Anxiety (particularly, separation anxiety)
- Emotional lability (extreme mood swings) and/or depression
- Irritability, aggression, and/or severely oppositional behaviors
- Behavioral (developmental) regression (e.g., talking baby talk, throwing temper tantrums, etc.)
- Deterioration in school performance
- Sensory or motor abnormalities
- Somatic signs and symptoms, including sleep disturbances, bedwetting, or urinary frequency.

3. Symptoms are not better explained by a known neurologic or medical disorder, such as Sydenham chorea, systemic lupus erythematosus, Tourette disorder, or others

Note: The diagnostic work-up of patients suspected of PANS must be comprehensive enough to rule out these and other relevant disorders. The nature of the co-occurring symptoms will dictate the necessary assessments, which might include MRI scan, lumbar puncture, or electroencephalogram (EEG) in some cases. More often, laboratory studies will be warranted and should include tests to determine if there is a current infection or ongoing immunologic dysfunction.

Reviewing the evidence, it appears that in some individuals (whose characteristics have not been defined by research), GAS infection (perhaps by certain strains) results in immune system activation such that brain tissue is affected, causing the behavioral and motor symptoms of PANDAS.

Agreeing on criteria for PANS allows researchers to investigate a defined population, hoping to lead to information about the mechanisms of, and treatments for, PANS and other mental health, neurological, and rheumatologic conditions.

Assessment
Clinical history

The medical and psychiatric history of the child's illness establishes the diagnosis of PANS/PANDAS. A history of frequent upper respiratory infections (sore throats, earaches, sinusitis), scarlet fever (blotchy red sandpapery rash that accompanies streptococcal infections), episodic tics, OCD, or overly frequent urination may be clues to a PANS/ PANDAS presentation. A very dramatic and severe development of anxiety, OCD, and tics within 1–2 days is another clue. A recent exposure to others who had been ill is suggestive of a possible trigger but is not conclusive.

Identification of GAS

For children with new onset symptoms, a throat culture will provide useful information and direct treatment of the infection, which will likely lead to tic or OCD improvement. Testing for influenza or *Mycoplasma pneumoniae* may also be indicated by the child's medical presentation.

Streptococcal antibody tests

A high titer does not mean that the child has PANDAS, and a low titer does not rule out PANDAS. A significant change in titer indicates that a GAS infection and a resulting immune reaction has occurred, but does not prove PANDAS either. Commonly used antibodies tested in commercial laboratories are anti-streptolysin O (ASO) and anti-deoxyribonuclease B (anti-DNase). In very young children and children with immune system deficiencies, antibodies may not be elevated. Elevations of these antibodies do not mean that the child has a current/active streptococcal infection but indicate that a GAS infection occurred at some point weeks to months earlier.

Medical evaluation

The primary care provider must obtain a detailed history to rule out other medical causes for emotional and behavioral changes. Specialists such as child psychiatrists, neurologists, cardiologists, rheumatologists, immunologists, infectious disease specialists, psychologists, and otolaryngologists may need to be consulted to rule out other disorders that may cause neurological, psychiatric, and other physical symptoms. A child with a very severe sudden onset of anxiety, tics, and heart murmur should be referred to a cardiologist to evaluate for, and rule out rheumatic carditis of ARF. The same is true of children with painful joints, who should be referred to a rheumatologist. The PANS consortium has published recommendations for evaluation of these children (Chang *et al.* 2015).

Treatment
Acute treatment for GAS
The first step in treating children with PANDAS is identifying and treating any infection. For treating all GAS pharyngitis, the American Academy of Pediatrics (AAP) and the American Heart Association (AHA) recommend penicillin as first-line treatment, with the AAP suggesting once-daily dosing of amoxicillin for ease of administration. Sinus infections, ear infections, and pneumonia must be treated with appropriate antibiotics. Children's symptoms may improve within days of starting antibiotics (Murphy and Pichichero 2002), suggesting that antibiotics may also help by modulating the immune response in addition to eliminating the bacterial infection (Obregon *et al.* 2012).

Prophylactic antibiotics for GAS
Repeated GAS infections place a child at risk for PANS recurrence and accelerating severity of symptoms on recurrence. One study found that PANDAS patients receiving preventative antibiotics (antibiotic prophylaxis for one year with either penicillin or azithromycin) had fewer GAS infections and fewer PANDAS recurrences (Garvey *et al.* 2005). The American Heart Association endorses penicillin prophylaxis for those with ARF for a minimum of 10 years and, depending on the case, sometimes for one's entire life (Gerber *et al.* 2009).

Tonsillectomy
Tonsillectomy may be indicated for individuals who have had frequent and severe pharyngitis and for those with sleep disorders due to large tonsils. While a number of case reports have noted improvement of and resolution of PANDAS symptoms following tonsillectomy, there is inadequate evidence to support tonsillectomies in every PANDAS

or PANS patient (Murphy *et al.* 2013). Since the 1960s, the rate of tonsillectomies has decreased dramatically.

Immune modulatory treatments

Clinically and anecdotally, over-the-counter anti-inflammatory medications (non-steroidal anti-inflammatory drugs (NSAIDs) such as ibuprofen and naproxen) have led to improvement of PANS/PANDAS symptoms in some children. Side effects may include stomachaches and, with long-term use, renal dysfunction. When allergies predispose children to infection, allergy medications may be helpful, too.

Two treatments used to treat other immune disorders, intravenous pooled immunoglobulin infusion (IVIG) and plasmapheresis (or plasma exchange), have been studied preliminarily in a small number of children with PANS/PANDAS. In IVIG treatment, purified immunoglobulins from many healthy individuals are given intravenously over many hours. This treatment is approved and indicated for several pediatric conditions, including common variable immunodeficiency (CVID), which has co-occurred with PANS in some cases. More common side effects include headache, flu-like symptoms, aseptic meningitis, blood vessel obstruction, and hemolysis. In plasmapheresis, blood is sent through a machine that separates blood cells from the rest of the blood (i.e., the plasma that contains, among other things, immunoglobulins) then returns the blood without the plasma and with a plasma substitute. Side effects from plasmapheresis may include low blood pressure, fluid-electrolyte imbalance, muscle cramps, paresthesia (tingling or prickling), pneumothorax (air between the lung and chest wall, leading to collapsed lung), blood clots in the blood vessels; and infection, immune system suppression, and bleeding due to using an anticoagulant. Each of these treatments can be especially challenging with a very sensitive and often agitated child, who must be in the hospital and remain still for the treatments for long periods of time. Despite the risks and difficulties, some children have improved significantly with these treatments.

One study compared plasma exchange (every other day for five days), IVIG infusion (over two days), and a placebo treatment in 30 children with PANDAS (Perlmutter *et al.* 1999). OCD, anxiety, depression, and tics improved in the plasma exchange and IVIG groups when measured at one month and at one year. At the time of this writing, however, adequate research aimed at establishing the exact indications for, effectiveness of, and optimal dosing and optimal timing of these treatments is absent. Obtaining insurance company approval for these expensive treatments is difficult, as well. Treatment with corticosteroids is an acceptable helpful treatment in SC and some other autoimmune disorders, but their use has not been studied in PANS or PANDAS. Research in the future will test additional treatments affecting the immune system.

Pharmacotherapy

The most effective medications for PANS are the ones that treat infection and inflammation. Few reports are available to suggest helpful psychiatric medication treatment for PANS. Case reports have described the usefulness of selective serotonin reuptake inhibiting antidepressants (SSRIs, fluoxetine and citalopram) and an atypical antipsychotic (risperidone) in adolescents with PANDAS (Coffey and Wieland 2007; Gabbay and Coffey 2003). One case report and anecdotal reports suggest that patients with PANDAS are particularly prone to the SSRI side effect of behavioral activation (which the patients already have), suggesting that one should begin with low doses and increase slowly (Murphy, Storch, and Strawser 2006).

In our experience in a PANS clinic, in general, using psychiatric medication to treat children's symptoms does improve symptoms as much as might be expected for children with the same symptoms not caused by PANS. However, children with PANS are more prone to side effects. Diphenhydramine (Benadryl) and melatonin may help sleep. Benzodiazepines (such as lorazepam) appear to be helpful for anxiety, agitation, and sleep symptoms.

Cognitive Behavioral Therapy (CBT)

CBT is a powerful therapy proven helpful for anxiety, OCD and depression in children. In CBT, one examines one's thoughts, emotions, and behaviors, works to think realistic thoughts, and tries to actively approach situations rather than avoiding them or doing a ritual to cope. These strategies help to desensitize oneself from anxiety. Participation in this anxiety-provoking work, CBT, requires motivation, either by a belief that the therapy will help or by a reward that the patient finds commensurate to the suffering. Rewarding effort, not bribing, is part of the therapy and rewards need not be material. In one study, even children with PANDAS-related OCD were treated with 14 sessions of family-based CBT over three weeks. Most were improved at the study's end and at the three-month follow-up (Storch *et al.* 2006). For children not presenting with extreme symptoms, evidence does support engaging children with PANDAS and their families in CBT for OCD. The child's symptoms may fluctuate with PANDAS flares, and it may appear that the ground gained doing CBT has been lost. However, clinical experience suggests that when the child is emotionally and cognitively available for a "teaching moment," the knowledge about CBT strategies and improvement in symptoms gained previously will return.

Whatever the status of the patient in his or her saw-toothed course of illness, it is useful for parents to become expert in both CBT and understanding behavior modification using strategies such as monitoring, ignoring, and rewarding behaviors. While it may be outside the scope of educators' knowledge and roles to become "expert" in these areas, it is essential for school staff to gain at least a working knowledge of how CBT works and to actively support students who may be participating in it. Frequent and proactive communication with parents, and with therapists where feasible, is important in this process. When possible, teachers and other school professionals should take particular care that reward and behavior management systems implemented in school are not in direct conflict with the goals of a student's CBT treatment, as such conflict is likely to confuse the student and result in reduced effectiveness for all strategies and therapies. For instance, if stopping hand-washing at school is part of the CBT plan, excusing the child from class to wash hands would work counter to the plan.

Course of illness

At this time, little research has been accomplished studying the course of PANS prospectively. Most children's PANS symptoms start at between seven and nine years of age and for most, unfortunately, some years have elapsed between symptom onset and diagnosis. Proximity to other children in classrooms, and the state of a child's immune system competence, increases the risk for infection. This does not mean that children with PANS should not attend school. It does mean that school staff, students, and parents need to be informed of the risk of GAS and of appropriate hand-washing technique. Treating physicians should inform school staff of the PANS diagnosis and suggested accommodations (see Appendix A for a sample letter).

Those children who meet diagnostic criteria have had a sudden, severe onset of symptoms, but careful examination of pediatric records may reveal episodes of infection followed by behavioral or emotional changes. Looking back, parents often report that their children have had many exacerbations or recurrences (flares) of PANS symptoms, precipitated by illnesses and other stressors. Some children appear to outgrow the recurrences, but the proportion of those has not been established. Some individuals return to their baseline function and some are left with residual symptoms of tics, OCD, anxiety, motor dysfunction, ADHD, sensory amplification issues, and cognitive dysfunctions.

When children and adolescents are in a flare, they are severely ill. Many miss school for a week or more; a proportion of these do not return to school or return with accommodations which are necessary for their participation. Often a parent has taken a leave of absence from work or quit work as a result of the child's illness. In our study, parents reported a higher stress level than that seen in parents of children with cancer (Frankovich *et al.* 2015). Interestingly, children often report that they do not remember much about the flares, but parents often report feeling traumatized by the fears that they have "lost a child" to the illness, by the difficulty in obtaining diagnosis and treatment (which may include being discounted by professionals unfamiliar with PANS/PANDAS), and by the difficulty of managing their child during the emotional and behavioral storm of PANS.

Key points to remember

In particular, school personnel should be mindful of the following considerations:

- Proper hand-washing technique should be reviewed with all school personnel and with classmates of students who have PANS/PANDAS. Frequent hand-washing, throughout the school day, may decrease the risk of exposure to infection.

- Children with PANS/PANDAS may have increased absences from school, due to infections and to recurrence of PANS/PANDAS symptoms following infection. The complexity of the underlying disorder may also lead to more frequent absences for physician appointments, therapy sessions, laboratory tests, and the like.

- In planning classroom seating arrangements and activities, school personnel should be mindful of the risks of exposure to infection for students with PANS/PANDAS. Additional precautions may include preferential seating for these students, wiping down desks and classroom surfaces between classes, and adjusting student groups so that students with PANS/PANDAS are not sitting in close proximity to peers who appear to be sick and potentially contagious (i.e., frequently coughing, sneezing, or sniffling).

- To the extent it is feasible and authorized by parents, frequent and open communication with a student's healthcare team may help school personnel to better understand symptoms and plan for any health-related issues that may arise.

Conclusion

PANS/PANDAS result from immune system dysfunction and can be triggered by infection with (or exposure to) GAS and other illnesses including influenza, mycoplasma, and the common cold. Given the complexity of presenting symptoms, it is essential for school personnel to have a basic understanding of these disorders: the typical course and symptoms associated with flares, the related stressors for children and families, and the health issues associated with school attendance for children with PANS/PANDAS.

References

Armstrong, C. (2010) 'AHA Guidelines on prevention of rheumatic fever and diagnosis and treatment of acute streptococcal pharyngitis.' *American Family Physician 81*, 3, 346–359.

Brimberg, L., Benhar, I., Mascaro-Blanco, A., Alvarez, K., *et al.* (2012) 'Behavioral, pharmacological, and immunological abnormalities after streptococcal exposure: a novel rat model of Sydenham chorea and related neuropsychiatric disorders.' *Neuropsychopharmacology 37*, 9, 2076–2087.

Chang, K., Frankovich, J., Cooperstock, M., Cunningham, M.W., *et al.* (2015) 'Clinical evaluation of youth with pediatric acute-onset neuropsychiatric syndrome (PANS): Recommendations from the 2013 PANS Consensus Conference.' *Journal of Child and Adolescent Psychopharmacology 25*, 1, 3–13.

Coffey, B., and Wieland, N. (2007) 'Tics, anxiety, and possible PANDAS in an adolescent.' *Journal of Child and Adolescent Psychopharmacology 17*, 4, 533–538.

Cunningham, M. (2012) 'Streptococcus and rheumatic fever.' *Current Opinion in Rheumatology 24*, 4, 408.

Dale, R.C. (2005) 'Post-streptococcal autoimmune disorders of the central nervous system.' *Developmental Medicine and Child Neurology 47*, 11, 785–791.

Dale, R.C., Merheb, V., Pillai, S., Wang, D., *et al.* (2012) 'Antibodies to surface dopamine-2 receptor in autoimmune movement and psychiatric disorders.' *Brain 135*, 1–16.

Frankovich, J., Thienemann, M., Pearlstein, J., Crable, A., *et al.* (2015) 'Multidisciplinary clinic dedicated to treating youth with pediatric acute-onset neuropsychiatric syndrome: presenting characteristics of the first 47 consecutive patients.' *Journal of Child and Adolescent Psychopharmacology 1*, 38–47.

Gabbay, V., and Coffey, B. (2003) 'Obsessive-Compulsive disorder, Tourette's disorder, or pediatric autoimmune neuropsychiatric disorders associated with Streptococcus in an adolescent? Diagnostic and therapeutic challenges.' *Journal of Child and Adolescent Psychopharmacology 13*, 3, 209-12.

Garvey, M., Snider, L., Leitman, S., Werden, R., and Swedo, S. (2005) 'Treatment of Sydenham chorea with intravenous immunoglobulin, plasma exchange, or prednisone.' *Journal of Child Neurology 20*, 5, 424–429.

Gerber, M., Baltimore, R., Eaton, C., Gewitz, M., *et al.* (2009) 'Prevention of rheumatic fever and diagnosis and treatment of acute Streptococcal pharyngitis: a scientific statement from the American Heart Association Rheumatic Fever, Endocarditis, and Kawasaki Disease Committee of the Council on Cardiovascular Disease in the Young, the Interdisciplinary Council on Functional Genomics and Translational Biology, and the Interdisciplinary Council on Quality of Care and Outcomes Research: endorsed by the American Academy of Pediatrics.' *Circulation 119*, 11, 1541–1551.

Kirvan, C., Swedo, S., Snider, L., and Cunningham, M. (2006) 'Antibody-mediated neuronal cell signaling in behavior and movement disorders.' *Journal of Neuroimmunology 179*, 1–2, 173–179.

Macri, S., Ceci, C., Proietti Onori, M., Invernizzi, R.W., *et al.* (2015) 'Mice repeatedly exposed to Group-A β-Haemolytic Streptococcus show perseverative behaviors, impaired sensorimotor gating, and immune activation and rostral diencephalon.' *Scientific Reports 5*, 13257.

Murphy, M., and Pichichero, M. (2002) 'Prospective identification and treatment of children with pediatric autoimmune neuropsychiatric disorder associated with group A streptococcal infection (PANDAS).' *Archives of Pediatrics and Adolescent Medicine 156,* 4, 356–361.

Murphy, T., Lewin, A., Parker-Athill, E., Storch, E., *et al.* (2013) 'Tonsillectomies and adenoidectomies do not prevent the onset of pediatric autoimmune neuropsychiatric disorder associated with group A streptococcus.' *Pediatric Infectious Disease Journal 32,* 8, 834–838.

Murphy, T., Snider, L., Mutch, P., Harden, E., *et al.* (2007) 'Relationship of movements and behaviors to Group A Streptococcus infections in elementary school children.' *Biological Psychiatry 61,* 3, 279–284.

Murphy, T., Storch, E., and Strawser, M. (2006) 'Selective serotonin reuptake inhibitor-induced behavioral activation in the PANDAS subtype.' *Primary Psychiatry 13,* 8, 87.

National Institute of Mental Health (NIMH) (2015) *Diagnostic Criteria for PANS.* Available at www.nimh.nih.gov/labs-at-nimh/research-areas/clinics-and-labs/pdnb/web.shtml, accessed on 3 March 2016.

Obregon, D., Parker-Athill, E., Tan, J., and Murphy, T. (2012) 'Psychotropic effects of antimicrobials and immune modulation by psychotropics: implications for neuroimmune disorders.' *Neuropsychiatry 2,* 4, 331–343.

Perlmutter, S., Leitman, S., Garvey, M., Hamburger, S., *et al.* (1999) 'Therapeutic plasma exchange and intravenous immunoglobulin for obsessive-compulsive disorder and tic disorders in childhood.' Lancet 354, 9185, 1153-1158

Perlmutter, S., Leitman, S., Garvey, M., Hamburger, S., *et al.* (1999) 'Therapeutic plasma exchange and intravenous immunoglobulin for obsessive-compulsive disorder and tic disorders in childhood.' *Lancet 354,* 9185, 1153–1158.

Singer, H., Gilbert, D., Wolf, D., Mink, J., *et al.* (2012) 'Moving from PANDAS to CANS.' *Journal of Pediatrics 160,* 5, 725–731.

Storch, E., Murphy, T., Geffken, G., Mann, G., *et al.* (2006) 'Cognitive-behavioral therapy for PANDAS-related obsessive-compulsive disorder: Findings from a preliminary waitlist controlled open trial.' *Journal of the American Academy of Child and Adolescent Psychiatry 45,* 10, 1171–1178.

Swedo, S. (1994) 'Sydenham's chorea. A model for childhood autoimmune neuropsychiatric disorders.' *Journal of the American Medical Association, 272,* 22, 1788–91.

Swedo S., Leckman, J., and Rose, N. (2012) 'From research subgroup to clinical syndrome: Modifying the PANDAS criteria to describe PANS (Pediatric Acute-onset Neuropsychiatric Syndrome).' *Pediatrics and Therapeutics 2,* 113, 1–8.

Swedo, S., Leonard, H., Casey, B., Mannheim, G., *et al.* (1993) 'Sydenham chorea: physical and psychological symptoms of St Vitus dance.' *Pediatrics 91,* 4, 706–713.

Swedo, S., Leonard, H., Garvey, M., Mittleman, B., Allan, A., *et al.* (1998) 'Pediatric autoimmune neuropsychiatric disorders associated with streptococcal infections: clinical description of the first 50 cases.' *American Journal of Psychiatry 155,* 2, 264-71. Erratum in *American Journal of Psychiatry 1998 155,* 4, 578.

Swedo, S., Leonard, H., Mittleman, B., Allen, A., *et al.* (1997) 'Identification of children with pediatric autoimmune neuropsychiatric disorders associated with streptococcal infections by a marker associated with rheumatic fever.' *American Journal of Psychiatry 154*, 1, 110–112.

Wei, F., and Wang, J. (2013) 'Sydenham chorea, or St. Vitus's dance.' *New England Journal of Medicine 369*, e25. Available at www.nejm.org/doi/full/10.1056/NEJMicm1303705, accessed on 3 March 2016.

World Health Organization (2005) *The Current Evidence for the Burden of Group A Streptococcal Diseases.* Geneva: WHO.

Chapter 5

PANDAS/PANS in the General Education Classroom

Creating a Brain-Friendly Learning Environment[1]

DARLENE FEWSTER, ED.D., AND PATRICIA RICE DORAN, ED.D.

Cindy, seven, was diagnosed with PANS when she experienced an onset of tantrums, anxiety, and restricted eating following a bout of flu in the spring of first grade. In addition to these behavioral symptoms, Cindy's class performance deteriorated; she was no longer able to write her name, and she could not finish simple addition problems that she had mastered months before. In class, Cindy would sometimes cower under her desk, hands over her ears, or curl up and try to get into the cubby where she was supposed to place her backpack and coat each morning. Cindy's teacher consulted her cooperating special educator and initiated a referral for evaluation to see if Cindy qualified for an IEP.

At the same time, the teacher asked multiple colleagues—the occupational therapist, school counselor, special educator, and other veteran first-grade teachers—how to make the classroom more accessible, and less anxiety-producing, for Cindy. Together, the team identified some simple fixes: providing sensory seat cushions, dimming the lighting slightly, and incorporating frequent stretches and brain breaks for all learners. Cindy's teacher made sure to alternate highly demanding activities with less demanding, more enjoyable ones throughout the day. While benefiting Cindy in particular, these fixes also helped several other students relax and perform better during the day. Even as Cindy's health improved and her PANS symptoms abated, her teacher kept these improvements in place for the entire class and saw improvements in many students' attention, behavior, and academic performance for the rest of the year.

Neuroscience and Learning Environments

Perhaps without realizing it, Cindy's teacher was applying principles of neuroscience in adapting the classroom environment to ensure Cindy was able to learn. Neuroscience has enabled educators to pair our rapidly developing understanding of the brain with new insights for instruction. As our knowledge of the brain expands, so too does our understanding of student behavior and learning environments. As we learn more about the brain—such as its proclivity for novelty and challenging stimulation (CAST 2014; Willis 2007)—we can extrapolate how best to design learning environments for students from birth through adulthood.

Brain basics: structure and functions

A detailed overview of the brain's complete structure is outside the scope of this chapter. However, it is helpful for teachers to know some fundamental concepts most relevant for brain functioning, particularly in children with PANDAS/PANS. The brain has several regions (NIH 2015). Frontal lobes (one on each side of the brain, or hemisphere) are located toward the front of the brain closest to the forehead. These are involved in executive function, judgment, abstract thought, some motor planning, and speech. Executive function is the cognitive processing of information that takes place in the left frontal lobe and prefrontal cortex that exercise conscious control over one's emotions and thoughts. This control allows patterned information to be used for organizing, analyzing, sorting, connecting, planning, prioritizing, sequencing, self-monitoring, self-correcting, assessment, problem-solving, and linking information to appropriate actions (Willis 2007).

Occipital lobes process visual input; parietal lobes, directly behind the frontal lobes, process sensory input and also are involved in some school-related functions such as reading and mathematical skills. The temporal lobes, below the occipital and frontal lobes, process auditory input and are thought to be involved in the creation of memories as well.

Additionally, some areas of the brain, distinct from these regions, are particularly important in the neurobiology of PANDAS/PANS. The basal ganglia are a center of neurons found toward the rear low center of the brain. Some scans have identified basal ganglia inflammation in children with PANDAS/PANS (Insel 2012); the basal ganglia typically are important to motor skills, emotions, and memory or routine learning. The amygdala has been found, in very recent research, to be implicated as well in models of PANDAS/PANS (Dileepan *et al.* 2016); this is an area of the brain which controls fear and our "fight or flight" reflex, often found to be hyper-reactive in children with PANDAS/PANS. For teachers, it is particularly helpful to keep these biological principles in mind when working with children who have PANDAS/PANS, as their reactions or behaviors are likely influenced by biological factors which are only beginning to be understood.

Brain plasticity

The brain is not fixed in its development; it continues to grow throughout childhood, adolescence, and even into adulthood. New connections can be forged, and new skills can be learned (Jensen quoted in Flannery 2015), although childhood is a time of particularly dramatic brain growth (Chugani 1998). Brain development continues throughout adolescence, with continued growth in executive functioning, judgment, and impulse control through early adulthood (Semrud-Clikeman n.d.). Given the brain's continued growth, and the concept of plasticity, there is ongoing debate among PANDAS/ PANS specialists as to whether PANDAS/PANS cause permanent impairment when untreated. However, there seems to be consensus, at the present time, that students with PANDAS/PANS who receive early identification and treatment can regain full neurological functioning without permanent impact (PANDAS Network 2015). Educators working with students who have PANDAS and PANS should keep in mind, though, that healing and recovery do take time. A student who experiences an acute PANS episode in October, is treated and does not relapse, may not have regained full neurological functioning by New Year or even by spring break. However, that student may be back to normal by the following school year.

Universal Design for Learning (UDL)

In considering implications of these concepts, it is helpful to be aware of frameworks for brain-friendly teaching, including Universal Design for Learning (UDL), a set of principles for creating instruction that benefits all learners (CAST 2014) by providing multiple means of representing concepts, multiple means of expressing ideas or interacting with content, and multiple ways of engaging student interest (CAST 2014). The UDL framework is based on analysis of three sets of networks within the brain, focused on recognition, strategies, and affective response. In a UDL framework, educators support students' varied backgrounds and skill levels regarding recognition, strategies, and affect and take these into account, considering students' strengths as well as needs in order to design activities, assessments, and means of engaging students that are uniquely suited to those students' needs. When implemented correctly, UDL can eliminate the need for complicated accommodations or adaptations, as accessibility and appropriate levels of challenge are already built into the curriculum (CAST 2014). Planning with UDL in mind can be particularly effective for students with PANDAS/PANS. Educators implementing UDL-based instruction focus on representing ideas and learning goals in a variety of ways, giving students options and choice for demonstrating what they know, and finding multiple avenues for helping students feel engaged, safe, and secure in the classroom. Ensuring the classroom is one in which activities are accessible, planned with students' needs in mind, can be a powerful first step toward helping students with PANDAS/PANS be included, regardless of their medical status on any given day.

A UDL-based approach also seeks to minimize student anxiety and stress, along with presenting information in new and exciting ways to maintain optimal brain functioning (CAST 2014). Lack of novelty can foster boredom, which neurologists and neuro-educators see as a neurobiological state rather than a student choice (Willis 2007). Boredom, along with other conditions, can lead to stress, which can reduce the likelihood that students will retain new knowledge (or follow behavioral guidelines) (Willis 2007). In fact, stress is known to have a variety of harmful effects on the brain (Medina 2014)—a key fact for teachers of students with PANDAS/PANS. Minimizing anxiety and stress is one of the most important steps a teacher can take to ensure success for a student with PANDAS/PANS.

Far from being opaque, the principles of brain-friendly teaching are surprisingly simple and, when embraced, can have powerful results. This may be particularly true for children with PANDAS and PANS, whose brain function is already affected by illness and who may enter the classroom in a state of stress. Brain-friendly teaching is particularly important to foster achievement for these students, even those who may not require significant other accommodations or modifications.

In recent years, brain-friendly teaching practices, neuro-education, and brain-based learning have become veritable buzzwords in educational theory and practice (Waldron and Jenner-Matthews 2015). Much of this recent interest is driven by the rapidly expanding base of knowledge in this area; tools such as functional magnetic resonance imaging (fMRI) allow scientists to gain unprecedented awareness of how different sections of the brain respond to specific stimuli. This knowledge can then be translated into practical guidelines and strategies for educators, who can maximize the natural physical tendencies of the brain to help students retain knowledge. In doing so, it is important to make decisions based on strong scientific research and evidence-based practice (Waldron and Jenner-Matthews 2015), reviewing all of the available findings on a topic before making decisions about curriculum or instruction. This concept, as applied to PANDAS/PANS, becomes trickier; there is a dearth of scientific research on learning and instruction of students with PANDAS/PANS (Rice Doran 2015). However, it is possible to consider what we know about the brain, what we know about how students learn, and what we have recently discovered about PANDAS/PANS in order to inform decisions educators make about classroom setup and instruction.

Classroom impact

Specific behaviors of concern reported by parents and teachers of children with PANDAS, in our experience, include the following:

Behavioral challenges

Behavioral symptoms may include defiance; yelling or screaming; hitting or kicking; eloping or running away; cursing (be careful not to confuse behavioral difficulties with verbal tics or coprolalia, which is an involuntary repetition of forbidden or taboo words); and avoiding school entirely. Shifting into "fight or flight" mode, particularly when stressed or threatened, is not uncommon among children with PANDAS/PANS. The need to perform compulsions, such as rubbing hands along the wall or walking through doors over and over, can be both disruptive to instruction and problematic in terms of peer attention. Some parents report teachers complaining about excessive noise-making, such as finger-tapping or humming; again, caution is urged here as these behaviors may be motor or vocal tics, and tics should never be treated as choice-based behaviors or addressed through a punishment-based framework. Drawing attention to a tic may increase anxiety and be counterproductive. For this reason, teachers should begin by carefully considering and analyzing their perceptions of challenging behaviors.

Academic challenges

As also discussed later in the book, children with PANDAS/PANS often experience academic difficulties as well. These may include difficulty completing work due to slow rate of progress; difficulty completing work due to concerns about having it all correct (a common manifestation of OCD); deficits in math, reading, or writing, including spelling; distractibility and attention. Perseverative behaviors such as re-reading a sentence, erasing a punctuation mark over and over to get it right, or repeating words may interfere with academic performance. Related to academic challenges, though distinct in some ways, are motor difficulties. These may range from clumsiness and lack of spatial awareness to severe limitations with handwriting, dressing, and other self-help skills. One parent of a seven-year-old with PANS reported that she would scan her daughter's face each day as she returned home from school; a messy face, and the fine motor issues that it indicated, typically correlated with academic struggles that day in school.

Social challenges

PANDAS/PANS, like many difficulties, can make peer relationships fraught. Children with PANDAS/PANS may experience severe social anxiety, and the difficulty they may have attending school can impact peer friendships as well. Children with PANDAS/PANS also may experience increased impulsivity, sensory seeking, and rage, all of which are problematic in peer relationships. This is particularly the case if peers are not aware of the child's diagnosis or needs. As with other disabilities, some families of children with PANDAS/PANS choose to disclose their child's condition to peers, and some are less comfortable doing so.

Other physical or family challenges

Some physical symptoms of PANDAS/PANS have potential to be quite disruptive in the classroom environment. These include fatigue and sleep issues, which may lead to excessive drowsiness or even narcolepsy in the classroom. Frequent urination is also common; some parents describe their children needing to leave the classroom to urinate twenty or thirty times in the course of a school day. Urinary or bowel incontinence may occur. As described in Chapter 2, featuring families' experiences, PANDAS/PANS can also be a source of significant stress for parents, siblings, grandparents, and other relatives. While less relevant to within-classroom functioning, family challenges associated with PANDAS/PANS can increase stress on all concerned and, also, can limit families' capacity to provide homework help or other support at home.

Brain-friendly strategies for students with PANDAS/PANS

The remainder of this book describes interventions and supports, some more intensive than others, for students whose PANDAS/PANS diagnosis may cause significant impairment in one or more school-related areas. However, not all students with PANDAS require significant intervention, nor are all students with this diagnosis served with an IEP or a 504 plan. Even among those who do require such intervention, their needs fall along a continuum and may vary with each illness-related flare. For this reason, teachers need a repertoire of classroom-friendly strategies, ideally ones that benefit all learners as well as those with PANDAS/PANS, that can ensure their classroom is brain-friendly and provide a foundation for implementing further supports and interventions. In schools implementing Response to Intervention (Fuchs and Vaughn 2012), such strategies might be considered Tier 1 supports (i.e., implemented for all learners within a general classroom setting).

Understanding how the child learns

It is important that teachers understand "how" their students learn. Are their students visual, auditory, or kinesthetic learners? Some researchers refer to these as three strong sensory channels for learning (Rose and Nicholl 1997). Although some refer to learning modality as a preference, others refer to it as a strength (Burke-Guild and Garger 1998). It is helpful for teachers to determine a student's preferred modality and if possible teach to all three modalities to reach all students.

The visual learner prefers to "see" the information to be learned— that is, in pictures, charts, graphs, maps, and videos. Basically, this type of learner absorbs the world through words and pictures. A learner who prefers to talk or listen is typically characterized as an auditory learner. This learner likes information presented orally. Books on tape and reports presented orally are ways in which the auditory learner prefers to acquire and remember information. Discussing what has been learned is an important strategy for this learner. The learner who needs to "do" or perform certain actions in a classroom is described as a kinesthetic learner.

Kinesthetic learners probably experience the most difficulties in our traditional classrooms (Sprenger 2007). Kinesthetic learners need hands-on activities that require movement. They benefit from movement, performing actions such as conducting a science experiment, or demonstrating how to perform a particular action. Such approaches may be particularly beneficial for students with PANDAS/PANS, for whom movement can provide a welcome distraction, minimize anxiety, and support focusing.

Managing the environment

As described in earlier chapters, PANDAS/PANS may result in behavioral difficulties in the classroom. These may exist along a continuum; teachers may notice mild fidgetiness in one student and full-scale meltdowns or violent rage in another. While different levels of support will certainly be appropriate for each, a brain-friendly approach to teaching will provide a framework to allow each student to succeed. Before considering specific classroom practices, teachers will also benefit from familiarizing themselves with the work of Dr. Ross Greene, a child development expert whose mantra "Kids do well if they can" (Greene 2014, p.9) is particularly applicable to PANDAS/PANS, as it reminds educators that challenging behaviors may not be a function of conscious choice but rather may express stress, anxiety, sensory overload, or inability to solve the problem at hand (Greene 2014). While more directly related to behavioral issues, this philosophy is helpful to keep in mind when planning brain-based instruction, where it becomes important to design environments that foster student learning, positive behavior, and social skills development.

One common, related, practice in supporting students with brain injuries is antecedent management of behavior (Kern and Clemens 2007). Managing antecedents, or conditions or factors that precede or trigger specific behaviors, requires shaping the learning environment in order to reduce those factors that could trigger problem behavior for students whose neurological state makes them unlikely to respond well. As an illustration, under a traditional approach toward behavior management, a student who exhibited challenging behavior (such as cursing at peers) when placed in a loud room might be given positive incentives to refrain from cursing or might receive a consequence (loss of recess, for example) each time she cursed. In an approach centered on managing environment and antecedents, the child's support team might instead find ways to reduce his or her exposure to noisy rooms in order to avoid triggering the behavior in the first place. More and more schools have adopted this approach in behavior intervention; it is highly appropriate for students whose behaviors may be partially or wholly out of their control due to neurological factors.

Last, having an organized classroom is crucial in providing students with stability and comfort. Kat, a student in fifth grade, states, "I feel most comfortable when I am learning in a safe, welcoming and organized learning environment. I feel as if when the room is clean, I focus more. At my school, my teachers make sure our classroom is as organized as it can be, 24/7. When the classroom is like that, I enjoy school and learning."

Purposeful decision-making

Brain-friendly classrooms do not occur spontaneously or accidentally. Teachers should take time, at the beginning of the year and periodically throughout, to assess tangible and intangible elements of their classroom environment that are conducive to learning (Hoge 2002). Physical classroom environment is an important, though not sufficient, element to consider in this process; class emotional climate and sense of well-being are equally important.

Emotional warmth and safety

When asked to identify important features of a classroom that would help her learn, Trish, a fifth-grader with PANDAS, wrote a list that consisted of one item: "Safe learning environment." All students need to feel both physically and emotionally safe; brain-friendly teaching is built around the idea that students should feel engaged and any perceived threats should be reduced (CAST 2014), and extensive research highlights the importance of emotional well-being in the learning process (Kovalik and Olsen 1998). But for students with PANDAS/PANS, this effect is heightened; overpowering anxiety is already a constant for many of these students, and therefore it becomes doubly important to have a friendly, low-pressure and safe classroom environment.

Student engagement

Keeping students engaged relates closely to classroom environment and sense of safety. Research demonstrates that high levels of student engagement increase interest and learning (CAST 2014; McGinty, Radin, and Kaminski 2013). Using games, interactive activities, computerized learning, and music and art are all ways to engage students; building on personal experience or positive memories can also be helpful, particularly with students who may experience excessive anxiety, and can channel positive emotions related to learning.

Movement and exercise

Movement is important for all learners, particularly those with PANDAS/PANS who may have pre-existing attention and sensory challenges. "I don't think you can always learn when you are moving, but I do think you should take breaks between learning, when you can do stuff instead of just sitting there all the time," says James, a seventh grader. Corroborating James' advice, studies have found that incorporating movement (both kinesthetic activities and tactile stimulation) can focus students' attention (Stalvey and Brasell 2006). Consider offering sensory stimulation and opportunities for small-muscle movement (fidgets, stress balls). Consider, also, allowing students to complete activities while walking instead of sitting (worksheet items can be rewritten on chart paper and students can circulate around the room to record answers) and to use alternatives such as exercise balls rather than remaining at desks.

Hydration and rest

Physical well-being, such as adequate food and hydration, are important for brain functioning (Sikora 2013). Additionally, both adequate rest (Jensen quoted in Flannery 2015) and sufficient downtime—not necessarily sleep—are important too. In fact, unstructured downtime may support development of varied thinking abilities, imagination, and social skills not developed during highly structured activities (Immordino-Yang, Christodoulou, and Singh 2012). Consider providing several quiet spaces in the classroom, with ambient lighting and comfortable seating.

Instructional routines, also, can be varied to allow multiple times for silent reflection throughout the day, facilitating students' development of reflective skills, metacognition, and self-regulation strategies. These reflection periods could even include breathing exercises, listening to music, or other calming activities, helping students with PANDAS/PANS to reduce stress at different points through the day.

Physical setting

Along the same lines, the physical environment of the classroom can help to support students' cognitive functioning and lower stress. Kaufeldt (1999) recommends careful selection of lighting and decorations to ensure the classroom feels inviting and welcoming, but not overwhelming. Decorations and wall posters or signs can be positive and can create a personalized and welcoming climate; however, teachers should take care to include sufficient blank space so that the walls do not seem overwhelming. Lighting can be varied in different parts of the room, perhaps including a table or floor lamp to offset harsh fluorescent lights.

Seating arrangements can help to minimize stress and allow for collaboration; a U-shape, clusters of desks, or even a V-shaped arrangement can offer opportunities to work with different partners (Sikora 2013). However, seating arrangements also offer pitfalls for students with PANDAS/PANS; the "pods" of four desks popular in many classrooms can increase students' exposure to peers' illness by placing them facing one another, within a distance of one or two feet.

Whatever seating arrangements are used, students with PANDAS/ PANS may need teachers to be flexible, rearranging seats and partner groupings so that those with PANDAS/PANS are not in close proximity to peers who are visibly ill (coughing, sneezing, etc.). In fact, the medical (if not social) needs of these students may have been better served by the traditional arrangement of having students in rows facing forward together rather than sneezing directly into one another's faces.

Activity and choice

Offering choice to students helps to facilitate engagement and deepen student interest in the topic (Erwin 2004), leading to stronger retention of content (CAST 2014). Collaborative work may help students to feel more engaged and more in control of their activity; however, teachers should be mindful that, for some students with PANDAS/PANS, collaborative work can also cause heightened anxiety and may trigger negative behaviors as a result.

Timing

All learners need frequent breaks, ideally every 10 minutes (Sousa 2001). These breaks need not take the form of time off-task, but can be changes in movement or activity, chatting with a peer about questions, or circulating to a new area of the room to continue learning activities. Sousa also suggests interspersing downtime or relaxed-pace activities with more cognitively demanding ones (2001).

For students with PANDAS/PANS, teachers should be aware of several variables specific to time. First, it is likely students will need extra time as a consistent accommodation, given the impact of PANDAS/PANS on cognitive functioning (Lewin *et al.* 2011). Additionally, certain times of day may be more challenging, based on medication schedules and each student's specific needs. Students with school attendance phobia, for example, may be well-served by a relaxing activity to complete when they enter the classroom in the morning. This also allows them some flexibility in the event they are late, a common occurrence for some students with PANDAS/ PANS due to separation anxiety. These students may be better able to complete challenging cognitive work after having an hour or so to adjust to school. The school nurse, counselor, and a student's health professional are likely to be able to provide more specific suggestions relevant to that student's particular profile.

Teaching to the modalities

Researchers (Sprenger 2007) have suggested ways in which teachers can design their lessons and facilitate a brain-friendly classroom environment by implementing the following strategies: (1) include each modality (visual, auditory, and kinesthetic) in every lesson; (2) begin each lesson with emphasis on a different modality, as this will help to increase interest and motivation in the lesson; (3) provide ample opportunities for the auditory learner to talk about information that was presented in the lesson or what was learned; (4) offer opportunities for kinesthetic learners to move about the classroom for a variety of reasons; (5) be aware of the learner's language (visual learners may use phrases such as "I see," while kinesthetic learners may say "I get it now!", and auditory learners may say "I heard what you were saying, but…"); and (6) observe what your students are relaying to you regarding how they learn.

Specific strategies for challenges encountered by students with PANDAS/PANS

Table 5.1 provides particular classroom-based considerations for children with PANDAS and offers suggestions of brain-friendly ways to address each. While subsequent chapters provide extensive discussion of academic, behavioral, and social difficulties, and offer supports of varying intensity, the intent of this chapter—and this table—is to provide ideas for strategies that can be easily implemented in the general education setting, with minimal outside support, consistent with principles of Tier 1 intervention.

Table 5.1 Brain-friendly solutions for PANDAS/PANS symptoms (see Chapters 8 and 9 for additional suggestions)

PANDAS/PANS symptom	Brain-friendly solutions
School anxiety and refusal	Create warm and safe classroom environment. Offer comforting beginning-of-school rituals. Use close collaboration with parents for school drop-off or classroom good-byes. Minimize stress during drop-off and transition.
Elopement or flight behaviors	Identify and minimize triggers. Work with student to define "safe spaces" to go if elopement occurs. Seat student purposefully, without easy access to doors. Confrontation, when a student is in "fight or flight mode," is likely to be unsuccessful.
Rage	Identify and minimize triggers. Provide student with self-calming strategies, with "safe space" outside classroom to visit when angry, and with positive behavioral supports for appropriate responses.
Obsessions, intrusive thoughts, persistent fears	Emphasize positive classroom support and warm, safe classroom climate. Distraction can be a useful tool for some intrusive thoughts or fears. Be mindful that repeated discussion of obsessions or persistent fears may reinforce the fear rather than ameliorating it—seek advice from student's treating professionals if applicable. For intractable fears, provide alternatives and minimize stress related to fear-inducing events.
Compulsions	Approach compulsive behaviors with understanding. Work with mental health or medical professionals in implementing plans to address or minimize compulsions. Be careful that classroom interventions do not reinforce compulsive behaviors. Use positive support, rather than punishment, to encourage desired behaviors and reduce undesirable ones. Threats ("If you touch the door one more time, I am calling home!") are generally not effective in reducing compulsive behaviors.
Tics (motor or vocal)	Tics are involuntary behaviors, generally outside a student's control. Ignore tics to reduce stress and embarrassment. If a student's tics are noticeable, consider asking student and family if they prefer to disclose to peers to facilitate peer acceptance of unusual behaviors. With students who have PANDAS/PANS, use care in distinguishing between tics and choice-based behaviors. Some parents report their children being disciplined for shouting profanities, for example, when this behavior was a tic.

Challenge	Strategies
Frequent urination	Frequent absences due to urinary accidents or excessive bathroom breaks can result in missed content. Be aware that frequent urination is a medical symptom and that, while repeated bathroom breaks may seem like task avoidance, they may reflect underlying physiological need. Technology and planning can reduce the amount of content students miss when leaving the class often (consider providing voice recording of lectures, SmartBoard notes, copies of notes, conference with peer buddy). Minimize disruption and embarrassment by providing student with a quiet signal to request a bathroom break rather than raising his/her hand and disrupting instruction. Consider seating student near the door for easy access (as long as elopement is not an issue).
Sensory challenges	Covered more fully in Chapter 7, sensory challenges can be addressed through UDL-based supports as well. Sensory stimulation at a student's seat (textured cushion, pencil grips, rubber bands around desk bottom) can be helpful. Consider allowing snacks or gum or other oral stimulation. A variety of seating in the classroom is helpful for students—this can include beanbags, sofas, and rocking chairs as well as traditional desks and floor cushions. Carefully consider lighting and sound. Consider using a white-noise machine at appropriate times.
Math difficulties	Provide calculator, manipulatives, and opportunities to redo work. Chunk problems and allow breaks between problems, problem sets, or problems of different types. Students with PANDAS/PANS may evidence regression across different areas of math skills; they may also evidence splinter skills, remaining strong in problem-solving while having challenges with computation, for example. Use frequent check-ups to informally measure areas of skill.
Reading difficulties, fluency, or comprehension	As with math, student difficulties may manifest in specific areas (decoding), or may manifest across different skill areas. Offer read-aloud options, e-books, or story summaries. Try sensory strategies for teaching decoding or grammar (tracing letters, fitting letter or word rods together).
Memory or recall difficulties	Short-term memory and routine, procedural learning can be affected by PANDAS. Provide prompts and supports for memory. Reduce demands for memorization and recall. Provide visual aids and supports. Offer visual schedules and visual directions.
Graphomotor (writing) difficulties	UDL-based solutions such as keyboarding, oral response options, or drawing responses can help to address writing difficulties. Provide options for different types of writing implements (pens, dry-erase markers, crayons, triangular crayons). More specific handwriting supports are discussed in Chapter 7.
Organizational challenges	If student is willing, use a peer buddy to help with organization. Color-code and texture-code folders, using stick-on covers that are soft, furry, or ridged (Mooney and Cole 2000).

PANDAS/PANS symptom	Brain-friendly solutions
Peer issues (conflicts, anxiety, withdrawal)	Provide frameworks for group work so expectations are clearly defined, reducing anxiety. Offer flexibility in partner selection when appropriate. Provide a variety of high-interest group tasks with varied partners or groups. Incorporate choice when possible. Be mindful of the role compulsions or fears may play when there is difficulty in peer relationships (a student may have irrational anxiety about being injured in a specific part of the room; the student's OCD may make him or her uncomfortable sharing writing utensils with peers), and address accordingly with family and professionals such as school social worker or counselor.
Fatigue	Create a calming classroom. Offer students frequent breaks. Plan up-tempo activities at low-energy times (after lunch, end of the day) and alternate physical movement with high-stress or sedentary work such as tests and worksheets. Brain breaks from a site such as GoNoodle.com can help students remain active and also provide sensory stimulation.
Sudden shifts in behavior	A calming classroom environment may help students regulate behavior. Provide break spaces in the classroom, sensory resources, and opportunities for self-reflection throughout the day. Recognize signs of impending difficulties and redirect student, or offer alternatives, when possible.
Inconsistent attendance	Technology-based solutions (electronic notes, video, Skype/FaceTime, online discussions) can help students remain included even when attending inconsistently.

Although the two hemispheres of the brain process information differently, research (Sousa 2001) has concluded that we learn best when both hemispheres are engaged. When designing lessons for students with PANS, it is suggested that teachers consider teaching to the whole brain. According to Sousa (2001), teachers can accomplish this goal by doing the following: (1) present concepts verbally and visually; (2) present effective visual aids, with information organized and positioned effectively; (3) discuss concepts logically and intuitively (concepts should be presented to students from different perspectives that encourage the use of both brain hemispheres); (4) be aware of the language used in the classroom to avoid conflicting messages; and (5) be sure to design activities and assessment for both hemispheres (implementing UDL principles).

Key points to remember

- PANDAS/PANS can affect multiple areas of the brain, but particular regions identified in research are the amygdala, which controls fear and the fight-or-flight reflex, and the basal ganglia, which are associated with motor skills, anxiety and emotions, rote learning, and procedural memory.

- The brain is plastic; new skills can be learned as well as lost, and students with PANDAS/PANS may regain skills affected during illness, though this often takes time.

- Reducing stress, and addressing anxiety in non-punitive ways, is critical for the success of students with PANDAS/PANS.

- Structuring classrooms in brain-friendly ways can help all students, including those with PANDAS/PANS, succeed.

Conclusion

Students with PANDAS/PANS have needs that span a continuum. Some of these needs will require intensive planning with educational experts from multiple fields, including counselors, behavior specialists, speech, physical or occupational therapists, and others. Some, though, can be met within the general education setting with minimal disruption to instruction, particularly when classroom instruction is compatible with UDL principles.

References

Burke-Guild, P., and Garger, S. (1998) *Marching to Different Drummers* (Second edition). Alexandria, VA: Association for Supervision and Curriculum Development.

CAST (2014) *What is UDL?* Available at www.udlcenter.org/aboutudl/whatisudl, accessed on 3 March 2016..

Chugani, H.T. (1998) 'Biological basis of emotions: Brain systems and brain development.' *Pediatrics 102*, 1225–1229.

Dileepan, T., Smith, E., Knowland, D., Hsu, M., *et al.* (2016) 'Group A *Streptococcus* intranasal infection promotes CNS infiltration by streptococcal-specific TH17 cells.' *Journal of Clinical Investigation 126*, 1, 303–317.

Erwin, J. (2004) *The classroom of choice: Giving students what they need and getting what you want.* Alexandria, VA: ASCD.

Fuchs, L.S., and Vaughn, S. (2012) 'Responsiveness-to-Intervention: A decade later.' *Journal of Learning Disabilities 45*, 3, 195–203.

Greene, R. (2014) *The Explosive Child: A New Approach for Understanding and Parenting Easily Frustrated, Chronically Inflexible Children.* New York: Harper Press.

Hoge, P. (2002) 'The integration of brain-based learning and literacy acquisition.' *Dissertation Abstracts International: Section A. Humanities and Social Sciences 63*, 11.

Immordino-Yang, M.H., Christodoulou, J.A., and Singh, V. (2012) 'Rest is not idleness: Implications of the brain's default mode for human development and education.' *Perspectives on Psychological Science 7*, 4, 352–365.

Insel, T. (2012) *Director's Blog: From Paresis to PANDAS and PANS.* National Institute of Mental Health. Available at www.nimh.nih.gov/about/director/2012/from-paresis-to-pandas-and-pans.shtml, accessed on 2 March 2016.

Jensen, E. (2003) *Tools for Engagement: Using States of Mind to Maximize Learner Success.* Thousand Oaks, CA: Corwin.

Kaufeldt, M. (1999) *Begin with the Brain: Orchestrating the Learning-Centered Classroom* (First edition). Chicago, IL: Zephyr Press.

Kern, L., and Clemens, N.H. (2007) 'Antecedent strategies to promote appropriate classroom behavior.' *Psychology in the Schools 44*, 65–75.

Kovalik, S., and Olsen, K. (1998) 'How emotions run us, our students, and our classrooms.' *NASSP Bulletin 82*, 598, 29–37.

Lewin, A.B., Storch, E.A., Mutch, P.J., and Murphy, T.K. (2011) 'Neurocognitive functioning in youth with pediatric autoimmune neuropsychiatric disorders associated with streptococcus.' *Journal of Neuropsychiatry and Clinical Neurosciences 23*, 4, 391–398.

McGinty, J., Radin, J., and Kaminski, K. (2013) 'Brain-friendly teaching supports learning transfer.' *New Directions for Adult and Continuing Education 2013*, 137, 49–59.

Medina, J. (2014) *Brain Rules: 12 Principles for Surviving and Thriving at Work, Home and School.* Seattle: Pear Press.

Mooney, J., and Cole, C. (2000) *Learning outside the lines: Two students with disabilities and ADHD give you the tools for academic success and educational revolution.* New York: Touchstone.

National Institutes of Health (2015) *Brain Basics: Know Your Brain.* Available at www.ninds.nih.gov/disorders/brain_basics/know_your_brain.htm, accessed on 3 March 2016.

PANDAS Network (2015) *What is PANDAS?* Available at http://pandasnetwork.org/understandingpandaspans/about-pandaspans/whatispandas, accessed on 3 March 2016.

Rice Doran, P. (2015) 'Sudden behavioral changes in the classroom: What educators need to know about PANDAS and PANS.' *Beyond Behavior 24*, 1, 31–37. Available at www.academia.edu/15102564/Sudden_Behavioral_Changes_in_the_Classroom_What_Educators_Need_to_Know_about_PANDAS_and_PANS, accessed on 2 March 2016.

Rose, C., and Nicholl, M.J. (1997) *Accelerated Learning for the 21st Century: The Six-Step Plan to Unlock Your Master-Mind.* New York: Dell.

Semrud-Clikeman (n.d.) *Student Learning.* American Psychological Association e-publication. Available at www.apa.org/education/k12/student-learning.aspx, accessed on 3 March 2016.

Sikora, D. (2013) *What Great Teachers Do (Or Should Do): Innovative Brain-Based Instructional Strategies.* Association for Career and Technical Education. The Free Library. Available at www.thefreelibrary.com/What+great+teachers+do+(or+should+do)%3a+innovative+brain-based...-a0345613798, accessed on 3 March 2016.

Sousa, D. (2001) *How the Brain Learns.* Thousand Oaks, CA: Corwin Press.

Sprenger, M. (2007) *Becoming a "Wiz" at Brain-Based Teaching: How to Make Every Year Your Best Year.* Thousand Oaks, CA: Corwin Press.

Stalvey, S., and Brasell, H. (2006) 'Using stress balls to focus the attention of sixth-grade learners.' *Journal of At-Risk Issues 12*, 2, 7–16.

Waldron, H., and Jenner-Matthews, A. (2015) 'Neuroscience in the classroom.' *IECA Insights, December 2015*, 15–18.

Willis, J. (2007) *Brain-Friendly Strategies for the Inclusion Classroom.* Alexandria, VA: ASCD.

Chapter 6

Collaborative Planning for Students with PANDAS and PANS

PATRICIA RICE DORAN, ED.D.

Tabitha's son was diagnosed with PANDAS and began treatment with a team of physicians at a well-respected medical center. His symptoms included rage, suicidal statements, self-harming behaviors, and severe OCD, as well as struggles across the board in school. Tabitha, who knew nothing about 504 or IEP plans, kept asking her son's teachers for extra help. As school staff became more familiar with her son's symptoms, they began to come more readily to Tabitha with questions or ideas for strategies. Eventually, after many discussions with school staff, the formal referral process was begun for her son. Though the school year was just ending, the team worked around some scheduling challenges and arranged a meeting with her son's teachers, the school's counselor and psychologist, and the school social worker (as well as the usual administrator and special educator). Tabitha brought medical records as well as letters from her son's neurologist and psychiatrist. While neither physician was present at the meeting, she gave consent for them to speak with school staff before or after the meeting to answer specific questions. When the team began to discuss a behavior intervention plan, Tabitha asked for a copy to forward to her son's neurologist and psychiatrist for their input. Eager for expert assistance with some of this student's more unusual symptoms, the team members agreed. The meeting, which addressed some challenging behaviors, academic difficulties, and health and attendance issues, ended on a cordial note as Tabitha thanked the team for their assistance.

As all educators know, not every meeting goes as smoothly as the one for Tabitha's son. In fact, many parents of children with a PANDAS or PANS diagnosis have reported challenges with the special education and school support processes, in large part because of issues such as teachers' lack of familiarity with the diagnosis and accommodations (Rice Doran, unpublished manuscript). Collaborative planning, both with families and with other professionals, is a bedrock part of the IEP process (Friend and Cook 2013). It is essential for all personnel on the IEP or 504 team to have strong relationships with families throughout the process, particularly when dealing with a disorder which may have significant impact on families (McClelland *et al.* 2015) and whose symptomatology may change throughout the process (Rice Doran 2015).

Supporting families: Awareness of stress and family's reality

Going through the special education process, or any formal process for supporting a student, can be daunting for any parent—particularly one also coping with sudden behavioral changes in his or her child. Hardman, Egan and Drew (2017) describe the intense emotions that families may experience when a child has a disability, ranging from anxiety and anger toward acceptance, coping and adapting to the new reality of the child's disability (Hardman *et al.* 2017). For parents of a child with PANDAS/PANS, these stages may be complicated by their realization that their child's levels of functioning may not remain static but may require continued adjustments as they vary through illness and treatment, requiring continuous adjustment on the part of parents as well. Parents may also be dealing with stress or trauma experienced by siblings of the child with PANDAS/PANS, who may need assistance coping with the abrupt changes in his or her functioning.

Staff working with families of children with PANDAS and PANS diagnoses should be aware of potential areas of challenge associated with the specific nature of the illness. McClelland *et al.* (2015) describe some family reactions, quoting families who describe their fears and their ongoing concerns that children will relapse (McClelland *et al.* 2015). Consistent themes in family experiences included fear, a sense of frustration, and the belief that professionals were not listening to or hearing concerns (McClelland *et al.* 2015). These findings are mirrored, in fact, in the stories that Wendy and Sarah shared in Chapter 2, in which they describe feeling alienated, shaken, and disbelieved by professionals at school and at physicians' offices.

Best practices for collaboration

In addition to taking time to understand the impact PANDAS and PANS may have on families, professionals should be familiar with best practices for collaboration and planning in general. Friend and Cook (2013) highlight specific considerations for educators that can facilitate successful partnership. Among these are communication, specifically proactive and positive conversations with parents about the child, and active listening. Collaborative problem-solving and team-based approaches, including co-teaching when possible, are often also recommended (Friend and Cook 2013) as these collaborative practices can ensure a student has access to a range of support implemented by a group of knowledgeable professionals who are all on the same page.

Plans for students with PANDAS and PANS

Planning for students with PANDAS and PANS may take several forms. A significant amount of teacher planning, as with many situations, may be informal and spur-of-the-moment; teachers often learn best from one another, sharing promising practices, effective adaptations, and new ideas. Such planning may take the form of casual hallway conversations, or questions asked and answered in the teachers' lounge.

All of these are productive and even essential for ensuring the success of students with PANDAS and PANS. In particular, the dynamic nature of PANDAS and PANS symptoms makes it particularly important for teachers to have well-developed collaborative relationships in place, so that they can seek timely advice from other professionals when symptoms shift suddenly.

However, the complex nature of PANDAS and PANS, and the likelihood of relapse or exacerbation for many students, often prompt teams to develop more structured supports and procedures than an informal, conversational process might yield. At a minimum, most students with active PANDAS or PANS symptoms will require a health plan, with many students also benefiting from the accommodations, modifications, and services that can be provided through a 504 plan or IEP. The most common plans that teams may create are listed below.

IEP

The bedrock document of special education is the Individualized Education Program (IEP). This comprehensive document lists challenges and needs (and sometimes strengths) a given student demonstrates; describes accommodations, modifications, supports, and services that will be provided to the student; specifies individualized curriculum goals that will drive the student's educational program; and documents the least restrictive environment for the student. Much of this chapter's discussion of process, collaboration, and multidisciplinary planning is focused specifically on IEP teams; therefore, IEP planning will be addressed more completely throughout this chapter.

In writing an IEP, teams must designate the primary disability under which the student qualifies for special education services. For most students with PANDAS and PANS, the category Other Health Impairments (OHI) is preferred due to the fluctuating nature of symptoms and the systemic physical challenges associated with PANDAS and PANS. However, some students with PANDAS or PANS may also have comorbid autism spectrum disorders or learning disabilities; these may be designated as the primary disability category. If a student's manifestation is primarily behavioral (particularly if the

IEP was created before the PANDAS/PANS diagnosis was received), a student may also qualify for special education services as having an emotional/behavioral disability. In selecting the primary category under which to qualify a student for an IEP, teams should carefully consider the comprehensive totality of a student's symptoms and the results of multidisciplinary assessments.

FBA/BIP plans

For students with behavioral challenges, functional behavioral assessments (FBAs) and behavior intervention plans (BIPs) should be created prior to formal identification of behavioral disabilities in the IEP. Many districts have moved to a framework of tiered interventions and support, in which increasing supports are provided to students as their behavior or academic needs may warrant. This process often leads naturally into an FBA and BIP for students whose behavioral challenges cannot be addressed via within-classroom differentiation and accommodation. An FBA is developed prior to the BIP, and the goal of the FBA is to identify specific challenging behaviors and analyze their causes and functions. Behavioral plans and supports generally are rooted in behaviorist principles, which assume that all behavior serves a function (to gain or avoid attention or sensory stimulation; to gain rewards, which may include preferred tasks and activities; to avoid non-preferred tasks; and so on).

Behaviorist principles have a long history of successful use in school settings, particularly for students with disabilities (Gable, Park and Scott 2014), and their use in behavioral planning has been validated with extensive evidence. Still, parents have reported concerns regarding behavior assessments and planning for their children with PANDAS and PANS. Many neurological symptoms associated with PANDAS, such as tics, may present as challenging behaviors but may in actuality be involuntary, beyond the student's control. Other behaviors may be within the student's control some days but not others, depending on the student's physical and neurological condition. One parent reported receiving a related service provider's report that her daughter's attention varied according to her mood and motivation; the role of her physical condition in affecting mood, motivation, and attention was not addressed. Omissions such as these make it difficult to plan accurately; educators may construct behavioral supports that are not appropriate, such as a reward system for students who control their tics. Educators may also evaluate the effectiveness of behavior supports erroneously, assuming a support is ineffective when, in actuality, the student may be experiencing a symptom exacerbation which changes his or her baseline level of functioning independent of any behavioral support.

One strategy to mitigate this concern is to ensure, as Tabitha's team did, that input from treating physicians was obtained and considered by the team. A physician or nurse practitioner reviewing a behavioral support plan may be able to give input about the appropriateness of behaviors targeted in the plan and methods of reinforcing desired behaviors. For example, a team may devise a plan that attempts to reduce a student's loud humming because it is disruptive, but may not consider the possibility that the humming is actually a verbal tic— input that may need to be given or corroborated by a medical provider. Similarly, a team may decide to use toy train pieces as a behavior reinforcement for a child obsessed with trains, not realizing that the child's therapist has directed the family to limit access to trains in order to reduce manifestation of that obsession. For these reasons, it is recommended that teams seek and thoughtfully consider input from healthcare professionals when feasible and appropriate in the planning process.

504 plans

Under federal law, students with disabilities may qualify for accommodations under Section 504 of the federal Rehabilitation Act (United States Department of Education 2013). Students whose disabilities substantially limit a "major life activity" (which can include learning) may be provided accommodations to ensure they have equal access and full opportunity to participate regardless of their disability. It is important to realize that 504 plans will not provide program modifications, services, or related curriculum (though, on some occasions, 504 plans may provide related services if they are needed to guarantee equal access) (USDOE 2013). Generally, 504 plans are appropriate for students whose needs can be met with accommodations and minor adaptations or adjustments.

Attendance plans

Sometimes, students with PANS/PANDAS will have frequent absences, tardiness, or early dismissals. These may be related to school anxiety, frequent illness, frequent physician or therapist appointments, or fatigue that makes a full day of school impossible for the student. Some districts may require formal discussion of the student's attendance issues and documented plans on file for those issues. Even in districts where such plans are not required, school staff should ensure that attendance considerations are taken into account as part of regular IEP, 504, or health planning. In districts where parents can be held criminally liable or reported to child welfare agencies for students' attendance issues, staff should also ensure that medical (and psychological) reasons for possible attendance issues are well documented. School staff also should take the initiative to explain attendance policies—those existing at the school, district or county, and state level—to parents so that there are clear lines of communication for later discussion of attendance issues as they may arise.

Health plans

Students whose PANDAS/PANS symptoms do not have specific educational impact, or cause substantial limitation, may be eligible for a school health plan. These plans are usually available for students who need school personnel to be aware of their medical issues. The documents may differ in form and substance from district to district, but typically contain a synopsis of the health issue, any treatment information that is relevant for school personnel, and specific action items or steps to be taken in school. Health plans may also state considerations in particular areas, such as attendance, extended breaks during the day, communication with medical personnel, and the like. Health plans are usually initiated by the school nurse's office; other school personnel may be involved in planning as appropriate, though there is not a specific legal process for developing health plans as with 504 plans or IEPs.

Transition plans

As discussed further in this book, students with PANDAS and PANS may transition frequently between settings. For example, students may move from a general education setting to a home and hospital setting and back. Students may move from a residential placement to a self-contained setting in the local public school. Students may transition from homeschool supervised by parents to home instruction provided by the district (sometimes referred to as "home and hospital," "homebound," or "concurrent home" teaching).

In one study, half of all parents of children with PANDAS/PANS interviewed reported their child had been placed, temporarily or permanently, in a homeschool or home and hospital setting (Rice Doran and O'Hanlon 2015). For children with a formal IEP or 504 plan, planning for transitions between settings or environments is likely to occur as part of the larger planning discussion. For students who do not have such plans, it is advisable for school personnel to initiate, either formally or informally, a conversation about whether such transitions are anticipated, and if so, what steps can be taken to ensure a positive outcome.

One parent discussed the value of allowing her child to return to school gradually from home and hospital care, participating first in school dances, then specials, then a half-day of classes, then a full day. She advocated this approach as a way to help her son manage his anxiety and, also, test his immune system to be sure he could tolerate the physical fatigue and exposure to illness that would accompany a return to school.

Special considerations and caveats for planning

RTI and MTSS

First authorized in 2004 in IDEA as an alternative method for identifying students with disabilities, response to intervention (RTI)

(Fuchs and Vaughn 2012), sometimes referred to as multi-tiered system of supports (MTSS), is a system of tiered interventions and supports in which an early screening process facilitates the identification of students who need additional academic and behavioral supports, which are provided rapidly and monitored consistently (Metcalf n.d.). Over time, students who do not show improvement in response to those additional supports and interventions may be referred for consideration of special education eligibility. Experts concur that RTI holds significant potential for improving standard operating procedure in special education (Fuchs and Vaughn 2012; Gargiulo and Metcalf 2012; Hoover 2012), as students need not wait to fail and, instead, can be provided flexible and evidence-based supports from the moment they are first determined to be at risk. This is particularly relevant for students with PANDAS, who may receive tiered interventions for learning or behavioral issues. The RTI process can provide valuable information about what works for those students and about what level of support they may need. That process may also be particularly beneficial for students with PANDAs and PANS because of the flexibility built into systems of multi-tiered supports; students can be provided more or fewer supports, of varying types, as their needs fluctuate.

At the same time, federal law is also clear that the existence of an RTI process should never be used to delay a student's pre-existing right to be evaluated for special education, should the parent request it (IDEA 2006). Frequently, parents may be unclear about their procedural rights—particularly when processing new terminology or acronyms such as those used here. If RTI is in place at a school, professionals should ensure parents are aware that, should a child's condition (or sudden change in condition) require it, referral for special education consideration need not be delayed simply because the school uses tiered supports and response to intervention.

Disability category

Most often, students with PANDAS/PANS will qualify for special education services under the category of Other Health Impairment (OHI), commonly used for physical, health, and other issues not listed in one of the other IDEA categories of eligible disabilities (Candelaria-Greene 2014). On some occasions, teams may qualify students for special education under other categories which are also relevant to a particular student's symptoms and presentation; these may include autism spectrum disorder (ASD), specific learning disability (SLD), or emotional and behavioral disorder (EBD). Young children may also receive services under the category of Developmental Delay (DD). These alternative categories may be particularly relevant when a student has a comorbid condition, such as a dual diagnosis of ASD and PANS. However, teams should use caution when qualifying a student under one of these diagnoses; given the complexity of symptoms in many cases of PANDAS or PANS, a label such as SLD or EBD may lead to an undue emphasis on some symptoms and may not capture the full spectrum of a student's needs and presentation.

Planning team composition

In considering team membership, professionals should assess the student's functioning across domains. Table 6.1 shows one instrument that may be used to facilitate this.

Table 6.1 Considerations for teams in planning
for students with PANDAS/PANS

1.	Are the student's symptoms episodic (relapsing/remitting) or constant? If relapsing/remitting, are there known triggers (allergies, strep exposure, etc.)?
2.	Are any of the following areas affected? If so, how?

     1.   Fine motor

     2.   Gross motor

     3.   Social-emotional

     4.   Psychological (may overlap with social-emotional)

     5.   Attention and executive function

     6.   Academics (specify area).

3.	For any areas listed in #2, what input or support is needed from school personnel? What further input is needed from parents/family members?
4.	Does the student experience sleep difficulties, and if so, do these impact school performance?
5.	Does the student experience urinary or bowel issues, and if so, do these impact school performance?
6.	Does the student experience difficulty with eating or food intake, and if so, how does this manifest during school? Is there an impact on school performance or a need for awareness or action on the part of school personnel? If so, describe.
7.	Does the student need sensory supports or aids? Is an occupational therapy evaluation appropriate?
8.	Does the student experience difficulty during transitions or departure from routine? If so, how? Is a functional behavior analysis in order?
9.	Does the student need to receive medication during school hours, and how frequently?
10.	Is it likely the student will miss a significant amount of school this year?
11.	What is the student's level of self-awareness and self-advocacy regarding PANDAS/PANS symptoms?
12.	Is further information needed from the student's family or healthcare team?

Teacher input about areas of specific difficulty may be used to guide selection of specialists who should attend; if teachers report issues with clumsiness, bumping into objects, or physical functioning, for example, input from physical or occupational therapists may be warranted. Additionally, the team's chairperson can review the list of frequent symptoms or diagnostic guidelines provided by the National Institute of Mental Health (NIMH n.d.) to ensure there are no potential areas of impact which are left unaddressed. Dahlia, parent of several children with PANDAS/PANS, reported that she was initially surprised to hear an occupational therapist had been invited to her daughter's 504 plan meeting.

At the meeting, the occupational therapist described reasons for assessing her daughter's handwriting, organization, and other areas of functioning. While Dahlia would not have thought to request her attendance, the occupational therapy assessment proved to be a valuable element in the overall plan.

One recent article recommends the school nurse be included in planning for students with PANDAS/PANS (Rice Doran 2015), a recommendation found also in earlier literature (O'Rourke 2003). While team members should always be selected based on the student's individual presentation, the following describes roles commonly represented at planning meetings:

- *Parent/family member
- *General educator
- *Special educator
- *School administrator
- Student (if appropriate).

Other specialists selected on the basis of the student's current profile, strengths, and needs include:

- School psychologist
- Counselor or social worker
- School nurse
- Occupational therapist
- Speech and language therapist/speech pathologist
- Physical therapist
- Reading specialist
- Interventionist or intervention teachers
- *Personnel qualified to interpret assessment results, if not listed above.

Note: Those indicated with a * are required by IDEA to be present for IEP process meetings.

Involving family members, healthcare specialists, and outside professionals

The multidisciplinary process of identifying a child for services or accommodations requires input from diverse individuals who represent multiple perspectives. For students with a complex medical diagnosis such as PANDAS or PANS, the input of family members and outside professionals (e.g., physicians, therapists, psychologists) is essential. To facilitate productive involvement of these individuals, the following suggestions may be helpful:

- *Create an environment of openness and trust.* Sharing the sensitive information that may accompany a PANDAS/PANS diagnosis can be difficult for families, particularly if such information includes protected health information, psychiatric diagnoses, and challenges such as eating disorders or behavioral anomalies. Creating an open and welcoming climate may help families to feel more comfortable sharing such information (Rice Doran 2015). Specifically, personnel should assure parents that any information shared will remain confidential and should respond in a nonjudgmental manner to whatever is shared before, during, or after the meeting.

- *Establish parameters for communication with outside professionals.* It can be challenging for teams, including families and professionals, to navigate requirements of federal laws such as the Health Information Patient Portability Act (HIPPA) and Federal Educational Records Protection Act (FERPA). Teams should discuss, openly, how all stakeholders view the information-sharing process. Are parents comfortable having their neurologist or psychiatrist communicate directly with the team? Is there information that teachers should provide to the student's outside therapist? If so, how will that information be gathered, shared, and followed up on? Clear discussion of these issues in advance will make for a more smooth communication.

- *Recognize that family situations may change.* As described earlier, PANDAS and PANS place tremendous stress on parents, siblings, and other family members. This stress can encompass emotional, physical, psychological, and financial challenges, among others. Family schedules may change rapidly depending on the need for medical appointments, treatment schedules, sibling illness, and other variables. Be understanding of families who cancel appointments or meetings with little advance notice for such reasons. Additionally, recognize that families come to the IEP table already under significant stress, a fact which may impact their availability and affect throughout the process.

Involvement of outside agencies

Frequently, families have recounted stories of meetings in which school personnel made the decision to involve social services, child protective services, or law enforcement as a result of concerns over a child's school attendance, aggressive behaviors in the school setting, or other concerns. As a matter of legal and professional responsibility, school personnel are required by relevant district policies and state law to decide whether such outside involvement is warranted; some policies leave school personnel little room for discretion. At the same time, school personnel should take time to ensure their decisions to involve outside authorities are based on an accurate understanding of the medical, neurological, and psychological implications of the student's diagnosis. A referral to law enforcement for violent behavior, for example, may be inappropriate if the violent behavior is an involuntary reaction, motor or vocal tic, or the like. Vocal tics involving profanity or violent language, self-injurious behaviors, and motor responses that result in unintentional injury to personnel would often fall into this category.

Communication with families in such situations should be respectful, direct, and clear, within the boundaries of what relevant policy or law allows; communication with treating professionals, if authorized by the parent, is encouraged as a way to clarify treatment plans and symptom presentation for school personnel. In this process, school personnel should also be mindful of the potential impact such decisions may have on the student's functioning and emotional state and, to the extent possible, should minimize such impact. More than one parent has described receiving visits from truancy officers or child protective services personnel based solely on their child's non-attendance at school. The stress caused by such visits may, in itself, increase anxiety for students. The impact of such interactions might easily be mitigated by a prior conversation between district officials and the school-level administrator or counselor working with the student, explaining the student's challenges and planning for a less stressful, more positive discussion regarding school attendance and/or home teaching. The impact might also have been mitigated by more frequent communication with the parent in order to share district attendance requirements and next steps for students with concerning attendance patterns.

On a more positive note, external agencies, such as social services or a state's bureau of mental health or disability services, can be a tremendous support for families. Information about local and statewide (or federal) resources can be shared with families at or before planning meetings. If the school's counseling or special education department has not yet created one, an IEP meeting for a student with PANDAS/PANS may be an excellent opportunity to compile a resource guide for families of available supports and agencies.

Areas for evaluation

Teams should also consider the nature, frequency, and type of evaluations for children with PANDAS/PANS. Table 6.2 summarizes some potential assessment areas and the purpose of using each as part of the evaluation process for a student with PANDAS/PANS.

Table 6.2 Assessment areas, purpose, and considerations for students with PANDAS/PANS

Instrument	Purpose	Special considerations/limitations
Intelligence/cognitive testing	May establish a baseline for cognitive functioning; useful for short- and long-term planning and for establishing patterns of aptitude and skill.	Baseline may be inaccurate if the student is in a current symptom flare; medical or psychological professional consultation about validity of results may be useful.
Academic/achievement testing	Provides a baseline for academic knowledge and skills. May assist with placement and short- and long-term planning.	As with cognitive testing, the baseline established by standardized measures may be inaccurate if the student is in an active symptom flare. Ongoing informal or curriculum-based measures, administered consistently over time, may provide a better indication of strengths, needs, and growth.
Behavioral and emotional health	Behavioral inventories can measure student's feelings, self-worth and self-efficacy, risk level, and behavioral strengths and needs. Assessment of social skills and interactions with peers is also important.	As with other measures, results may vary according to a student's medical status. Behavioral assessments may establish symptoms or behavioral patterns consistent with such disorders as ADHD, autism spectrum disorders, adjustment disorders, and the like. While PANDAS/PANS have a unique medical etiology, establishing symptom characteristics may help to guide decisions about placement, planning, services and goals. The anxiety typical of students with PANDAS/PANS, for example, may impact peer relationships, fight or flight responses, interactions with adults, and a multitude of other behavioral reactions.

Instrument	Purpose	Special considerations/limitations
Motor skills (fine and gross)	Fine motor involvement is common in cases of PANDAS/PANS (Chang et al. 2015). Gross motor symptoms may result as well, particularly in students whose symptoms are more characteristic of Sydenham chorea.	The nature of motor assessment may change as students become older; concerns about handwriting and sensory needs may predominate in the upper grades. Fine motor skills are often reported by parents to fluctuate significantly (Rice Doran and O'Hanlon 2015), and research on PANDAS criteria and symptoms has borne this out (Swedo, Leckman, and Rose 2012; Chang et al. 2015).
Speech	Patterns of speech may be affected by PANDAS/PANS. Involvement may extend to pragmatics as well as fluency, rate, and pitch (Swedo et al. 2011).	Speech therapists should exercise care to distinguish speech and language issues from vocal tics. One parent recalls her daughter receiving speech therapy for months to improve her "vocal hygiene," when her daughter's unusual vocalizations were actually tics.
Health	School nurses may undertake general health screening or assessment. This assessment is generally holistic, using data from multiple sources, and is focused on understanding a student's needs in order to ensure she or he has appropriate supports during the day.	Complete information from parents and families will make this assessment most accurate and useful. Clearly communicating the purpose of health assessment to families, including the ways that the process can be helpful to the child, is one effective strategy to build trust and ensure they feel comfortable disclosing sensitive information.
Attendance	Many districts or states have attendance policies which mandate a certain number of days in school or which stipulate penalties (retention in the current grade, referral to truancy divisions or child protective services) for specific numbers of absences. These policies are often enforced by means of record review, where students with a set number of absences are identified and then referrals are initiated.	In addition to regular review of records, it is essential for school personnel to consider extenuating factors with respect to attendance. As with a student undergoing chemotherapy, immunotherapy, surgery, or other intensive medical intervention, school attendance for students with PANDAS/PANS is likely to be inconsistent. Frequent tardiness and multiple or lengthy absences are not uncommon.

As with any assessment and evaluation, results should be shared with parents prior to the meeting and discussed at the meeting in order to answer parents' questions—particularly if the assessment report uses a great deal of technical language. Fish (2006) found that parents often felt school personnel were condescending to them or did not adequately explain technical terms to them; taking the time to paraphrase technical language, in a mutually respectful way, can ameliorate some of these concerns.

Facilitating planning meetings for students with PANDAS/PANS

Some logistical recommendations for planning and running the IEP or 504 meeting are:

1. It is helpful to ensure all team members have a working familiarity with the general nature of PANDAS and PANS. At a minimum, all team members should review the brief information sheet included in Appendix B as well as current information from the National Institute of Mental Health (NIMH 2015) and other medical sources available.

2. Team members who are less familiar with the student and his or her family will also benefit from a brief pre-meeting conference with colleagues who have more day-to-day involvement with the student. This conference may cover the student's specific PANDAS/PANS presentation and the day-to-day impact of the most common symptoms.

3. If the PANDAS/PANS diagnosis is recent or if team members are not familiar with the family, consider a brief pre-conference or "listening session" before the meeting, in which family members can share with one or more team members some specifics about their child's needs, symptoms, and health history, as well as describing how the condition may impact family functioning. As school schedules tighten and many educators report being asked to fit IEP meetings into ever shorter blocks of time, it becomes more and more challenging to make time for this type

of communication within the parameters allotted for a meeting. Hearing family members' concerns in advance may clear a path for more productive conversation during the meeting itself and may allow school personnel to anticipate what information is most essential for their colleagues during the decision-making process.

4. If the student will be in attendance, it is essential both to take any health-related precautions necessary (sanitizing the room in advance, for example) and to consider specific steps that may reduce student anxiety and stress (carefully selected seating; comfortable chairs; ambient lighting). Family members and team members alike can prepare the student for what will be involved in the meeting; walking into a room of teachers, administrators, and specialists can be intimidating for any student, particularly one who experiences anxiety or school phobia.

5. Be mindful of parent stress. As discussed in Chapter 4, parents of children with PANS/PANDAS were found to exhibit higher stress levels than those of parents whose children had cancer (Frankovich *et al.* 2015). It is important to take steps to minimize stress on families where possible. Such steps may include opening the meeting with positive comments, using active listening strategies with parents, and taking the time to ensure parents' questions are answered and concerns are heard (Diliberto and Brewer 2014; Friend and Cook 2013).

Implementing the IEP

For children with PANDAS/PANS, many of the same principles hold true for implementation of the IEP that are true for children with other disabilities. Collaboration, empathy, progress monitoring, and frequent communication with families and treating professionals (as appropriate) are all important for smooth, successful IEP implementation (Friend and Cook 2013; Hardman *et al.* 2017). The particular nature of PANDAS/PANS will likely make flexibility, collaboration, and consistent progress monitoring particularly important:

1. *Flexibility.* Flexibility may be needed both in implementation and in progress monitoring. One teacher interviewed on this topic described adjusting students' work on-the-go each morning, based on the state of his or her neurological and social functioning. Some days, the student would spend an hour or two sorting books, meeting both his sensory and social needs. Other times, the student might be entirely ready for what the school task might be. Teachers might consider using a brief inventory or student self-rating scale each morning, where the student can respond to indicate his or her mood, level of functioning, and readiness for work. One example of such a scale is shown in Table 6.3.

2. *Collaboration.* This chapter opened with discussion of the importance of collaboration and communication. Planning for a student with a complex medical and psychological disability is a near-impossibility without the involvement of multiple professionals, both in school and out of it. Educators should build in time to contact all relevant professionals frequently for updates and feedback. In this author's experience, the status of a child with PANDAS/PANS may change rapidly. While IEP and 504 meetings are typically mandated once a year, this author has found more frequent meetings to be helpful. Consider scheduling a beginning-of-year and mid-year check-in meeting where family members and professionals can communicate, both about any medical changes and about educational goals and progress. As stated earlier, a proactive and positive approach can help to build that collaborative relationship.

3. *Progress monitoring.* For a student with PANDAS/PANS, progress monitoring takes on a particularly important role. Progress monitoring, for a student with PANDAS/PANS, should in fact include not just formal assessment or curriculum-based measurement, but ongoing attention to less formalized indicators that are correlated to PANDAS/PANS symptoms. These may include handwriting changes, attention and focusing, skills measured on classroom assessments, social behaviors, eating habits, fatigue, and behavioral changes. Behavioral changes may

be dramatic or, for students experiencing minor flare-ups with ongoing treatment, less dramatic but still disruptive.

For example, Nancy, mother of a third-grader with PANS, had contacted her child's teacher to mention that some family members had been ill lately, thinking that might impact her child's academic performance. She was surprised to hear from the teacher that her son had been having verbal conflicts at recess with other students, something quite uncharacteristic for him. While Nancy's son had not been formally disciplined, this small behavioral change appeared to be correlated to illness at home. Without the teacher's careful noting of behavior (and without proactive communication from both), neither Nancy nor the teacher would have had the knowledge necessary to address the student's behavior. Given his PANDAS/PANS diagnosis and anxiety over "getting in trouble," they opted to address his conflicts through positive encouragement, informal conferences with peers, and adult support to mediate conflicts for the next week or so.

Table 6.3 Elementary-grade student self-rating scale

Directions: Circle the picture that shows how you feel today

Glad to be here	Still waking up	Not happy
Ready to work!	Ready to work in a few minutes	I need some space for now

Key points to remember

For educators working with students who have PANDAS/PANS, input from both families and professionals is likely to be essential, given the multifaceted presentations of either disorder. In particular, the following principles may be a useful guide:

- Best practices for collaboration are important for teachers of all students with disabilities, but particularly those with PANDAS/PANS.

- As PANDAS/PANS are medical diagnoses, Other Health Impairments (OHI) is often a category used to qualify students for special education services.

- Flexibility and strong communication can benefit relationships with families and colleagues.

- Various types of plans may be developed and implemented for students with PANDAS/PANS.

- Minimizing parent/family and student stress will have beneficial effects in the planning and implementation of services or accommodations.

Conclusion

As the remaining chapters indicate, collaboration is a necessary but not sufficient element for support of students with PANDAS/PANS. Appropriate adaptations and accommodations, particularly for academic, motor and sensory, and behavioral functioning, are also critical. These are discussed more fully in Chapters 7–9.

References

Candelaria-Greene, J. (2014) *Considerations Regarding Academic Accommodations/ Compensatory Strategies, and Services for Students with PANDAS/PANS.* Available at http:// pandasnetwork.org/wp-content/uploads/2014/09/School-Considerations-2014. pdf, accessed on 7 March 2016.

Chang, K., Frankovich, J., Cooperstock, M., Cunningham, M.W., *et al.* (2015) 'Clinical evaluation of youth with pediatric acute-onset neuropsychiatric syndrome (PANS): Recommendations from the 2013 PANS Consensus Conference.' *Journal of Child and Adolescent Psychopharmacology 25*, 1, 3–13.

Diliberto, J.A., and Brewer, D. (2014) 'Six tips for successful IEP meetings.' *Teaching Exceptional Children 47*, 2, 128–135.

Fish, W. (2006) 'Perceptions of parents of students with autism towards the IEP meeting: A case study of one family support group chapter.' *Education 127*, 1, 56–68.

Frankovich, J., Thienemann, M., Pearlstein, J., Crable, A., *et al.* (2015) 'Multidisciplinary clinic dedicated to treating youth with pediatric acute-onset neuropsychiatric syndrome: presenting characteristics of the first 47 consecutive patients.' *Journal of Child and Adolescent Psychopharmacology 1*, 38–47.

Friend, M., and Cook, L. (2013) *Interactions: Collaboration skills for School Professionals* (Sixth edition). Upper Saddle River: Pearson.

Fuchs, L.S., and Vaughn, S. (2012) 'Responsiveness-to-Intervention: A decade later.' *Journal of Learning Disabilities 45*, 3, 195–203.

Gable, R.A., Park, K., and Scott, T. (2014) 'Functional behavioral assessment and students at risk for or with emotional disabilities: Current issues and considerations.' *Education and Treatment of Children 37*, 111–135.

Gargiulo, R.M., and Metcalf, D. (2012) *Teaching in Today's Inclusive Classrooms: A Universal Design for Learning Approach* (Second edition). Belmont, CA: Wadsworth.

Hardman, M., Egan, W., and Drew, C. (2017) *Human exceptionality: School, Community and Family.* Boston: Cengage.

Hoover, J. (2012) *Linking Assessment to Instruction in Multi-Tiered Models: A Teacher's Guide to Selecting Reading, Writing and Mathematics Interventions.* Upper Saddle River: Pearson.

IDEA (2006) *Individuals with Disabilities Education Improvement Act (IDEA), Final Regulations (2006)*, 34 CFR 300 *et seq.* Available at http://idea.ed.gov/download/finalregulations.pdf, accessed on 2 March 2016.

McClelland, M., Crombez, M., Crombez, C., and Wenz, M. (2015) 'Implications for advanced practice nurses when Pediatric Autoimmune Neuropsychiatric Disorders Associated with Streptococcal Infections (PANDAS) is suspected: A qualitative study.' *Journal of Pediatric Health Care 29*, 5, 442–452.

Metcalf, T. (n.d.) *What's Your Plan? Accurate Decision Making Within a Multi Tier System of Supports: Critical Areas in Tier 1.* RTI Action Network. Available at www.rtinetwork.org/essential/tieredinstruction/tier1/accurate-decision-making-within-a-multi-tier-system-of-supports-critical-areas-in-tier-1, accessed on 7 March 2016.

National Institute of Mental Health (NIMH) (n.d.) *Information About PANDAS.* Available at www.nimh.nih.gov/labs-at-nimh/research-areas/clinics-and-labs/pdnb/web.shtml, accessed on 2 March 2016.

National Institute of Mental Health (NIMH) (2015) *Diagnostic Criteria for PANS.* Available at www.nimh.nih.gov/labs-at-nimh/research-areas/clinics-and-labs/pdnb/web.shtml, accessed on 3 March 2016.

O'Rourke, K. (2003) 'PANDAS syndrome in the school setting.' *School Nurse News, September 2003*, 34–35.

Rice Doran, P. (2015) 'Sudden behavioral changes in the classroom: What educators need to know about PANDAS and PANS.' *Beyond Behavior 24*, 1, 31–37. Available at www.academia.edu/15102564/Sudden_Behavioral_Changes_in_the_Classroom_What_Educators_Need_to_Know_about_PANDAS_and_PANS, accessed on 2 March 2016.

Rice Doran, P., and O'Hanlon, E. (2015) *Families' Experiences with PANDAS and Related Disorders.* Poster session at Council for Exceptional Children Convention, San Diego, April 2015.

Swedo, S., Latimer, E., Kovacevic, M., and Leckman, J. (2011) *PANDAS/PANS Symptom Scale, Parent Version.* Available at http://pandasnetwork.org/wp-content/uploads/2012/11/pandas_pans_scale.pdf, accessed on 7 March 2016.

Swedo, S., Leckman, J., and Rose, N. (2012) 'From research subgroup to clinical syndrome: Modifying the PANDAS criteria to describe PANS (Pediatric Acute-onset Neuropsychiatric Syndrome).' *Pediatrics and Therapeutics 2*, 113, 1–8.

United States Department of Education (2013) *Protecting Students with Disabilities. Frequently asked questions about Section 504 and the Education of Students with Disabilities.* Available at www2.ed.gov/about/offices/list/ocr/504faq.html, accessed on 2 March 2016.

Chapter 7

Academic Accommodations and Supports for Students with PANDAS/PANS

AMY MAZUR, ED.D.

Classroom teacher: "Jasmine, you have been out of school for two months. Please listen to me and stop making that annoying clicking sound with your throat. We have finished the story and now it is time to answer questions about what we have read. The questions are on the board. Please read all eight questions, copy them from the board, and get started with your written response. We just finished lunch and recess and you are asking to go use the bathroom again. If you wash your hands one more time they may start to bleed. When are you going to get started?"

Jasmine looks at the board. She gets paper from her desk but cannot find a pencil, so she takes everything out of her desk. To the teacher she appears to be disorganized, unfocused, and late in starting work. After three minutes of copying from the board, she rips up her paper and starts again, saying that her writing is "not easy to read" and "looks messy." She tells the teacher that she can't remember the whole story and can't answer the questions.

Classroom teacher: "You will never finish the assignment. Did you read the book at home? Why are you taking so long? You have to keep up with the rest of the class. You haven't even copied the questions yet, and what you have copied I cannot even read. You need to try harder if you want to stay in this class."

Introduction

Students with PANDAS/PANS frequently have difficulty with social, emotional, and medical issues. These issues may include, among others, separation anxiety, severe physical or vocal tics, difficulties with focusing, intrusive and obsessive thoughts, fatigue, or other neurological or cognitive symptoms. Despite these difficulties, there are frequently extended periods of time when these students are able to successfully attend school. For some, this period of time may be a week, a month, a semester, or even years. While well-meaning teachers may be aware of the problems that impact the student's school attendance, it is often assumed that, when a student is present in the classroom, he or she should be able to follow the daily classroom agenda without any adaptations or modifications. This, however, is often not the case, as the vignette at the start of this chapter illustrates.

We know that learning does not occur in a vacuum; each of us brings our feelings, fears, obsessions, anxieties, behaviors, and beliefs to the learning environment. This is true of our students as well. The degree and frequency with which they can control these potentially debilitating behaviors greatly impacts their success in the classroom. When educators are aware of how each student's PANDAS/PANS symptoms interfere with their academic learning, they are better able to identify appropriate accommodations and modifications.

The areas that impact a particular child's success should be identified in his/her 504 plan or IEP, if one is needed, so as to facilitate the understanding of how to best plan for that child's school success. Educators and families need to frequently revisit identified goals to assess what the child has achieved and which goals have not been accomplished and thus may need further assessment and task analysis. While it is important to measure behavioral and academic accomplishments, it is not realistic to anticipate a linear trajectory of improvement. For instance, exposure to others who are carriers of strep may cause flares in those whose PANDAS symptoms had seemed to subside; students with PANS, whose illnesses are triggered by other infections than strep, may flare during flu season or when a classmate has a cold.

During flares, a student who was performing at his/her developmental level both academically and emotionally may suddenly look like a different child, causing those around him/her to wonder if the behaviors are within the child's control or if the child still belongs in the classroom. For this reason, it is critical for educators to understand symptoms of PANDAS/PANS, how they will affect performance, and what might be appropriate modifications.

General recommendations for academic supports

Student success depends upon the teacher's understanding of their strengths and needs, their prior knowledge, and their educational, medical, and behavioral history. Therefore, even before planning specific accommodations, teachers should be careful to address the following:

- *Maintain clarity about the goal of a lesson or assessment.* If, for example, a teacher is trying to assess a student's knowledge of a particular subject area, do not demand that they complete an assessment whose format will interfere with their performance. For instance, requiring students to copy problems from the board will produce unreliable results on an assessment of fraction multiplication. Copying from the board is likely to slow students down and may result in inaccurate copying, yielding inaccurate answers. Rather, consider how to assess this skill in a way that is compatible with the strengths and needs of the student.

- *Use various strategies to teach and assess.* Consider the materials used, the avenue of input of instruction, and the grouping. Consistent with UDL, as discussed in Chapter 5, provide multiple means of representation, action and expression, and engagement for all learners (CAST 2014). Alternative means of assessment, minimizing anxiety or other barriers, are particularly important for students with PANDAS/PANS.

- *Create a supportive socio-emotional climate.* Students must be supported in academic, social, and behavioral terms. Positive peer relationships, frequent teacher praise and reinforcement, and other accommodations can help to ensure a classroom is warm, welcoming, and accessible.

- *Understand that PANDAS/PANS may not result in a quick "cure" with a straight upward trajectory.* Educators must look at each child through an individual lens. As with all students, those identified as having PANDAS/PANS may not all exhibit the same behaviors and, if they do so, it may not be to the same degree or with the same frequency. Recovery may be uneven and inconsistent, with regression during periods of exacerbation or symptom flares.

- *Know each student's strengths and needs.* As with all students, a person with PANDAS/PANS has his or her own unique behaviors, skills and feelings. Knowing this allows one to maintain the integrity of the general curriculum while guiding modifications to instruction.

- *Implement necessary accommodations, modifications, or services.* Because of the neurologically based deficits caused by PANDAS/PANS, appropriate strategies and classroom supports are often needed. Teachers must recognize that what works at one point, for one student, may not work for the next; each teacher needs an extensive repertoire or "bag of tricks" from which to draw instructional strategies. It is important to recognize, also, that students with PANDAS/PANS may need accommodations or other supports in the midst of a symptom flare but may not need them when symptoms subside. As indicated in Chapter 4, PANDAS and PANS can be chronic conditions with an unpredictable trajectory, and therefore communication among team members and with family members is essential.

Identifying and implementing appropriate accommodations, modifications, services or supports

In a study of how parents of children with PANDAS/PANS described their children's accommodations, Rice Doran and O'Hanlon (2015) found that the accommodations most frequently reported, across grade levels, included:

- flexible attendance and flexible school schedules

- access to "safe spaces" in schools

- specialized behavior plans

- sensory supports such as special seating, lighting, or fidgets

- extended time

- use of keyboards and laptops

- expedited transitions to home teaching.

General areas for teams to consider include the four main areas of accommodations: presentation of materials, including alternative formats; setting for instruction and assessment; timing, including pacing, breaks and extended time limits; and response method, including response by alternative modalities (United States Office of Special Education Programs n.d.). These accommodations are designed to ensure equitable access and mitigate the effects of PANDAS/PANS (or other disabilities). Accommodations do not, in and of themselves, alter the curriculum but rather guarantee access to it. Program modifications may alter or reduce curriculum expectations (US OSEP n.d.). Most states or districts list frequently accessed accommodations, modifications, and services or supports on their state IEP forms.

When using such forms to identify appropriate supports for students with PANDAS/PANS, it can be helpful to consider the areas of skill or development that are often impacted by PANDAS/PANS and identify accommodations and supports accordingly. Lewin *et al.* (2011) found that children with PANDAS exhibited consistent deficits in visual-spatial reasoning. In particular, those with elevated strep titers (suggesting recent exposure to infection) evidenced decreased fine motor, neurocognitive, and executive function skills. Such impairment is consistent with the diagnostic criteria for both PANDAS and PANS, which emphasize neurological abnormalities, fine motor challenges, obsessive compulsive symptoms, and, sometimes, sudden declines in school performance (Chang *et al.* 2015; Swedo, Leckman, and Rose 2012). Brendan, father of several children with PANDAS, described each of his children's exacerbations as being accompanied by declines in their usual school grades: from As and Bs to Cs, Ds, and sometimes Es. Variables such as support with organizational skills, chronic fatigue, and emotional needs may significantly impact the learning experience.

Candelaria-Greene (2014) identified areas of development that are described as being potential roadblocks to success with the general education curriculum in the general education classroom, including visual processing, memory, executive functioning, and other areas. The list given in Table 7.1, which identifies potential accommodations and strategies for classroom implementation by category, is based on the categories of impact identified by Candelaria-Greene. When using this list, keep in mind that, although these accommodations and modifications may be necessary for students with PANDAS/ PANS, good teaching is good teaching. That is to say, providing other students with the use of class notes, scratch paper, or a book on tape not only allows each student to participate in the way he or she best learns, but it also helps to de-stigmatize the student who has PANDAS. Such practices are consistent with principles of UDL (CAST 2014), as discussed in Chapter 5.

Table 7.1 Accommodations, adaptations, and strategies by skill area

Skill	Accommodations, adaptations, and strategies
Fine motor skill/visual motor integration	Shorten assignments and assessments to reduce handwriting or computer fine and visual motor demands.
	Provide access to manipulatives in math, science, or other relevant classes. Recognize that some manipulatives may be difficult for students with PANDAS/PANS to utilize or keep track of.
	Put fewer questions per page, leaving white space between each problem or question.
	For computerized testing, offer students scratch paper and pencil.
	Provide extended time on classroom and standardized tests.
	Recognize that copying content from the board requires visual motor integration and minimize or eliminate this requirement.
	Ensure that worksheets and homework, particularly math, do not require students to copy or line up numbers.
	Offer access to a scribe and/or dictation programs in lieu of writing.
	Consider providing sentence strips that the student dictates and then assembles to create his or her response (or computer-generated sentences that the student can select).
	Use "green and red light" start and stop highlighter to indicate the left and right side of page and margins. Allow the student use of adaptive pencil and/or pencil grip(s).
	Allow the student to select/use the writing utensil (pen, marker, pencil, etc.) they prefer (discourage a "must be in pen/no erasing" rule).
	Consider reducing the writing workload or allowing use of short answers/incomplete sentences.
	Grade on content, rather than neatness, spelling, or grammar. (Undue emphasis on mechanics can feed into students' anxiety and perfectionism, making it difficult for a student to complete work.) If a student's writing is illegible, ask them to read the answer back to you or paraphrase his or her thoughts. See additional fine motor accommodations and suggestions in Chapter 8.
Visual processing	Provide less writing, larger print, and larger margins on handouts. Ensure there is sufficient space between items to facilitate visual differentiation.
	Consider using books with raised-line drawings or diagrams.
	Structure handouts with visual cues, such as bold type, outlines, reduced text, and bullet points.
	Offer graphic organizers, providing multiple options rather than requiring use of one that may not work for the student, and teach students how to use them.
	Ensure preferential seating to minimize visual distraction from both within the classroom and outside (consider windows, glaring light, activities of others in hallway, etc.). Use window shades, curtains, or study carrels to control the lighting, glares, and visual environment. Provide handouts with clearly marked, visually accessible, written directions.

Receptive language, including auditory processing	Offer headphones or earbuds to minimize distraction.
	Provide written instructions to accompany all verbal instructions. Provide samples or model in all directions. When possible, actively model desired behavior or task to the class or for the student in question. Ask students to restate directions or model the desired behavior back.
	Provide opportunities for assessment that do *not* rely on quick processing of language (e.g., class math facts, flash card games, or quiz-style competitions). Such activities may significantly increase students' anxiety.
	Provide extra wait time for responses.
	Use personal notebooks or individualized vocabulary journals to support reading, as expectations for these can be adjusted easily during PANDAS/PANS exacerbation.
	Consider providing reading services, in a push-in or pull-out setting. Consider the student's anxiety level and the psychological impact/organizational disruption of pull-out; if pull-out services are appropriate, plan with teachers and family to minimize disruption.
Expressive language	Allow students to select pictures, diagrams, or other visuals to respond rather than using words.
	Writing prompts such as sentence starters, skeletal paragraphs or cloze stories (partially completed stories) can provide effective language supports.
	Encourage students to develop their own list of vocabulary words meaningful to them (coordination with parents and school counselor or nurse is recommended for students with restricted or obsessive interests). For some students whose OCD leads them to focus on a particular topic (such as dinosaurs or space exploration), teachers will need to consult with others to determine when, if at all, to redirect students away from areas of obsession.
	Similarly, encourage students to keep both academic and personal journals. These can be a valuable tool for reinforcing learning, a helping therapeutic aid, and an avenue for communication among home, school, and student. Students with writing difficulties may type and print journal entries or select images instead.
	Provide appropriate wait time for students with PANDAS/PANS, both in read-alouds, in class discussions, and during oral exams.
	Provide opportunities, other than through spoken language, for students to show their knowledge (e.g., have students point to the correct answer rather than verbally restating the correct answer).
	Teach students to use keywords in directions to identify what to do first, second, and so on when completing writing tasks.
	Provide students in upper grades with lecture notes.
	Provide an outline of each lesson in advance.
	Select a classroom note-taker whose notes will be shared with others in the class, including the student(s) with PANDAS/PANS.

	Provide the opportunity for team writing projects where 3–4 students collaborate to complete a writing project, each using their strengths. Be mindful of concerns or issues, such as OCD or social anxiety, that may make participation a challenge for students with PANDAS/PANS.
	Consider pull-out or push-in support with writing, expressive language, or speech. Be mindful of considerations outlined under "Receptive language" in determining the appropriate structure and setting for services.
Visual and auditory memory	Provide visuals (chart or graphic organizer) to guide students through the writing process.
	When teaching or assessing, tell students what information to listen or look for as you introduce the activity. For example: "Listen for the number of children that are sharing the four apples," or "Look at the picture to see how many children have to share the four apples."
	Provide fact sheets, equations, lists of key vocabulary or dates, and other information so that students do not need to rely on memory during assessments.
	Visual and auditory memory are particularly important for math skills, and students with PANDAS/PANS frequently struggle in math. Consider providing supplemental math-related services, support, or instruction, subject to considerations described under "Receptive language" and "Expressive language" for planning and implementing such services.
	Consider shortening work and reducing expectations for memory-related tasks. Spelling tests, for example, are often required by the curriculum but may feel like an exercise in futility for students with significant memory (and fine motor) challenges; target academic demands at the level of the student's current functioning.
Executive functioning skills	Prior to assigning the work, explicitly teach the use of calculator, graph paper, graphic organizers, and other tools or supports needed for task completion. For each new tool or implement introduced, teach the student an organizational method to manage it.
	Teach specific strategies, particularly for reading, writing, and math, allowing time to practice each one before introducing a new one. Provide time for practice and review of (new) concepts.
	Provide a calendar indicating assignments and timeline. Have students cross off work as it is completed.
	Consider offering support from an occupational therapist (OT) or special educator for organization and cognitive functioning.
	Task-analyze projects, identifying each stage or step and providing students opportunities for feedback and revision at each step.
	Maintain a class webpage or online homework journal so that students and families can plan for upcoming assignments and projects.

Offer preferential seating in an area with few distractions. This may be near the front of the room if instruction usually occurs from this platform. Consider the seating most appropriate for the particular student's needs. Students needing frequent bathroom or school nurse visits, for example, should be seated near the door to minimize disruption and travel time.

Teach and provide verbal or visual cues to use during transitions or when behavioral feedback is needed.

Provide sufficient transition time between activities. Students with PANDAS/PANS may benefit from a few minutes of additional transition time. Provide breaks between tasks and choices for use of the "break time."

Pre-teach vocabulary and concepts, and provide students with the opportunity to practice using and listening for important words or concepts.

Offer positive, nonthreatening reinforcement for remaining on task. As discussed in Chapter 5, stress can significantly impede performance.

Consider shortening homework, providing it in an alternative format, or waiving it entirely.

Provide for shortened classroom assignments.

Use a "feelings board" or other chart where students can indicate their mood, feelings, and readiness for work. Explicitly teach methods and strategies for recognizing and voicing feelings.

Sensory integration	Schedule opportunity for movement during and between activities.
	Provide access to fidgets, textured seating, varieties of writing utensils, and appropriate sensory environments (such as a beanbag chair, a room with ambient lighting, or a white noise machine).
	Minimize sensory demands or tasks when these will be challenging. For example, avoid asking a student to listen to verbal instructions, copy a math problem from the board, solve the problem, write the answer in a small space, and then explain to the class how the problem was solved. Rather, support the student in using one or two sensory modalities to be successful (e.g., responding, in sufficient space, to a pre-printed problem or prompt and then providing a brief explanation or justification in writing or orally).
	Consider the need for OT services, as well as the nature and delivery of those services.
	See additional sensory integration strategies in Chapter 8.

Academic assessment and careful analysis of information

As discussed in Chapter 6, academic or cognitive assessments to determine strengths and needs should be performed carefully, with attention to potential limitations due to PANDAS/PANS. Candelaria-Greene (2014) recommends making decisions about placement or performance level with several data points, never with one isolated piece of data, because of the risk that PANDAS/PANS symptoms may interfere with assessment performance. Informal classroom assessments may be less anxiety-producing than standardized tests and may provide better data for decision-making purposes (Candelaria-Greene 2014). Educators must look at each child through an individual lens. As with all students, those identified as having PANDAS/PANS may not all exhibit the same behaviors and, if they do so, it may not be to the same degree or with the same frequency. A student's health status may significantly impact his or her performance on any given assessment, a fact which should be taken into account in the planning process. In fact, what works at one point for one student might not work during the next lesson, the next day, or the following week. For this reason, it is necessary for members of the team to own a wide repertoire of skills—"a bag of tricks"—from which to draw instructional strategies.

It is beneficial to recognize that many students with PANDAS/PANS may need accommodations and supports when in the midst of a flare but do not need them when symptoms subside or disappear. For many students, PANDAS/PANS can be chronic conditions whose trajectory may be unpredictable. It is important that all those participating in the instructional team are observant and note the student's presenting needs as they engage in an ongoing dialogue about the most appropriate supports.

As with all instruction across developmental levels, effective teachers of students within the general education population consider the *timing and pacing of instruction* as well as the *physical and psychological demands of learning*, in conjunction with the academic content. However, unlike many students in the general education population, those with PANDAS/PANS are less likely to be incidental learners; they often need specific, targeted, and purposeful instruction during symptomatic periods (though research suggests students' intelligence and academic achievement are comparable to those of students without PANDAS/ PANS) (Lewin *et al.* 2011). Teachers cannot rely on the student to independently piece together the fabric of an assignment, draw inferences about "next steps," or make uninterrupted transitions from one space to the next, one class to the next, one teacher to the next, or one assignment to the next.

The role of observation in identifying and addressing PANDAS/PANS symptoms

All involved must consider the student's particular behavioral symptoms, whether at home or at school, in order to discern what environment is therapeutic for each child's learning. This discernment relies on accurate observation and assessment of student behaviors. For instance, the best planned instruction is likely to fail when teachers do not recognize that the student is fatigued, whether from physical issues, an overabundance of sensory input, writing demands, or a host of other challenges. Recognizing behaviors such as these would allow one to plan for a break in the instructional routine, for a few minutes, a period, or the entire day. If fatigue, rage, tics, or OCD behaviors arise three-quarters of the way through every day, the team might question whether an abbreviated school day or school week might work best for this individual.

Not only must the team members be willing to adjust or modify curricula, they must often be able to help students navigate their social emotional needs and facilitate interaction with others in their environment. A student with germ-related phobia, for example, may refuse to share materials, work with, or sit near another student whom he/she may suspect is likely to spread germs. Teachers who recognize this characteristic in some students with PANDAS/PANS can plan accordingly and mitigate chances of this interfering with class dynamics and relationships. Again, a nuanced understanding of PANDAS/PANS and the ability to look objectively at behavior are critical here in ensuring that instruction continues without disruption.

Additional academic indicators that may signal a PANDAS/PANS exacerbation may include (but are not limited to):

- complaints of significant headaches, fatigue, or joint pain during school

- difficulty organizing self and materials

- difficulty completing tasks

- presence of tics

- presence of, or increase in, OCD-related symptoms (may be indicated by concerns about sitting by peers; frequent erasures on papers; lining up items or needing to walk on/step on/touch particular surfaces; needing to get work "just right"; rage over minor issues; changes in eating habits; intrusive or disruptive worries; repetition of words, ideas, or concerns)

- gut-related symptoms, anxieties, or disorders

- difficulty focusing (may affect ability to understand, begin work, or complete it)

- increase in processing (auditory and/or visual) challenges

- new challenges with math, handwriting, or expressive writing

- new speech challenges

- changes in test performance (or study habits)

- challenges with transitions

- sudden increase in the ability to make both horizontal and vertical transitions.

Considerations for specific age and grade levels

PANDAS/PANS are often considered to begin in early childhood, but onset has been reported in later years as well. Additionally, even after treatment, PANDAS/PANS can continue to affect functioning into adolescence or even adulthood depending on the degree of symptom resolution experienced with treatment. For this reason, it is very important for educators, along the continuum of education from preschool to higher education, to think developmentally when planning for accommodations. While developmental skills may build on each other, it is possible, during a PANDAS/PANS flare, for a student to revert to lower levels of development or academic skill. The accommodations and supports suggested thus far are, for the most part, generalizable across grades and subject areas. Additional considerations specific to age and grade levels are presented below.

Early childhood

Entering a stimulating, multi-sensory classroom is often very challenging for a young child with PANDAS/PANS. Separation anxiety, not atypical for the age, can be intensified for such children. To ease these feelings, it is suggested that the teacher make a home visit to meet the child prior to the time he/she enters the classroom. During that time a special toy or blanket can be selected to serve as his/her transition toy to help the child bridge the home environment to school. (It may be suggested that the parent purchase a duplicate item to keep at home in case one should be misplaced or lost.)

It is also important to provide for transitions within the classroom. It is suggested that the teacher select a designated cubby for the child to use that is the first space closest to the entrance. This will minimize other visual distractions within the cubby area and be most likely to facilitate use of the space during each day as he/she is required to go to that area to find his/her coat, lunch, show and tell, and so on. A picture of the child can also be taped to the assigned cubby to support the child's visual memory and perceptual skills.

An early childhood setting is often a busy place with much purposeful movement. Visually and physically designating the various areas of the room for different activities and selecting materials to be used in each area-specific activity can promote the child's understanding of what activity happens in each space, thus promoting organizational success. Additionally, using clear, picture-labeled containers in each area supports access to the materials needed in each center/area. Teachers might also utilize large picture organizers to indicate each day's activities (to be shared with the group every morning at the opening/circle time); use of picture symbols to identify class schedule; timer to indicate when transitions between play/work centers are to occur, providing advance warning; or posting pictures of the activity center and a numeral at each center so children can identify the center to which they intend to go as well as the number of children that can optimally play in that center at one time (encouraging the development of self-monitoring skills).

Elementary school

Elementary schools present increasing organizational, as well as academic, demands. The number of children per class typically increases and there is usually more space to navigate both within the classroom and school. The use of preferential seating is suggested to support the student's learning style.

It is at the elementary school level that students are also responsible for getting and keeping track of materials. Small desks with little visual interior access can make it hard to gather necessary work/materials for each activity or transition between activities. Delayed auditory processing, and the need for visual or kinesthetic modeling of tasks and expectations, can further complicate a student's readiness to begin an assignment. In response to this challenge, it can be helpful to assign other classmates to serve as the "material delivery helpers," providing class members with papers, crayons, glue, or whatever is needed for a particular task. "Cleanup helpers" can assist with putting these materials away after an activity ends, providing support not only to the student with PANDAS/PANS but, in the spirit of UDL, to the entire class and reducing overall transition time.

An extra set of books or instructional materials that stays in the student's home is recommended to increase the likelihood that books will not get misplaced or lost and that completed assignments will be returned to school. The use of an extra set of books also minimizes fatigue, particularly in later elementary (or middle or high) school, when books become larger and heavier.

Picture charts taped to a student's desk can identify each step of a task or assignment. Bernard, a nine-year-old with PANS, uses a picture chart created by his third grade teacher to help him organize his folder each morning and pack up each afternoon.

Additionally, older students familiar with computer use and able to read can follow a homework website identifying homework, long-term assignments, using the program to complete a checklist of completed activities, thus facilitating their ability to self-monitor their performance and identify what is needed.

As in later years, medical interventions and treatment for PANDAS/ PANS may cause frequent absence; systems should be put into place to ensure a student can keep up with class learning even if he or she is unable to complete work during treatment. More discussion of these concerns is found below under "Middle school" and "High school," as frequent absence can place a student at greater academic risk in those levels.

Middle school

Transitioning to middle school presents new challenges; students from one or more elementary schools merge together in a building that may be two to three times larger than the student's elementary school setting. Many new organizational challenges presented at this level are the result of this change, especially for students with PANDAS/PANS.

Some potential student challenges to be considered that may not have been addressed at the elementary level include: navigating movement through the school so as not to get lost and facilitating the ability to arrive at classes in a timely manner; planning for similar teacher expectations and methods of communication from all involved in the team; access to books and materials within each classroom for the student with PANDAS/PANS so he/she does not have to be responsible for carrying all texts and notebooks with him/her from class to class in a backpack; access to a laptop or computer within each class so as to facilitate use of technological supports such as computer instructional programs or voice-activated writing programs.

Transition from class to class may take more time for students with PANDAS/PANS and may require early release from one class to get to the next. Until the student is comfortable and ready to navigate the building alone, a peer buddy, also going to the same class, may be identified to support class-to-class transitions.

With the expectation that each class addresses a new subject area, it is a good idea to color-code subject area notebooks and the corresponding textbook and instructional materials. At this level, the student can rely on the use of course websites to identify the daily homework calendar as well as the timelines for long-term projects and assignments within each course.

School-based educators working with students at all developmental levels must realize the impact medical intervention may have on the performance of their students with PANDAS/PANS. This becomes even more significant for students who prioritize attending school—often a consideration as academic rigor increases in upper grades and students' peer relationships become more important. Being in a larger building, exposed to more potential illness, may cause challenges for some students; these can be particularly stressful during middle school years when students are often focused on peer approval. Some students may have severe migraine headaches and nausea for three to four days following IVIG and yet still try to be present in the classroom; plasmapheresis may necessitate absence during hospitalization and recovery; students may experience steroid side effects such as anxiety, appetite increase, urinary changes, or aggression. These physical changes may exhaust students, requiring schedule adjustments or reduced workload during treatment as well as empathy from teachers and peers.

High school

Once a student arrives at the high school level there is frequently an assumption that they have the organizational skills necessary to succeed, and this is often not the case for the student with PANDAS/ PANS. Transitions are even more difficult to handle at the high school level where the pace of learning is more rapid, independent learning is often required, and there is little, if any, practice or review of basic skills. Teachers need to be aware that these needs still exist even though the student is older and may appear able to manage the demands of a typical school day.

If a student does not have an IEP case manager, it can be helpful to identify a counselor, academic coach, or other support person who can meet with him or her weekly to review progress meeting timelines, implementation of accommodations and identification of "next steps" such as application for accommodations on PSAT/SAT and other college entrance exams.

In high school, it is appropriate for a student to become more vocal and accept more responsibility for requesting feedback from, and providing feedback to, counselor, teachers, and family about his or her needs. This provides good practice for college, where self-advocacy is essential. Offering a student some support (workshops, one-on-one mentoring, and so on) in developing self-advocacy is appropriate and, for students with IEPs, should be built into the transition plan. This process may also involve planning and discussion of academic skills required for college.

As in earlier grades, frequent absences are likely, whether as a result of illness, IVIG treatment, or even plasmapheresis. Providing a buddy who can keep records of homework, or even audio record lectures in the student's absence, can be helpful.

Postsecondary education

While the focus of this book is on PK–12 schooling, postsecondary education merits a brief mention as well. Postsecondary education for students with disabilities, in the U.S., is covered primarily by Section 504 (as well as the Americans with Disabilities Act), referenced in Chapter 6. (In other countries different laws apply, but protections are typically provided to students pursuing higher education.) As an adult beyond high school, a student can choose whether or not to identify himself/herself to the University's Disability Support Services office and can decide whether, and when, to request accommodations in classes. By law, a student's family is not part of the process unless the student elects to involve them and signs a release to that effect. Accommodations typically depend on outside documentation which must be reviewed and approved by a college or university's Disability Support Services office. Once it is approved, the student is usually assigned an advocate who works with the student to determine what supports should be put into place. This plan can be modified as needs change and might include, for example, any of the following: access to course lecture notes or class notes from a peer; extended time for assignments and assessments; reduction of written requirements and flexibility in manner through which knowledge is measured; ability to audio record lectures or classes; access to private test-taking spaces; allowances for medically excused absences. This list, of course, is not exhaustive; supports and accommodations are determined by the student's advocate and the student, with input from instructors when unique situations (for example, how to implement accommodations in an internship or field-based class) might arise.

Again, students at this level must serve as their own advocates, sharing information of their changing needs as they move through each class, each semester. They must learn time management and monitor their own progress as no one is there to monitor overall academic progress until grades are posted at the conclusion of each semester.

Key points to remember

While this chapter addressed multiple aspects of academic supports for students with PANDAS/PANS, the following key ideas are particularly important:

- Students with PANDAS/PANS may be impacted academically in various ways.

- Specific areas of impact may include visual, motor, and visual-motor skills, memory, expressive and receptive language, and executive function.

- Accommodations, modifications, and services, along with basic good teaching, can address needs in each of these areas.

- Needs may vary across grade levels, from early childhood through college.

Conclusion

Although many companies promote the sale of custom-made programs, materials, or "one-size-fits-all" interventions, expensive packaged materials are not necessary for most accommodations, modifications, or services. Rather, what is needed is creativity, patience, and empathy, which may "cost" time and effort rather than money. The real cost, however, is to the lives of our students when we don't work to create the supportive environment necessary for them to access curricula and acquire successful life skills.

References

Candelaria-Greene, J. (2014) *Considerations Regarding Academic Accommodations/ Compensatory Strategies, and Services for Students with PANDAS/PANS.* Available at http:// pandasnetwork.org/wp-content/uploads/2014/09/School-Considerations-2014. pdf, accessed on 7 March 2016.

CAST (2014) *What is UDL?* Available at www.udlcenter.org/aboutudl/whatisudl, accessed on 3 March 2016.

Chang, K., Frankovich, J., Cooperstock, M., Cunningham, M.W., *et al.* (2015) 'Clinical evaluation of youth with pediatric acute-onset neuropsychiatric syndrome (PANS): Recommendations from the 2013 PANS Consensus Conference.' *Journal of Child and Adolescent Psychopharmacology 25,* 1, 3–13.

Lewin, A.B., Storch, E.A., Mutch, P.J., and Murphy, T.K. (2011) 'Neurocognitive functioning in youth with pediatric autoimmune neuropsychiatric disorders associated with streptococcus.' *Journal of Neuropsychiatry and Clinical Neurosciences 23,* 4, 391–398.

Rice Doran, P., and O'Hanlon, E. (2015) *Families' Experiences with PANDAS and Related Disorders.* Poster session at Council for Exceptional Children Convention, San Diego, April 2015.

Swedo, S., Leckman, J., and Rose, N. (2012) 'From research subgroup to clinical syndrome: Modifying the PANDAS criteria to describe PANS (Pediatric Acute-onset Neuropsychiatric Syndrome).' *Pediatrics and Therapeutics 2,* 113, 1–8.

United States Office of Special Education Programs (OSEP) (n.d.) *Accommodations Manual: How to Select, Administer, and Evaluate Use of Accommodations for Instruction and Assessment of Students with Disabilities.* Available at www.osepideasthatwork.org/toolkit/ accommodations_manual_b.asp, accessed on 8 March 2016.

Chapter 8

Sensory and Motor Considerations for Students with PANDAS/PANS

JANICE TONA, PH.D., OTR

Have you noticed that the child in your classroom with PANDAS or PANS suddenly seems to be overly sensitive to sounds, light, smells, and textures? Is the child complaining about the feeling of his waistband or the seam in his socks? Is the child becoming aggressive or even running away in stimulating environments including art class, the cafeteria, and the school bus? Have you noticed that the child seems much clumsier and has lost the penmanship that she was developing?

These changes are not uncommon during PANDAS/PANS exacerbations. Six-year-old Alejandro had a history of sinus infections and his parents had met with Mrs. Smith, the first grade teacher, in September to let her know that in the past he seemed to have trouble in school when he had a sinus infection. In January, Alejandro came to school and just seemed out of sorts after a long weekend. His class work was difficult to read and when his teacher compared his work to the work completed in September, his handwriting was noticeably worse in January. He seemed fidgety and kept closing his eyes and rubbing them with his hands. In physical education, Alejandro had difficulty keeping up with his classmates during soccer, and his classmates laughed when he tried to kick the ball but lost his balance and landed on the ground. His teacher was confused about this as well, as he played soccer outside of school on a team. Over the next few days, Alejandro seemed to complain about many things. He covered his ears during free time because it was too noisy; he complained that his classmate punched him when the classmate claimed he had just bumped into him accidentally; and he refused to complete the finger painting project that was going to be displayed in the main lobby next month. He also complained about his clothes— his shoelaces were too loose or too tight, and the waistband on his pants was constantly bothering him.

At the end of one day he refused to put on his hat and scarf when going out in the cold Minnesota weather, resulting in a meltdown. Alejandro ran from his cubby into the hallway and had to be physically stopped by another teacher and brought to the principal's office to calm down and have his parents pick him up. When his parents arrived they met with Mrs. Smith and the principal and heard about Alejandro's unusual behavior and handwriting deterioration over the previous few days. The parents took Alejandro to an Ear, Nose, and Throat doctor. A CT scan revealed a large sinus infection in a small area of the sinuses. He was put on medication for the sinus infection, and the parents were referred to a doctor who specializes in PANS. Alejandro was diagnosed with PANS and the family and teacher started learning the best ways to support Alejandro both medically and educationally.

Alejandro's story is not unique among children with PANS. Many studies have identified problems in sensory processing and handwriting during exacerbation (Bernstein *et al.* 2010; Murphy *et al.* 2012; Murphy *et al.* 2015; Swedo, Leckman, and Rose 2012; Swedo *et al.* 1998; Tona and Bhattacharjya 2017) and parents have reported problems in coordination and gross motors skills as well. Teachers and caregivers who understand these symptoms can help children to develop tools and strategies to deal with sensory and motor changes while the exacerbation is treated medically (Candelaria-Greene 2014).

Overview of sensory and motor systems

The sensory and motor systems are integral parts of information processing for all people. The sensory system acts as a highway with lanes bringing information to the brain where it is processed and used to make decisions about how to act, move, and feel (see Figure 8.1). Before we even begin a movement, the sensory system is exploring the environment to know what challenges are present and is also exploring our own bodies so we know where our body parts are in space, how heavy they are, and how fast they are moving. All of this information is organized in the brainstem and brain to prepare us to interact with our world. The brain then sends a command away from the brain to the muscles through the motor system to tell them to contract to make a movement—much like a car moving on a highway in the opposite direction of the incoming sensory input. In order for us to adapt to different environments and learn, we also have sensory input that comes back into the brain during and after the movement, called feedback. This lets us fine-tune our movements and also lets us know if the movement went as planned and if we were successful. All of this information is used for learning and continued development of movement.

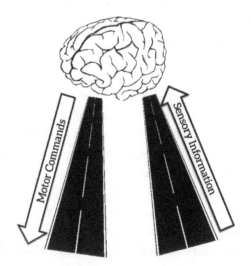

Figure 8.1   Sensory and motor systems as highways

Children with PANDAS/PANS are thought to have dysfunction in their brain during exacerbation. While we do not yet know all of the areas that are involved, studies have implicated the basal ganglia area as an area of dysfunction during exacerbation (Giedd *et al.* 2000; Kirvan *et al.* 2006). The basal ganglia is an area of the brain that helps us to fine-tune our movements, and it also sends information to the thalamus. The thalamus is the part of the brain that receives all of the sensory input from the body and relays this to the proper part of the brain for us to understand everything that is happening in our environment. Therefore, it is quite likely that the sensory and motor problems children experience with PANDAS/PANS are due, in part, to basal ganglia dysfunction, and may also be due to problems in other areas that have not yet been investigated. If we want to help children with PANDAS/PANS during and after exacerbation we need to understand how to help the sensory and motor systems to act more efficiently even when the brain is not functioning well.

Sensory systems for PANDAS/PANS

The sensory systems comprise seven senses—the five you learned about as a child (seeing, touching, hearing, smelling, tasting), and two hidden senses you may not have heard of called proprioception and vestibular sensations. Proprioception is sensory input that comes from our muscles and joints and moves toward the brain. It tells us how long our muscles are, how tightly they are contracting, and the angle of our joints, to allow our brain to make a mental map of our body. This lets us know where our body is in space and how it is moving through space, and it is very important for coordination. Vestibular input comes from our inner ear, where our semicircular canals and otolith organs, all filled with fluid, respond to the pull of gravity and movement of our head in various directions. This helps us know where our head is in space: if we are standing up or lying down and if we are spinning. The vestibular system works with the proprioceptive system and the visual system to tell us if we are falling and to initiate balance reactions to keep us upright (Desmond 2004).

Much like the lanes of a highway, each of these sensory systems travels in different pathways to get to the brain. Also like lanes of a highway that merge onto new roads leading to new destinations, information traveling along pathways toward the brain may synapse with other parts of the nervous system, sending information to additional areas along the way. Some of these pathways tend to be more excitatory or arousing, and some tend to be more inhibitory or calming. We all need to be aroused enough to be awake, alert, and attentive in school and throughout the day. However, if we become over-aroused, we have difficulty controlling our behavior. For children, this often results in meltdowns, and/or fight or flight reactions such as hitting other people, biting, hiding under a desk, or running out of the room. If we understand these pathways, we can use sensory input to help our children to become more awake and aroused when they are sluggish, or to help calm them when they are very aroused or over-responsive to sensory input.

Table 8.1 shows some of the sensory systems and the types of input that tend to be arousing or calming. It is very important to note that these are generalities, and individual children may have unique reactions that are different from the chart.

Table 8.1 Arousing and calming inputs (Bundy, Lane, and Murray 2002; Maddocks-Jennings and Wilkinson 2004; Umphred 2013)

Sensory system	What it does	Excitatory/ arousing input	Inhibitory/ calming input
Auditory	Hearing: localization of sound; focusing on what someone is saying as opposed to the background.	The buzz of fluorescent lights or background noise such as a television, radio, or other people chattering; upbeat music.	White noise, ocean sounds, music (the type of music is very individual).
Gustatory	Taste: exploring new tastes; eating foods from a variety of food groups; refraining from eating non-food items.	Bland tastes; favorite or familiar tastes.	Strong tastes; sour tastes; citrus tastes.

Olfactory	Smell: enjoying pleasurable scents; ignoring scents that are somewhat unpleasing; recognizing dangerous odors.	Familiar smells; lavender oil, rose oil.	Citrus scents; chemical scents.
Proprioceptive	Information from muscles and joints about where our bodies are in space and how we are moving; information about how much our muscles are being resisted when we move.	Proprioceptive information is unique in that it seems to *modulate* our system— or put it right where it needs to be. It is excitatory when we are sluggish and it is calming when we are over-stimulated. Good examples are working out with weights, pushing or pulling heavy items, wheelbarrow walking on our arms, using putty or play dough or kneading bread dough for resistance, jumping on a trampoline, running or riding a bike.	
Tactile	Touch: information from every part of our skin and the inside of our mouths about the texture, temperature, dampness, and physical properties of everything we come in contact with including our clothing, food, and other people who touch us.	Light touch tends to be very arousing, as does anything that touches our hair. Colder touch tends to be arousing. Sharp or painful touch is arousing.	Deep pressure tends to be calming, such as a pressure vest or a snug-fitting Lycra t-shirt. Warmth tends to be calming, such as a warm blanket or a warm bath.
Vestibular	Inner ear movement: information about where our head is in space from the pull of gravity, and information about how our head is moving through space.	Fast, angular movements tend to be arousing, for example an amusement park ride, fast elevator, fast-moving swing, skateboard or scooter ride, or a spin on a "sit-'n'-spin."	Slow, straight-line, rhythmic movement tends to be calming, for example a rocking chair, slow swing on a porch, or swaying back and forth.
Visual	Seeing: understanding the world from a distance without physical contact; understanding how things move in the world and how we are moving within space.	Incandescent lights can be very stimulating.	Natural light from the window tends to be calming; dim lighting can be calming when someone is very upset.

Sensory problems during PANDAS/PANS exacerbations

Children with PANDAS/PANS exacerbations are frequently reported to have sensory processing problems during exacerbation. Most frequently, families report that children suddenly become very sensitive to touch, sounds, tastes, smells, and movement. It is important to note that sensory information from different systems is combined to result in overall over- or under-arousal (Anzalone and Lane 2012). For example, a child may be able to tolerate having a friend touch him during class if he is wearing a snug Lycra t-shirt, is wearing noise-reducing headphones, has fluorescent lights turned off and only natural light in the room, and has a cardboard divider blocking his view of all the wall hangings and other children moving about. However, that same child may react with a fight or flight response if he is touched in the very same way when wearing a shirt with a scratchy tag on the back, is dealing with the background noise and background visual movement of his classmates, and has the fluorescent lights turned on with a background hum and bright reflection.

In this way, the nervous system can be likened to a barrel that becomes filled with sensory input throughout the day (Figure 8.2). When the barrel is empty, a little stimulation is easily tolerated; when the barrel is nearly full, just one bit of stimulation is like one last drop of water, and the barrel overflows, resulting in a fight or flight response. One way to prevent such an "overflow" is to decrease the amount of stimulation going into the barrel, such as having the child wear noise-reducing headphones, removing annoying tags from shirts and wearing comfortable clothing, and using a paint brush or gloves for sticky art projects. Another way to prevent spillover is to provide calming stimulation. Calming stimulation acts like a spigot that removes the effects of arousing stimulation without a fight or flight response.

Items found in the "calming" section of Table 8.1 are all ways to prevent overflow into a fight or flight response. Spending time wrapped in a warm blanket, reading a book in a makeshift tent in the classroom, using muscles to climb on a jungle gym or push a weighted cart to a room across the building, and wearing a snug Lycra undershirt for deep touch pressure are all ways to provide calming stimulation and reduce the likelihood of overflow and a fight or flight response. For children who are over-responsive during exacerbation, the trick is to keep the "barrel" as empty as possible by avoiding stimulation that is arousing, and supplying stimulation that is calming.

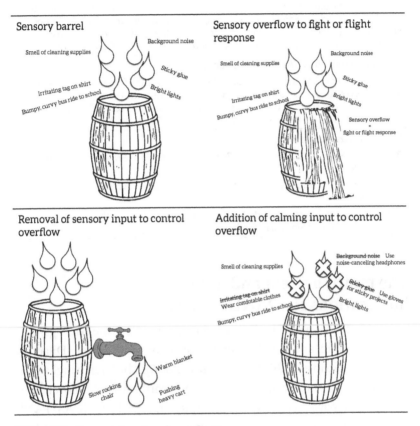

Figure 8.2   Sensory input and overflow

The guidelines provided in this chapter are general guidelines for sensory tools to help professionals with instruction and service delivery, particularly in the classroom setting. Not all children react to sensory input in the same way, and supporting children with sensory processing problems can be a puzzle requiring some detective work to understand. It is strongly recommended that teachers seek assistance from their school's occupational therapist if it appears that a child has sensory processing problems, to develop a "sensory diet" for that individual child that will provide appropriate input throughout the day to maintain the just-right level of alertness. Resources for additional information on sensory challenges can be found in Table 8.2.

Table 8.2 Resources on sensory dysfunction

Henry OT Services: www.ateachabout.com
Provider of continuing inter-professional education in sensory integration for all members of the education team. Also provider of *Sensory Tools* handbooks including *Toolchest for Teachers, Parents and Students; Tools for Parents; Tools for Tots: Sensory Strategies for Toddlers and Preschoolers; Tools for Infants*; and *SI Tools for Teens: Strategies to Promote Sensory Processing*. Products also include CDs and DVDs.
SPD Foundation: http://spdfoundation.net
Foundation dedicated to research, education, and advocacy for sensory processing disorder. Website includes information about SPD, continuing education for practitioners, information on current research, and an impressive library of articles related to sensory processing, located in the Resources tab.
Books for parents and educators
Biel, L., and Peske, N. (2009) *Raising a Sensory Smart Child*. New York: Penguin Random House.
Kranowitz, C., and Miller, L. (2006) *The Out of Sync Child*. New York: TarcherPerigee.
Miller, L.J. (2014) *Sensational Kids: Hope and Help for Children with Sensory Processing Disorder*. New York: TarcherPerigee.

The motor system and motor implications for PANDAS/PANS

PANDAS/PANS exacerbations are thought to affect the basal ganglia area of the brain, and possibly other areas of the brain as well (Dileepan *et al.* 2006; Giedd *et al.* 2000; Kirvan *et al.* 2006). The basal ganglia is an area that refines motor movement and prevents unwanted movements. Researchers have yet to study the full impact of PANDAS/PANS exacerbations on motor skills, but unwanted tics and deterioration in handwriting are two motor implications of PANDAS/PANS that are well documented. Additionally, in one study approximately 34 percent of families identified problems in children's walking pattern (gait), approximately 28 percent identified problems in muscle strength, and approximately 31 percent identified problems in endurance during exacerbation, though few practitioners look for these problems (Tona, Bhattacharjya and Calaprice 2017).

These motor changes, coupled with the frequent obsessive thoughts around perfection or doing things "just right," impact daily living for individuals with PANDAS/PANS to a very large extent, with approximately 28 percent of families reporting that children were not able to fully participate in physical education in school, and

50 percent reporting children unable to participate in extracurricular activities. A full 70 percent of families reported that children were unable to participate in community activities or organized activities outside of school, such as bowling or going to the movies, during exacerbation (Tona, Bhattacharjya and Calaprice 2017).

Also, families frequently report that the children are very fatigued during PANDAS/PANS exacerbations, further limiting their physical activity. It is important that school personnel are cognizant of these possible changes, as a sudden change in athleticism or physical activity could be an early sign of an infection or PANDAS/PANS exacerbation.

To date, there are no research studies to tell us the best ways to approach motor problems in children with PANS. It has been suggested that professionals provide accommodations and support during exacerbation, and then provide remedial activities to improve motor skills after exacerbation (Tona and Posner 2011).

Interventions for fatigue

Children who experience fatigue may need to utilize concepts of energy conservation and work simplification during PANDAS/PANS exacerbations. These concepts are frequently taught to individuals with chronic medical conditions. Energy conservation involves using devices to decrease the amount of energy expended during activities, and work simplification involves reducing the number of steps in activities. For example, when Ashley, a middle school student, goes to school in the morning she gathers all her books and notebooks from the homeroom until lunch and then carries these in front of her, in her arms, from class to class. Placing her books and supplies in a backpack would simplify the job of gathering the materials after each subject. Using a rolling backpack would conserve the energy used to carry heavy supplies. Ideas for energy conservation and work simplification include the following:

Rearrange the classroom

- Keep frequently used items in easily accessible places. Avoid over-reaching and bending by keeping often-used items within easy reach.

- Keep heavier items at arm level. Put heavy hardcover books on middle shelves and lighter weight paperback books on higher shelves.

- Move desks so that the child is able to look straight ahead to see the board or screen for presentation; avoid side-facing desks.

Eliminate unnecessary effort

- Have the child sit in a chair or lie on the floor for work, rather than stand.

- Use adaptive equipment such as a rolling cart or a rolling book bag.

- Encourage the child to use both arms and hands when carrying, pushing, and pulling.

- Encourage good posture and body mechanics.

- Do not have child lift items when they can be more easily pushed or pulled.

Plan ahead

- Help the child to gather all the supplies needed for a task or project before starting, so everything is in one place.

- Work rest breaks into activities as often as possible; have the child take a break before getting tired.

- Schedule enough time for activities—rushing takes more energy.

- Try having the child keep a daily activity journal for a few weeks to identify times of day or certain tasks that result in more fatigue.

- Alternate between heavy and light tasks throughout the day or week.

Prioritize

- Eliminate or reduce tasks that are not necessary and consider giving a reduced homework or schoolwork load (for example, doing only the odd numbered math problems on the page instead of every problem).

(Adapted from Advance for Occupational and
Physical Therapy Practitioners 2016)

Gross motor implications

During PANDAS/PANS exacerbations, accommodations may need
to be made in physical education and in the classroom for the child
to have periods of rest, engage in simple, non-competitive games
that do not demand high levels of coordination or agility, and have
periods outside of the classroom desk and seat when the child can
be positioned, for example, sitting in a bean bag chair or lying on
his tummy over a wedge to read a book. If changes are seen in gait,
physical agility, muscle strength, or balance, a referral to physical
therapy should be considered—especially if these changes continue
after the major exacerbation has ended. Children may need to change
to modified or adapted physical education (Candelaria-Greene 2014)
and a period of rehabilitative exercises may be needed to help the
child return to pre-exacerbation functioning.

Fine motor implications

Small motor skills with fingers or hands are frequently problematic
during PANDAS/PANS exacerbations. In fact, the first paper
identifying the term PANDAS/PANS suggests practitioners use
handwriting samples as a means of measuring a child's level of
exacerbation (Swedo *et al.* 2012). Families also indicate that children
frequently have difficulty fastening buttons, zipping coats, even using
utensils to eat. It is important to remember that motor skills rely on
adequate sensory information before, during, and after movements.
This sensory information includes good visual perception and spatial
awareness of the environment and the task at hand before a movement
begins; sensory feedback from vision, muscles, and the inner ear during
the movement; and feedback about the success of the movement after
the movement is completed by visually seeing results and from verbal
feedback from others. These sensory aspects are particularly important
in fine motor skills, where reliance on touch and proprioception are
necessary for success.

Fine motor skills generally progress from proximal (near the trunk) to distal (near the fingers) and from ulnar (near the pinky finger) to radial (near the thumb and index finger). By the time a child reaches elementary school, he or she should be using the pads of the thumb and index finger (pincer grasp) or pads of the thumb, index, and middle finger (three-jaw grasp) for most activities. The child should have enough strength to use these patterns when playing games with tweezers, such as the games "Bedbugs" and "Operation," when picking up coins or beads, and when buttoning buttons or zipping a zipper. The child should also be able to move objects around within the hand without using the other hand, such as moving a coin from the fingertips to the palm or palm to fingertips. This is called in-hand manipulation. You may see the child revert to a more proximal grasp (in the palm) and/or a more ulnar grasp (on the pinky side of the hand) when performing activities that require more strength such as squeezing glue from a bottle (Case-Smith and Exner 2015).

During a PANDAS/PANS exacerbation, children may have difficulty using the thumb, index, and middle fingers for fine motor tasks. They may seem clumsy and imprecise or may need to use two hands to move small objects around rather than using in-hand manipulation. They may not know exactly where their fingers are in space without looking, so fine motor skills that should be able to be completed without vision (such as buttoning the top buttons on a shirt without looking) may need the help of visual input (such as standing in front of a mirror).

Similarly, during a PANDAS/PANS exacerbation many children also present with handwriting changes that may be related to motor changes and/or to problems with visual perception of the paper and the space available. Difficulty with motor execution may be seen as letters appearing sloppy, jittery, misshapen, and not completely closed, making it difficult, for example, to distinguish a lower case *a* from a lower case *u*. Visual perceptual problems, including difficulty with visuospatial skills, often present as margin drift or spacing problems above and below the line and between letters and words. Additionally, the obsessive-compulsive thoughts prevalent during exacerbations often result in children writing over their work, filling in open circles in letters, or erasing to the point of tearing the paper. Figure 8.3 shows the handwriting of a child with PANS.

Seven-year-old boy in PANS exacerbation with sudden-onset dysgraphia. Notice the poor spacing between words and poor letter placement between lines.

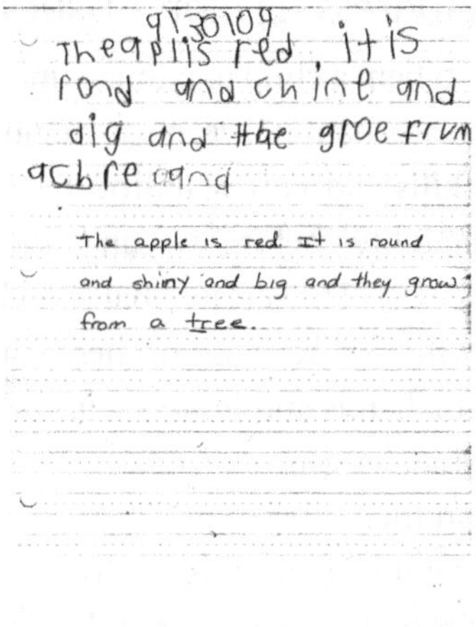

Same child four months later as the PANS exacerbation continued. Notice excessive erasures and re-drawing, letters consistent with obsessive-compulsive behaviors.

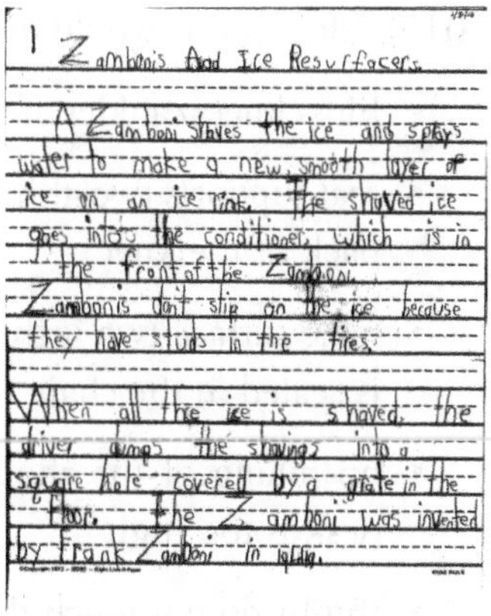

Same child two months later while on steroids. Notice the clear letters, even spacing, and limited erasures.

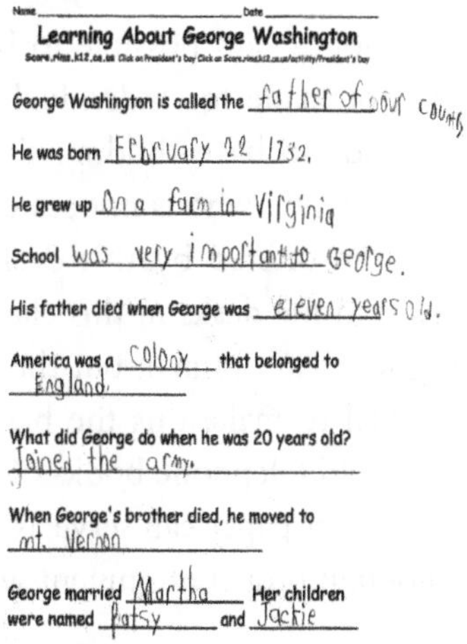

Figure 8.3 Handwriting of a seven-year-old boy in different phases of PANS exacerbation

Addressing motor issues in handwriting

To help a child maximize fine motor abilities during a PANDAS/PANS exacerbation, we must begin by looking at the child's gross motor skills and core stability. Therapists often say that we need "proximal stability" before we can have "distal mobility" (Case-Smith and Exner 2015). This means that if a child's core is weak or unstable, the child will tend to tense up her hands and fingers and have difficulty using the hands and fingers with fine, distinct movements. Children who are slouching in their chairs, lay their heads down on the desk, or lean on their elbows may have improved fine motor skills if their proximal stability is increased. To begin, the child should be positioned in a properly sized chair and desk (Boyle 2008; Schneck and Case-Smith 2015). Ideally, this would include:

- hips/knees/ankles at 90 degrees

- seat supports two-thirds of the thigh but does not press into the back of the knee

- table surface two inches above the flexed elbow when the child is seated in the chair

- no hiking of the shoulder or leaning to one side because the desk is too high

- thighs do not touch the underside of the desk.

It is not always possible to have ideal seating in school, since desks are not made for individual children. However, every effort should be made to have children sit in the best seating possible. Figure 8.4 shows a boy who is not seated in the ideal position, but is in the best position offered by this desk. The deep configuration of the book space in the desks in this classroom make the writing surface slightly higher than optimal, but the teacher and occupational therapist have worked to make this the best position possible for this child. Many times old telephone books of varying thicknesses covered in duct tape or contact paper can serve as adequate foot supports or back supports to obtain proper alignment when chairs are too tall or too deep.

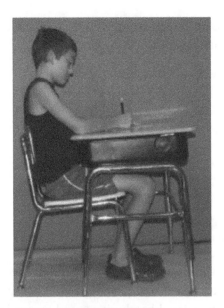

Figure 8.4   The best position offered by this desk

As a child moves out of exacerbation, physical or occupational therapy to address trunk stability may be needed. Extracurricular activities such as yoga, t'ai chi, tae kwon do, and other martial arts may also be beneficial as a child regains trunk strength. Coloring and drawing on vertical surfaces, such as an easel or chalkboard, is beneficial for building trunk and shoulder strength. Coloring a mural taped to the underside of a table, while lying on their backs on a mat underneath the table, is a fun way to rebuild shoulder strength.

The concept of stability applies not only to the trunk and shoulders, but also to the elbows and wrists. During exacerbation, children who have difficulty maintaining stability in the elbow or wrist may benefit from writing on a slightly inclined surface, such as a slant board. A slant board generally holds the paper at about a 15–20 degree angle (Figure 8.5). This is thought to place the wrist in slight extension during writing, so providing some degree of stability (Schneck and Case-Smith 2015). Some slant boards have a clip on top to hold the paper steady, and this can also be helpful for children who have trouble coordinating the two sides of their bodies to hold the paper steady with one hand while moving the pencil with the other hand.

Some people use a three-ring notebook, turned sideways, if a slant board is not available in the classroom.

Figure 8.5   Slant board (https://funandfunction.com)

Once the child's posture and proximal stability have been addressed, it is important to look at the pencil grasp. Pencil grasp alone is not an indicator of functional handwriting, and many children with very legible handwriting have unusual pencil grasps. However, for children who have difficulty with handwriting, having an inefficient pencil grasp can make the writing process even more difficult. Pencil grasp generally follows a developmental progression that is similar to other fine motor progression in that the pencil moves from the palm to the finger tips (proximal to distal) and from the pinky side to the thumb side (ulnar to radial) as the child develops skill (Schneck and Henderson 1990). Figure 8.6 shows progression of the pencil grasp in a typical child. The most advanced grasp is the dynamic tripod grasp, where the pencil is held between the pad of the thumb and index finger while resting against the side of the middle finger and the web space, and the child moves the fingers and wrist (not the wrist and elbow) to form letters.

(A) Palmar Supinate
(Toddler)

(B) Digital Pronate
(Early preschool)

(C) Four Fingers Grasp
(Late preschool)

(D) Tripod (School-aged)

Figure 8.6   Progression of the pencil grasp in a typical child. (a) (b) (c) (d)

Children with PANS may revert to an earlier grasp pattern during exacerbation. Some children have been successful using various rubber or silicone grips on pencils to encourage a tripod grasp and there are a variety of pencil grips on the market designed to place the pad of the thumb and index finger and side of the middle finger around the pencil near the tip. The Twist-N-Write (Figure 8.7) is a tool that some families have found very beneficial during exacerbation.

Figure 8.7   The Twist-N-Write (https://penagain.net)

Consultation with an occupational therapist for adaptive techniques to aid handwriting can be very beneficial during exacerbation. As a child moves out of exacerbation, occupational therapy to address finger dexterity may be needed. Resistive activities that require use of the small muscles of the hand can be very beneficial, especially activities such as kneading play dough, rolling small balls of dough between the fingers, pulling coins, small beads, or other small objects out of putty, pushing beads onto pipe cleaners as part of a craft project, and using tweezers to pick up small objects in games and crafts. Additionally, writing using small bits of chalk, crayons cut in half, or small pencils similar to golf pencils helps children learn to use the thumb, index, and middle finger and develop strength in this grasp pattern in preparation for a tripod grasp.

Children with visual spatial difficulties often have difficulty with margin drift when writing, whereby the left margin gradually becomes wider and wider as the child progresses down the page. Visual spatial deficits may also be seen with poor alignment of letters within words, or difficulty creating uniform spaces between letters and words. Children with spatial difficulties may find it beneficial to write in small boxes, such as graph paper, during exacerbation. Children can easily place one letter in each box and skip a box between words to provide uniform spacing when writing. Some therapists and teachers have found it beneficial to use a vertical line template (VLT) when writing (Figure 8.8). A vertical line template is made by printing dark, horizontal lines on a paper using landscape orientation (Ranade 2007). The paper is then turned to portrait orientation to become vertical lines and is placed behind the child's standard portrait-oriented paper, creating the illusion of boxes. Children write with one letter in each box and skip a box between words. When the child is finished, the vertical line template is removed and the child's work may be read easily and displayed in the classroom or shared with others without anyone knowing that the vertical lines were used. In this way, the child's work retains the look of the work of the other students.

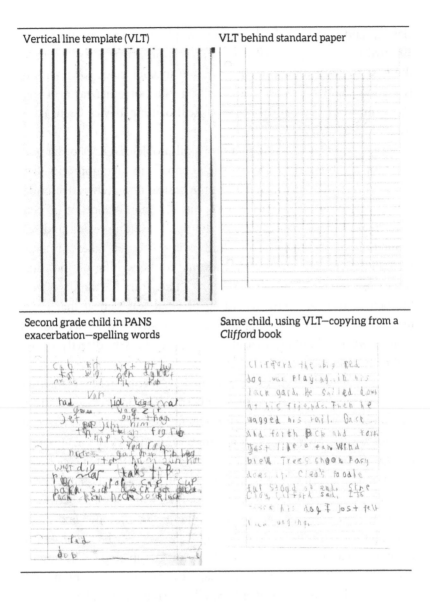

Figure 8.8   Vertical line template

Sometimes children are not able to write functionally despite adaptive interventions. In these cases, accommodations for handwriting may be needed, such as having an aide or a classmate act as a scribe, providing older children with a copy of the teacher's notes, audio recording classes, and allowing keyboarding in place of handwriting. The assistive technology specialist in your school can help to determine the best solution for individual children in your class. Keyboarding is a good solution for many children: an iPad or other tablet if that is the norm of the classroom, or a keyboarding device such as an Alpha Smart.

Some children, due to fine motor skill problems, OCD, or fatigue, may not be able to actively use the keyboard to take notes. In such cases, a Livescribe Smartpen may be the best solution (www.livescribe. com/en-us/smartpen). This device has the appearance of a pen, but actually has a small camera in the tip in addition to ink and has a microphone built in. As the child writes, the pen takes an audio recording of the lecture and matches that to the writing on the page. Afterward, the child only has to touch the writing on the page with the pen to hear an audio recording of what was said at that point in time. Smartpens are being updated regularly, and newer models include wi-fi technology that allows notes to be sent directly to the child's computer.

Children with PANDAS/PANS who have inconsistent presentation in school but who own a smartphone may benefit from accommodations that allow them to use their smartphones in class. Snapping a picture of a complex diagram on the chalk board or of the homework assignment for the night increases accuracy when reviewing the items at home while reducing fatigue and frustration in school. Similarly, most smartphones are capable of recording lectures, which are also beneficial when a child returns home in the evening. Smartphones and iPads also offer the opportunity to utilize applications, which are constantly being updated. For example, SnapType for Occupational Therapy by Brendan Kirchner (https://itunes.apple.com/us/app/snaptype-for-occupational/id866842989?mt=8) allows students to take a picture of worksheets and documents or import them from their device. They can complete the worksheet using the iOS keyboard and save, print, and email as needed. Notability, by Ginger Labs (www.gingerlabs. com) is a low-cost app that allows users to create notes by drawing, handwriting, typing, audio, or pictures. Work can be saved and sent via Google Drive, email, and Dropbox. Sonocent Audio Notetaker, a software program, allows students to capture audio information, have phrases displayed as color-coded chunks of information, annotate the display, organize the information, and share the finished product with others (www.sonocent.com/en-us/audio-notetaker).

Sonocent Audio Notetaker also integrates with Dragon Naturally Speaking by Nuance, a speech-to-text program for students who are unable to write legibly and have difficulty with the motor coordination required for keyboarding. This enables students to compose age-appropriate word documents independently (www.nuance.com/dragon/index.htm).

The physical stamina and stability required to maintain the trunk and head, and keep eyes steady while reading can tax weakened muscles. Note-taking for research or study adds another layer of difficulty. Text-to-speech applications offer a variety of features that allow students to highlight each word as it is read aloud; highlight and copy text to create vocabulary lists, study guides, and research notes; proofread written work to hear what was actually written; and access reference tools including thesaurus, dictionary, and homonyms. Text-to-speech applications are developed and updated regularly and an internet search will provide information regarding the most current products and features. Some examples of applications that offer both text-to-speech and speech-to-text are: Read&Write Gold by Text Help (www.texthelp.com/en-us), Voice Dream Reader (www.voicedream.com/reader), and Claro Read (www.claroread.com/category/claro-apps.php). Most of the programs can be downloaded for a free trial (Henning 2015).

Key points to remember and Conclusion

Sensory and motor changes experienced during a PANDAS/PANS exacerbation can be unsettling for children and confusing for parents, teachers, and other caregivers. Accommodation and adaptation during exacerbation can help children with PANDAS/PANS to remain functional during a flare, and remediation after exacerbation can help children move toward pre-exacerbation functioning and develop skills to prepare for possible future exacerbations. Children must continue to learn, participate, and develop—despite PANDAS/PANS exacerbations. As educators and caregivers, we are in a unique position to maximize a child's ability to function in school during these difficult times.

References

Advance for Occupational and Physical Therapy Practitioners (2016) *Energy Conservation Tips.* Available at http://physical-therapy.advanceweb.com/sharedresources/AdvanceforOT/Resources/DownloadableResources/OT_051503_energy_patient.pdf, accessed on 8 March 2016.

Anzalone, M.E., and Lane, S. (2012) 'Sensory Processing Disorders: Feels Awful and Doesn't Sound Very Good Either!' In S. Lane and A. Bundy (eds) *Kids Can Be Kids.* Philadelphia: FA Davis.

Bernstein, G.A., Victor, A.M., Pipal, A.J., and Williams, K.A. (2010). 'Comparison of clinical characteristics of pediatric autoimmune neuropsychiatric disorders associated with streptococcal infections and childhood obsessive-compulsive disorder.' *Journal of Child Adolescent Psychopharmacology 20,* 4, 333–340.

Boyle, M. (2008). *Effectiveness of an Online Tutorial to Improve Teacher Knowledge of Seating for Elementary School Students.* Available at ProQuest Dissertations and Theses, http://search.proquest.com/docview/275585750, accessed on 8 March 2016.

Bundy, A.C., Lane, S.J., and Murray, E.A. (eds) (2002) *Sensory integration: Theory and practice (Second edition).* Philadelphia: F.A. Davis.

Candelaria-Greene, J. (2014) *Considerations Regarding Academic Accommodations/Compensatory Strategies, and Services for Students with PANDAS/PANS.* Available at http://pandasnetwork.org/wp-content/uploads/2014/09/School-Considerations-2014.pdf, accessed on 7 March 2016.

Case-Smith, J., and Exner, C. (2015) 'Hand Function Evaluation and Intervention.' In J. Case-Smith and J. O'Brien (eds) *Occupational Therapy for Children* (Seventh edition). St Louis, MI: Elsevier/Mosby.

Desmond, A. (2004). *Vestibular Function: Evaluation and Treatment.* New York: Thieme Medical Publishers.

Dileepan, T., Smith, E., Knowland, D., Hsu, M., et al. (2016) 'Group A Streptococcus intranasal infection promotes CNS infiltration by streptococcal-specific TH17 cells.' *Journal of Clinical Investigation 126,* 1, 303–317.

Giedd, J.N., Rapoport, J.L., Garvey, M.A., Perlmutter, S., and Swedo, S. (2000) 'MRI assessment of children with obsessive-compulsive disorder or tics associated with streptococcal infection.' *American Journal of Psychiatry 157,* 2, 281–283.

Henning, M. (2015) *Beyond the Pencil Box: Strategies and Tools to use when Neuropsychiatric Symptoms affect Learning.* New York State Occupational Therapy Association, Spring CE Day. [PowerPoint slides]

Kirvan, C.A., Swedo, S.E., Snider, L.A., and Cunningham, M.W. (2006) 'Antibody mediated neuronal cell signaling in behavior and movement disorders.' *Journal of Immunology 179,* 173–179.

Maddocks-Jennings, W., and Wilkinson, J. (2004) 'Aromatherapy practice in nursing: Literature review.' *Journal of Advanced Nursing 48,* 1, 93–103.

Murphy, T.K., Patel, P.D., McGuire, J.F., Kennel, A., *et al.* (2015) 'Characterization of the pediatric acute-onset neuropsychiatric syndrome phenotype.' *Journal of Child and Adolescent Psychopharmacology 25*, 1, 14–25.

Murphy T.K., Storch, E.A., Lewin, A.B., Edge, P.J., and Goodman, W.K. (2012) 'Clinical factors associated with pediatric autoimmune neuropsychiatric disorders associated with streptococcal infections.' *Journal of Pediatrics 160*, 314–319.

Ranade, D. (2007) *The Effect of a Vertical Line Template and a Slant Board on Printing of Children with Handwriting Difficulties.* Available at ProQuest Dissertations and Theses, http://gradworks.umi.com/14/40/1440045.html, accessed on 8 March 2016.

Schneck, C., and Case-Smith, J. (2015) 'Prewriting and Handwriting Skills.' In J. Case-Smith and J. O'Brien (eds) *Occupational Therapy for Children* (Seventh edition). St Louis, MI: Elsevier/Mosby.

Schneck, C., and Henderson, A. (1990) 'Descriptive analysis of the developmental progression of grip position for pencil and crayon control in nondysfunctional children.' *American Journal of Occupational Therapy 44*, 10, 893–900.

Swedo, S., Leckman, J., and Rose, N. (2012) 'From research subgroup to clinical syndrome: Modifying the PANDAS criteria to describe PANS (Pediatric Acute-onset Neuropsychiatric Syndrome).' *Pediatrics and Therapeutics 2*, 113, 1–8.

Swedo, S.E., Leonard, H.L., Garvey, M., Mittleman, B., *et al.* (1998) 'Pediatric autoimmune neuropsychiatric disorders associated with streptococcal infections: clinical description of the first 50 cases.' *American Journal of Psychiatry 155*, 2, 264–271.

Tona, J., and Posner, T. (2011) 'Pediatric autoimmune neuropsychiatric disorders: A new frontier for occupational therapy intervention.' *OT Practice 16*, 20, 14–19.

Tona, J., Bhattacharjya, S. and Calaprice, D. (2017) 'Impact of PANS/PANDAS Exacerbations on Occupational Performance: A Mixed-Methods Study.' *American Journal of Occupational Therapy, 71*, 3 (in press).

Umphred, D.A. (2013) *Umphred's neurological rehabilitation.* St. Louis, Mo: Elsevier/Mosby.

Chapter 9

Emotional and Behavioral Impact of PANDAS/PANS

Considerations for Planning and Practice

KANDACE M. HOPPIN, ED.D.

Comments collected from interviews with families of students with PANDAS/PANS:

"...He doesn't have fatigue. He has hyperactivity. And he's young, he's still learning self-control..."

"...The teachers try to understand but it's not as clear cut. He has OCD symptoms and fears, fears of drugs, running to the bathroom every five minutes, and they think he's trying to escape the classroom and it's behavioral..."

"...He just needs breaks, he has so much anxiety. I think the teacher kind of sees if he's having a flare. His body language is different. His teacher recognizes that now..."

"...School issues [are] cited such as 'can't focus,' 'I can't give him enough time,' 'daydreaming,' 'not using time wisely'..."

"...Teachers thought he was fidgeting and trying to disrupt class, but those were tics that were hard to recognize as such..."

"...It made a difference that her teachers were willing to go out of their way and think out of the box to assess her during exacerbations..."

The descriptions from families listed on the previous page provide some insight into the array of behavioral and emotional challenges students with PANDAS/PANS may experience in school. This chapter aims to identify and address the impact of these emotional and behavioral concerns and provide suggestions for strategies and accommodations for school personnel working with these students.

The abrupt, dramatic onset of obsessive-compulsive disorder (OCD) or severely restricted food intake is the first diagnostic criterion for PANS (Chang *et al.* 2015). However, there is great variability in the nature of the symptoms accompanying the OCD (IOCDF 2014).

The second major criterion for PANS (Chang *et al.* 2015; Swedo, Leckman and Rose 2012) is the concurrent severe and acute onset of additional symptoms from at least two of the following categories:

1. Anxiety

2. Emotional lability and/or depression

3. Irritability, aggression, and/or severely oppositional behaviors

4. Behavioral/developmental regression

5. Sudden deterioration in school performance (related to attention deficit/hyperactivity disorder [ADHD]-like symptoms, memory deficits, cognitive changes)

6. Sensory or motor abnormalities

7. Somatic/physical signs and symptoms. These may be sleep disturbances, enuresis, or urinary frequency.

The third PANS criterion is that symptoms are not better explained by a known neurologic or medical disorder.

By definition, these individual PANDAS/PANS symptoms overlap with a variety of other psychiatric disorders. However, the acuity of onset and simultaneous presentations of these symptoms is what differentiates PANDAS/PANS from these psychiatric conditions (Chang *et al.* 2015).

The acute onset of these symptoms can have a significant impact on academic, behavioral, social, and emotional school experiences for a child with PANDAS/PANS (PANDAS Network 2015). As such, it is important for school personnel working with these children to understand the impact and implications, as well as to be aware of strategies and accommodations they can employ to provide support. Characteristics of PANDAS/PANS specifically related to emotional and behavioral concerns that will be discussed in this chapter include the acute onset of OCD, extreme anxiety, and rage and aggression.

Understanding OCD in the classroom: Impact, strategies, and useful accommodations

Impact and implications

One common concern with PANDAS/PANS is a dramatic onset of OCD symptoms. OCD—obsessive-compulsive disorder—is a psychiatric disorder that has a neurobiological basis. As its name suggests, OCD has two aspects: the intrusive thoughts, images, or impulses, known as obsessions; and the behavioral compulsions people engage in to relieve the anxiety these obsessions cause. When an individual perceives and/or feels that something is not "just right" or "complete," the compulsive behavior needs to be repeated until things do feel just right or complete. Obsessions and compulsive behaviors tend to take up considerable amounts of time and create distress in the lives of individuals with OCD to the point that they interfere with their daily functioning, schoolwork, and/or relationships (IOCDF 2014). Experts estimate that PANDAS/PANS may account for up to 25 percent of all cases of OCD (Westly 2009).

Obsessions and compulsions can take many forms. Obsessions might relate to fears of contamination and illness, worries about harming others, and preoccupations with numbers, patterns, morality, or sexual identity. Compulsions can include excessive cleaning or double-checking, particular arrangement of objects, or walking in predetermined patterns. Individuals with OCD might understand the relationship between their obsessions and compulsions quite well. However, being unable to avoid these thoughts and actions despite being aware of their irrationality is part of the reason why OCD is so distressing (IOCDF 2014).

It is important to understand that OCD is not something children or adolescents choose to have, and is not a behavioral choice. When OCD is untreated, young people frequently do not have any control over how OCD affects them or how they react to it. However, children with OCD can learn to manage their obsessions and compulsions with treatment and interventions—an important component of which may be educational support (Chaturvedi, Murdick, and Gartin 2014).

Although many children will experience times they feel anxious, for children who exhibit symptoms of OCD, anxiety related to obsessions and compulsions can significantly interfere with their classroom experiences (Adams 2004). Depression, agitation, feelings of shame, and stress (due to their time-consuming rituals) can contribute to social, emotional, and behavioral difficulties for these students on a daily basis. Additionally, OCD symptoms tend to worsen when children are stressed, tired, or ill. Students with OCD may feel isolated from their peers, partly because their compulsive behavior leaves them little time to interact or socialize with their classmates. They may avoid school because they are worried that teachers or peers will notice their odd behaviors. When asked "why" a behavior is repeated, students might only say, "It doesn't feel right" and be unable to explain a real "why." Some examples of how OCD symptoms may affect a child in the classroom include (Adams 2011):

- seeking reassurance from the teacher(s) due to self-doubt and self-criticism of their efforts

- appearing distracted because they are focused on an obsessive thought

- counting and re-counting objects, or arranging and rearranging objects on their desk

- seeming agitated or anxious because they want to perform a compulsive behavior, but also want to comply with classroom rules to stay in a set location/space

- unfinished classwork and/or homework because they feel a need to cross out, rewrite, or check and re-check work

- tardiness and/or absences due to trouble arriving on time because they need to get ready for school in a very specific, ritualistic way

- requesting frequent trips to the bathroom and asking to leave the classroom to avoid certain activities, places, objects, or persons.

Strategies and useful accommodations

It is important to note that symptoms of OCD frequently do not respond to traditional behavior modification principles. For example, many school personnel may believe that when a student has a behavioral problem, it must be linked to student motivation. As such, behavioral modification approaches using positive and negative consequences to alter motivation in order to reduce negative behaviors may be implemented. However, a child with OCD may not respond to positive and negative consequences, as their obsessions and compulsions are the function of their OCD; they are not willful behaviors that can be stopped simply by altering motivation. Attempting to use this approach to alter the motivation of a student with OCD who is already extremely anxious because they are stuck in a compulsive behavior ritual at school could very likely increase the student's anxiety and worsen symptoms (Dyches *et al.*2010).

Behavior plans for students with PANDAS/PANS and the acute onset of OCD symptoms need to consider that the student cannot suppress these behaviors consistently, even if they are highly motivated to do so. Students may sometimes be able to control or suppress their OCD symptoms for a period of time, although suppressing symptoms may result in higher levels of anxiety or stress. However, if the student cannot suppress them continuously, applying positive or negative consequences is likely to *increase* stress, make symptoms *worse*, and possibly create *new* behavioral problems (Chaturvedi *et al.* 2014). These children—like all children—are motivated to earn rewards and avoid punishment; they want to be successful. When an attempt is made to alter their truly involuntary OCD symptoms, students may try to modify their own behavior—expending large amounts of time and energy trying to suppress a ritual, experiencing high levels of stress and fatigue—which comes at a great cost for the student (Woolcock and Campbell 2005).

Despite concerns associated with positive and negative consequences, *positive reinforcement* may be effective for students with OCD. For example, verbal praise and rewards may be effective when trying to teach a student to use and maintain a behavior that replaces an inappropriate or interfering OCD behavior. It is helpful to notice and reinforce students for making progress on improving their OCD symptoms and even for making the effort to fight their OCD.

Some general strategies for school personnel working with students with PANDAS/PANS and the acute onset of OCD symptoms include:

- learn about OCD symptoms and access resources

- partner with the student's family

- bring awareness to the classroom and create a safe environment.

Taking these initial, proactive steps as school personnel can go a long way in providing ongoing supports to the student experiencing these symptoms, and also creating a classroom environment of understanding and tolerance as you implement more specific classroom strategies. Reading up on information about PANDAS/PANS and associated OCD symptoms—provided in this chapter, along with additional print and online resources—can provide school personnel with more knowledge, confidence, and strategies for supporting these students.

Partnering with a student's family will allow you to get a broader picture of how OCD symptoms are impacting their overall experiences, and you can hear how related behaviors are dealt with at home (Adams 2011). How you bring awareness to your classroom about OCD and create a safe environment could be specific or broad; with a parent's and student's permission to disclose, there might be an opportunity for the student—depending on age and comfort level—to share what they are going through and how their peers can be supportive. More generally, school personnel can focus on fostering a classroom community that values safety, support, tolerance, and understanding about differences and disabilities overall (Chaturvedi *et al.* 2014).

Some additional strategies for school personnel to consider when working with students with PANDAS/PANS and the acute onset of OCD symptoms include:

- Be attentive to changes in the student's behavior and try to recognize and reduce "triggers" that often result in compulsive behaviors.

- Accommodate situations and behaviors that the student has no control over; be patient and try to recognize these tough spots, without drawing extra attention.

- Try to *redirect* the student's behavior, rather than using consequences.

- Be flexible and provide adjusted expectations:
  - Allow options, when possible, for students to choose how they would like to complete assignments (e.g., handwritten, orally, or typed).
  - Allow the student to receive full credit for late work.
  - Allow the student to redo assignments to improve scores or final grades.

- Post the daily schedule and details in a highly visible place so the student knows what to expect each day.

- Provide extra time and advance notice for the student to prepare for transitions throughout the school day.

- Be positive, provide reassurance, and reward even small successes and improvements.

- Allow breaks to defuse anxiety and provide a relaxing space; breaks could be in the classroom, out of the classroom, or with another adult. Develop a private signal or cue to use with the student that is non-disruptive and will not draw attention when they need a break.

- Implement a buddy system to provide the student with a peer resource to check in with during classwork, after returning from breaks, and when arriving late to class.

- Consider a Functional Behavioral Assessment (FBA). Understanding the triggers of the student's OCD behaviors can help you respond with effective interventions and proactive strategies.

Other anxiety-related issues: Impact, strategies, and useful accommodations

Impact and implications

Anxiety is another common characteristic in children with PANDAS/ PANS. While occasional anxiety is a normal part of life, extreme anxiety involves more than temporary worries or fear. Anxiety in children with PANDAS/PANS could take many forms, including unrealistic worries about a range of topics and situations, social anxiety and isolation, separation anxiety, and/or irrational fears.

Children with PANDAS/PANS experiencing symptoms of generalized anxiety might worry about a range of topics, including world affairs, harm to self or others, school performance, or the future. Other worries may include perfectionist concerns or everyday concerns, such as saying the wrong thing. Physically, these children may experience muscle tension and restlessness. To ease their worries in the moment, children with anxiety often avoid activities and/or situations that trigger feelings of anxiety. They may also engage in excessive reassurance-seeking, asking questions aimed at mitigating their excessive worries (Benjamin *et al.*2011).

Children with social anxiety and fears have an excessive fear of being negatively evaluated by others. They often experience extreme distress in performance and social situations; avoidance of these situations is common for children with social anxieties. This avoidant behavior can result in fewer friends and strained peer relationships, and can result in decreased academic performance as the student tries to avoid class participation (Kearney 2005).

Children with separation anxiety experience an irrational fear of being separated from a caregiver or group of caregivers. In anticipation of such separation, children with separation anxiety experience extreme distress. They may cry, throw a tantrum, or report physical symptoms of anxiety (e.g., headaches, nausea). Children experiencing separation anxiety exhibit a range of avoidant behaviors aimed at minimizing time spent away from their caregivers. As such, it is difficult for these children to separate from their parents for school and social activities. Because of separation concerns, these students often have fewer friends and intermittent school attendance (Beesdo, Knappe, and Pine 2009).

Anxiety in children with PANDAS/PANS may also present as irrational fears or phobias related to a specific object or situation. In anticipation of encountering the fear, children experience extreme distress, sometimes expressed through tantrums or crying. Avoidance of fearful stimuli is highly characteristic of this type of anxiety (Ollendick *et al.* 2009).

Students with PANDAS/PANS may experience distressing levels of anxiety even when presented with seemingly low-threat situations, causing them to avoid these situations or endure them with distress during the school day. For example, a child with social anxiety may perceive answering questions in class as disproportionately threatening; this student's fear of negative evaluation by their peers may result in avoidance of class participation, or refusing to go to school. This level of anxiety experienced in children can significantly interfere with their daily school activities—not only academically, but also socially. They may experience a loss of friends, feelings of isolation, and/or low self-esteem and self-worth (Beesdo *et al.* 2009). Students with PANDAS/PANS experiencing extreme anxiety, worries, and fears on a daily basis may not be able to explain these worries, and they might not understand themselves why they are so anxious. They might also experience an inability to control or stop the worry, despite teachers' reassurances. Anxious thoughts are experienced internally, and do not always present with a verbal or physical behavior that can be "seen" (Bernstein *et al.* 2005). These students might try hard to hide their anxiety, especially if they experience worry and fears related to school and social situations. Although symptoms of anxiety may be difficult to recognize in school, this ongoing anxiety can take an emotional and physical toll. In addition to restlessness and muscle tension, these children may also experience involuntary anxious tics, headaches, nausea, feeling sick, and/or trouble sleeping due to their anxiety.

Some examples of anxiety-related issues and behaviors that can affect a child in the classroom include (Swan *et al.* 2014):

- expressing self-criticism and low self-esteem

- expressing fear of being embarrassed, humiliated, or failing

- seeking constant reassurance from teachers regarding directions, homework, classroom expectations, daily schedule, etc.

- refusal to join in social activities or partner/group work with peers

- extreme fear of new situations/activities, routines, and changes in school schedule

- taking longer to finish work/projects than other students, and/ or refusing to start work/projects, due to fear they can't do anything right

- becoming easily frustrated while attempting to complete classwork/homework, leading to unfinished work

- frequent tardiness and/or absences due to avoidance of school activities and/or refusal to attend

- requesting frequent trips to the bathroom and asking to leave the classroom to avoid certain activities, places, objects or persons.

Strategies and useful accommodations

Students with PANDAS/PANS experiencing extreme anxiety perform best in a calm and supportive, but organized classroom. Change and uncertainty can be unsettling for these students, so a structured classroom, calmly, consistently, and patiently managed, allows students to feel safe and know what to expect. The potential impact of anxiety-related issues on social and academic experiences in school can create a cycle of fear and failure, increased anxiety, and avoidance, which can lead to more absences from school (Beesdo *et al.* 2009). Thus, teachers leading a classroom with reason and respect, rather than fear of punishment, can help reduce anxiety, and also establish a trusting relationship with the student. As such, school personnel should proactively work to lessen students' anxiety by creating safe, supportive, and tolerant classroom environments (Bernstein *et al.* 2005). As similarly noted above regarding OCD symptoms, students with anxiety may not respond to the traditional use of positive and negative consequences to alter motivation and reduce negative behaviors. These students' anxious behaviors are based on their anxious feelings, which they often cannot explain and actively try to relieve. School personnel should implement strategies and accommodations that focus on ways to reduce the students' anxiety, rather than just reducing the behaviors—which are the result of their anxiety.

Connecting with the students' family and establishing a strong relationship and open communication are also early steps school personnel should take to address the anxiety-related issues a student with PANDAS/PANS may be experiencing. Families can provide helpful information to school personnel regarding their child's anxiety-related symptoms, anxiety triggers, and anxiety-reducing strategies that have been successful in the home setting (Swan *et al.* 2014).

Some additional strategies for school personnel to consider when working with students with PANDAS/PANS experiencing extreme anxiety include:

- Establish a daily check-in with the student upon their arrival to school to provide them with details at the start of the day and lessen anxiety about any new or unexpected events.

- Consistently post details and clear visuals for the daily schedule, classroom expectations, routines and procedures, and so on throughout the classroom so the student knows what to expect each day.

- Be attentive to changes in the student's behavior and try to recognize and reduce "triggers" that often result in excessive worry, fear, or avoidance.

- Try to *redirect* the student's behavior, rather than using consequences.

- Be flexible and provide adjusted expectations for completing assignments and tests, such as extra time/flexible due dates, options to work with a peer, alternative activities, and/or options for how to complete an assignment.

- Accommodate late arrivals, and provide extra time and advance notice for the student to prepare for additional transitions throughout the school day.

- Be positive, provide reassurance, and reward even small successes and improvements.

- Encourage, model, and practice positive self-talk with the student.

- Provide support and assistance with peer interactions, particularly during unstructured activities (e.g., recess, lunch room).

- Develop, teach, and practice using relaxation techniques to reduce anxiety in school; encourage the student and family to provide input on these techniques.

- Develop a consistent anxiety de-escalation procedure familiar to all staff working with the student.

- Identify a safe place where the student may go to reduce anxiety during stressful periods; establish clear expectations with the student and staff on how to use the safe place.

- Implement a buddy system to provide the student with a peer they are comfortable checking in with during classwork, after returning from breaks, and when arriving late to class.

Rage and aggression: Impact, strategies, and useful accommodations

Impact and implications

In addition to the acute onset of OCD symptoms and extreme anxiety, children with PANDAS/PANS may also exhibit sudden rage, aggression, and/or severely oppositional behaviors. Some oppositional behaviors may occur throughout the day for a child with PANDAS/PANS; however, rage and aggressive behaviors often occur suddenly and without any provocation. While some children may recognize their irrational behavior and experience remorse after an outburst, other children may have no memory of the episode or their behavior (PANDAS Physicians Network n.d.).

For a child with PANDAS/PANS, the onset of sudden rage and aggressive behavior can be in strong contrast to the child's typical disposition and demeanor. For example, a child who is typically happy and calm may suddenly lash out in anger, and become physically aggressive with individuals close to them (PPN n.d.). In the classroom, sudden outbursts of rage and aggression can impact the student with PANDAS/PANS, as well as the student's peers. Experiencing frequent aggression in the school setting has been shown to have a significant negative impact on both aggressors' and victims' short-term and long-term psychosocial outcomes (Card *et al.* 2008; Ladd 2006; Thomas and Bierman 2006). These students may experience feelings of loneliness, low self-worth, alienation, and be disliked by their peers (Hoff *et al.* 2009; Neal 2010). This negative impact may be exacerbated for students with PANDAS/PANS who exhibit co-occurring symptoms of extreme anxiety and/or OCD tendencies, in addition to their outbursts of rage and aggression.

Strategies and useful accommodations

Students with PANDAS/PANS exhibiting outbursts of rage and aggression may feel out of control and unable to explain this sudden behavior (PPN n.d.). The student may not be able to explain why the behavior occurred, or what trigger seemed to cause it. While this may be frustrating for school personnel, they must keep in mind that PANDAS/PANS is interfering with the student's normal neurological activity and behavior. School personnel should be observant of factors, circumstances, or events that seem to trigger the student's rage and aggression. During an aggressive outburst, school personnel should stay calm and insure that the student with PANDAS/PANS and their peers remain physically safe. Using calming language and providing reassurance may help individuals settle back down; however, they will likely need time to decompress physically and emotionally from the outburst (Lochman *et al.* 2006).

As noted previously, interventions and strategies to address the behaviors of students with PANDAS/PANS should not rely on positive and negative consequences to alter motivation and reduce negative behaviors. These students' rage and aggressive behaviors are intense reactions to triggers related to their PANDAS/PANS which they often cannot explain, identify, or predict (Bagian and Hartung 2015). These sudden outbursts may be in stark contrast to the student's typical demeanor, and thus are not likely to be due to lack of motivation to perform positively. Rather than focusing solely on reducing the rage and aggressive behavior of the student with PANDAS/PANS, school personnel should try to implement strategies and accommodations focused on reducing the triggers, events, and feelings that appear to prompt these aggressive outbursts.

For students who can recount their outbursts and are remorseful, school personnel can talk through the events that occurred and discuss with the student whether there were any internal or external trigger(s) that may have caused their sudden rage and aggression. For other students who may not have any recollection of the recent outburst, school personnel can talk through the events that occurred and try to relieve any confusion or frustration the student may feel. School personnel should also talk through events as needed with the student's peers, who may be feeling anxious or fearful about interacting with the student with PANDAS/PANS after an outburst. Implementing supports and opportunities for positive student interactions may prevent peers from alienating the student after they have experienced sudden rage and aggression (Thomas and Bierman 2006).

Some additional strategies for school personnel to consider when working with students with PANDAS/PANS exhibiting sudden rage and aggression include (MADI Resource Center n.d.):

- Acknowledge the student's intense feelings of anger and rage.

- Provide the student with an opportunity to describe his/her perception of events that occurred during their outburst.

- Identify a safe "break" area where the student can go during and/or after outbursts to decompress and regroup.

- Help the student identify any underlying feelings of anger and/ or anxiety that may have triggered their sudden aggression.

- Devise a consistent cue/language to redirect the student to avoid potential triggers during the school day.

- Recognize and reinforce the student's collaborative and prosocial efforts with peers.

- Positively reinforce appropriate behaviors throughout the school day when the student *is* in control of their behavior.

- Involve the student in reciprocal activities with school peers that encourage feelings of belonging and support self-worth.

Key points to remember and Conclusion

Additional information and research is needed specific to the impact of PANDAS/PANS in the school setting. As identification and awareness increase, school personnel will become more experienced and knowledgeable about how best to support students with PANDAS/ PANS.

While there is a lack of evidence-based research addressing specific PANDAS/PANS accommodations for schools, using existing knowledge of the disorders and accommodations discussed in this chapter can help school professionals address behavioral and emotional needs of students with PANDAS/PANS. Some key take-aways for school professionals addressing the emotional and behavioral functioning of students with PANDAS/PANS include (Candelaria-Greene 2014; IOCDF 2014; O'Rourke 2003; Scholder 2015; Tona and Posner 2011):

- Establish trusting relationships early on with the family and student.

- Engage in ongoing communication and collaboration with the family to help identify and monitor emotional and behavioral symptoms of PANDAS/PANS in the school setting.

- Create safe, supportive, and responsive classroom environments where expectations are clear, "triggers" are reduced, flexible options are provided, and positive reinforcement is utilized.

- Rather than focusing on reducing behaviors, focus on interventions and strategies that can help reduce the *feelings*, *emotions*, and *triggers* that lead to certain behaviors.

- Keep in mind the complex ways the emotional and behavioral symptoms of PANDAS/PANS can interact and change over time, and may possibly overlap with common symptoms of other disorders.

References

Adams, G.B. (2004) 'Identifying, assessing, and treating obsessive-compulsive disorder in school-aged children: The role of school personnel.' *Teaching Exceptional Children* 37, 2, 46–53.

Adams, G.B. (2011) *Students with OCD: A Handbook for School Personnel.* Champaign, IL: Research Press.

Bagian, K., and Hartung, S.Q. (2015) 'Is it PANS, CANS, or PANDAS?: Neuropsychiatric pediatric disorders that are not black and white – implications for the school nurse.' *NASN School Nurse 30*, 2, 96–104.

Beesdo, K., Knappe, S., and Pine, D.S. (2009) 'Anxiety and anxiety disorders in children and adolescents: Developmental issues and implications for DSM-V.' *Psychiatric Clinics of North America 32*, 3, 483–542.

Benjamin, C.L., Beidas, R.S., Comer, J.S., Puliafico, A.C., and Kendall, P.C. (2011) 'Generalized anxiety disorder in youth: Diagnostic considerations.' *Depression and Anxiety 28*, 173–182.

Bernstein, G.A., Layne, A.E., Egan, E.A., and Tennison, D.M. (2005) 'School-based interventions for anxious children.' *Journal of the American Academy of Child and Adolescent Psychiatry 44*, 1118–1127.

Candelaria-Greene, J. (2014) *Considerations Regarding Academic Accommodations/ Compensatory Strategies, and Services for Students with PANDAS/PANS.* Available at http:// pandasnetwork.org/wp-content/uploads/2014/09/School-Considerations-2014. pdf, accessed on 7 March 2016.

Card, N.A., Stucky, B.D., Sawalani, G.M., and Little, T.D. (2008) 'Direct and indirect aggression during childhood and adolescence: A meta-analytic review of gender differences, intercorrelations, and relations to maladjustment.' *Child Development 79*, 5, 1185–1229.

Chang, K., Frankovich, J., Cooperstock, M., Cunningham, M.W., *et al.* (2015) 'Clinical evaluation of youth with pediatric acute-onset neuropsychiatric syndrome (PANS): Recommendations from the 2013 PANS Consensus Conference.' *Journal of Child and Adolescent Psychopharmacology 25*, 1, 3–13.

Chaturvedi, A., Murdick, N.L., and Gartin, B.C. (2014) 'Obsessive compulsive disorder: what an educator needs to know.' *Physical Disabilities: Education and Related Services 33*, 2, 71–83.

Dyches, T.T., Leininger, M., Heath, M.A., and Prater, M.A. (2010) 'Understanding obsessive-compulsive disorder in students: Symptoms and school-based interventions.' *School Social Work Journal 34*, 2, 35–55.

Hoff, K.E., Reese-Weber, M., Schneider, W.J., and Stagg, J.W. (2009) 'The association between high status positions and aggressive behavior in early adolescence.' *Journal of School Psychology 47*, 6, 395–426.

International OCD Foundation (IOCDF) (2014) *Sudden and Severe Onset OCD (PANS/PANDAS) – Practical Advice for Practitioners and Parents.* Available at https://iocdf.org/pandas, accessed on 9 March 2016.

Kearney, C.A. (2005) *Social Anxiety and Social Phobia in Youth: Characteristics, Assessment, and Psychological Treatment.* New York: Springer.

Ladd, G.W. (2006) 'Peer rejection, aggressive or withdrawn behavior, and psychological maladjustment from ages 5 to 12: An examination of four predictive models.' *Child Development 77*, 822–846.

Lochman, J.E., Powell, N.R., Clanton, N., and McElroy, H.K. (2006) 'Anger and Aggression.' In G.G. Bear and K.M. Minke (eds) *Children's Needs III: Development, Prevention, and Intervention.* Washington, DC: National Association of School Psychologists.

Mood and Anxiety Disorders Institute (MADI) Resource Center (n.d.) *Mental Health in the Classroom: School-based Interventions.* Available at www2.massgeneral.org/schoolpsychiatry/inter_conduct_opposition.asp, accessed on 9 March 2016.

Murphy, T.K., Kurlan, R., and Leckman, J. (2010) 'The immunobiology of Tourette's disorder, pediatric autoimmune neuropsychiatric disorders associated with streptococcus, and related disorders: A way forward.' *Journal of Child and Adolescent Psychopharmacology, 20*, 317–331.

National Institute of Mental Health (NIMH) (n.d.) *Information About PANDAS.* Available at www.nimh.nih.gov/labs-at-nimh/research-areas/clinics-and-labs/pdnb/web.shtml, accessed on 2 March 2016.

Neal, J.W. (2010) 'Social aggression and social position in middle childhood and early adolescence: Burning bridges or building them?' *Journal of Early Adolescence 30*, 1, 122–137.

O'Rourke, K. (2003) 'PANDAS syndrome in the school setting.' *School Nurse News 20*, 4, 34–35.

Ollendick, T.H., Raishevich, N., Davis, T.E., Sirbu, C., and Ost, L.G. (2009) 'Specific phobia in youth: Phenomenology and psychological characteristics.' *Behavior Therapy 41*, 133–141.

PANDAS Network (2015) *PANDAS/PANS Fact Sheet: Compilation of Treatment Guidelines and Anecdotal Evidence.* Available at http://pandasnetwork.org/pandaspans-fact-sheet-2015, accessed on 9 March 2016.

PANDAS Physicians Network (PPN) (n.d.) *PPN PANS Diagnostic Guidelines.* Available at www.pandasppn.org/ppn-pans-diagnostic-guidelines, accessed on 9 March 2016.

Scholder, L. (2015) *To the New-to-PANDAS-PANS Family and Practitioner: Understanding the Impact of Symptoms, a Psychologist's View.* Available at http://pandasnetwork.org/wp-content/uploads/2015/08/Scholder-11x17-FINAL-final-2.pdf, accessed on 9 March 2016.

Swan, A.J., Cummings, C.M., Caporino, N.E., and Kendall, P.C. (2014) 'Evidence-based Intervention Approaches for Students with Anxiety and Related Disorders.' In H.M. Walker and F.M. Gresham (eds) *Handbook of Evidence-Based Practices for Emotional and Behavioral Disorders: Applications in Schools.* New York: Guilford Press.

Swedo, S., Leckman, J., and Rose, N. (2012) 'From research subgroup to clinical syndrome: Modifying the PANDAS criteria to describe PANS (Pediatric Acute-onset Neuropsychiatric Syndrome).' *Pediatrics and Therapeutics 2*, 113, 1–8.

Thomas, D.E., and Bierman, K.L. (2006) 'The impact of classroom aggression on the development of aggressive behavior problems in children.' *Development and Psychopathology 18*, 2, 471–487.

Tona, J., and Posner, T. (2011) 'Pediatric Autoimmune Neuropsychiatric Disorders: A new frontier for occupational therapy intervention.' *OT Practice, November 2011*, 14–22.

Westly, E. (2009) 'From throat to mind: Strep today, anxiety later?' *Scientific American*, 5 January 2009. Available at www.scientificamerican.com/article/from-throat-to-mind, accessed on 2 March 2016.

Woolcock, E., and Campbell, M.A. (2005) 'The role of teachers in the support of students with obsessive-compulsive disorder.' *Australian Educational and Developmental Psychologist 22*, 54–64.

Chapter 10

Transition Considerations for Students with PANDAS and PANS

KATHLEEN STEIN, PH.D.

Elliott, a five-year-old with a PANS diagnosis, attends preschool in an early childhood special education program, in which he is placed in a classroom with five other students who have developmental and neurological disabilities. His IEP team, working with his family, has determined he is likely to be successful in a general education kindergarten classroom next year. In May, they hold a transition meeting, which is attended by his current early childhood teachers, his future kindergarten teachers, and his occupational and speech therapists, as well as his parents. The team discusses strategies to support Elliott—and meet his health needs—as he transitions into a regular education setting with a much larger peer group.

Donna, a ninth-grade student with PANDAS, has spent her fall semester on homebound instruction following several rounds of plasmapheresis in an inpatient setting. With her PANDAS symptoms well controlled, she is looking forward to returning to school, but she, her parents, and her physicians have concerns about the physical demands of a school day and the services she may require in the event of a relapse. Donna's IEP team crafts a plan to help her return to school on a modified, shortened schedule, with the goal of gradually lengthening her school day. In the meantime, they address other strategies to support her during the day and help her adjust to high school, including checking in and checking out with a counselor in the morning and afternoon; support of a peer buddy; and academic accommodations for testing.

Eric is a twelfth-grade student who has completed college applications and been accepted to college. Eric has received treatment for PANS throughout middle and high school. He considers himself "recovered," in his words, but still has mild to moderate anxiety and OCD. When physically ill, he sometimes experiences worsening of these symptoms, along with difficulties with focusing and memory. Eric is an A and B student who receives accommodations in high school. His IEP team has worked with Eric, and his family, to create and update his transition plan throughout high school. Eric has received support with organization and metacognition so that he can recognize his own learning patterns along with training in self-advocacy, a skill that his family feels he will need to utilize with his future professors and perhaps his roommates as well.

Elliott, Donna, and Eric are all experiencing some type of transition, made more challenging by their health conditions. In an educational context, *transition* refers to the process of moving from one status or place to another, and can be minor (e.g., moving from an academic activity to recess or lunch) or major (e.g., graduating from high school). Children and young adults experience a variety of transitions throughout their school careers.

Kagan (1992) identified two types of transitions: horizontal and vertical. *Horizontal transitions* involve movement across settings within the same time frame. For example, students move from classroom to classroom and academic to social settings on a daily basis. Some students, particularly those with disabilities, may experience additional transitions, such as movement from a general education to special education setting and vice versa, often daily or multiple times throughout a school week. Moreover, children and young adults with significant health needs, like Donna, may move back and forth between settings such as hospital or home and school throughout a semester or academic year.

Whereas horizontal transitions occur within a particular time frame, *vertical transitions* occur over time and involve age and developmental benchmarks, such as movement from home to preschool, preschool to elementary school, elementary to secondary schools, and secondary to postsecondary settings. This chapter presents specific considerations for both horizontal and vertical transitions for students with PANDAS/PANS.

Transitions, especially those involving major changes, are difficult for most individuals, and can be particularly challenging for those with additional academic, behavioral, or health needs. Moreover, children and young adults with PANS or PANDAS contend with distinctive challenges due to the complex nature of the illness (Rice Doran 2015). In order to enable smooth transitions throughout a child's academic career, it is necessary for stakeholders to be aware of relevant legislation regarding transition for individuals with disabilities, understand the demands of the various transitions children and young adults with PANS or PANDAS experience, the challenges these changes present, and strategies teachers and other service providers can utilize to provide supports to students with PANS or PANDAS as they navigate the numerous transitions during their academic careers.

Relevant legislation

Federal laws, such as the Individuals with Disabilities Education Improvement Act (IDEA 2004), the Rehabilitation Act of 1973 (2006), and the Americans with Disabilities Act of 1990 and Americans with Disabilities Amendments Act of 2008 (ADAA 2009) provide various mandates regarding assistance, services, and accommodations for individuals identified as having a functional impairment due to a qualifying disability. Furthermore, these laws address, either directly or indirectly, transition programming or supports either during transition periods or in specific settings.

Individuals with Disabilities Education Improvement Act and transition programming

The Individuals with Disabilities Education Improvement Act (IDEA 2004) addresses two vertical transitions for students with disabilities. The first involves the transition from the Program for Infants and Toddlers with Disabilities, covered under Part C of IDEA, to special education, under Part B. The other addresses secondary transition, which occurs when students exit the birth-through-21 system. The 2004 reauthorization of IDEA outlines requirements for coordinated transition plans or programs, the role of service coordination, sources of support for transmittal of records, interdisciplinary personnel training to conduct effective transitions, paraprofessional training, the duties of the state interagency coordinating council, technical assistance, dissemination of research findings, parent involvement, parent training and information, and competitive grants for research to improve transitions. Furthermore, IDEA 2004 underscores the importance of effective transitions for positive child outcomes (Rous 2004).

Part C of IDEA: The Program for Infants and Toddlers with Disabilities

Part C of IDEA, or the Program for Infants and Toddlers with Disabilities, is a federal grant program that assists states in operating a comprehensive statewide program of early intervention services for infants and toddlers (birth through three years). Services are identified in the *Individualized Family Service Plan (IFSP)*, which is developed by an early interventionist and the family of the child. IDEA (2004) outlines the transition procedures for children moving from Part C to Part B (special education), and includes the following components (Rous 2004):

- *Review of program options.* The plan must review program options for the toddler for the period from the toddler's third birthday through the remainder of the school year.

- *Involving the family in the transition plan.* The lead agency must include the family in the development of the transition plan.

- *Timeline requirement.* The lead agency must establish a transition plan in the IFSP not fewer than 90 days, but at the discretion of all stakeholders up to nine months, before the child's third birthday.

- *Transition.* The transition plan in the IFSP must include any appropriate steps for the toddler to exit the Part C program and any transition services needed by that toddler and his or her family.

In some states, children who are aged three or older and who have participated in Part C services may continue to participate in the early intervention (infants and toddlers) program, until they enter, or are eligible to enter, kindergarten. In this case, the child continues to receive services under an IFSP rather than an IEP. The timeline for the transition process as delineated above is adjusted accordingly.

Secondary transition

In 1990, IDEA mandated the formulation of a transition program for youth receiving special education services beginning no later than the first *Individualized Education Program* be in effect after the student turns 16, or younger if determined appropriate by the IEP team. According to the law, the transition section of the IEP must include a statement of:

1. appropriate measurable postsecondary goals based upon age-appropriate transition assessments related to training, education, employment, and where appropriate independent living skills;

2. the transition services (including courses of study) needed to assist the student in reaching those goals (34 C.F.R. 300.320 [b]; 20 U.S.C. 1414 [d] [1] [A].

In addition, "the LEA must invite a student with a disability to attend the student's IEP Team meeting if a purpose of the meeting will be the consideration of postsecondary goals for the student and transition services needed to assist the student in reaching those goals under 3000.320b" (34CFR 300.321[b])(20 U.S.C. 1414[d] [1] [B]). The inclusion of this statement emphasizes the importance of student involvement, and allows the student's voice to be heard, which encourages self-determination and self-advocacy skills (Konrad and Test 2004). Transition services are defined as:

A *coordinated* set of activities for a student with a disability that:

1. is designed to be within a results-oriented process, that is focused on improving the academic and functional achievement of the student with a disability to facilitate the student's movement from school to post-school activities, including: postsecondary education, vocational education, integrated employment (including supported employment), continuing and adult education, adult services, independent living or community participation;

2. is based upon the individual student's needs, taking into account the strengths, preferences, and interests and;

3. includes instruction, related services, community experiences, the development of employment and other post-school adult living objectives, and if appropriate acquisition of daily living skills (34 C.F.R. 300.43.(a);20 U.S.C.1401(34)).

Transition services should also address domains such as community experiences, employment and other post-school objectives, instruction, daily living skills, and functional vocational evaluations (Frank and Sitlington 1997).

Civil rights legislation

The Americans with Disabilities Act (ADA) and the Rehabilitation Act are pieces of civil rights legislation designed to protect individuals with disabilities from discrimination and provide reasonable accommodations, when appropriate. Specifically, Section 504 of the Rehabilitation Act of 1973 prohibits discrimination based on disability in all institutions that receive federal funds, including most colleges and universities (PL 93-112, 1973; PL 102-569, 1992). In addition to prohibiting discrimination towards individuals with disabilities, both Title II of the Americans with Disabilities Act and Section 504 of the Rehabilitation Act require academic institutions to provide reasonable accommodations to students with disabilities (Collins, Bybee, and Mowbray 1998).

Furthermore, Section 504 requires postsecondary institutions to inform applicants of the availability of academic accommodations, services, auxiliary aid, and the person or office responsible for coordinating these services. For rights afforded under both ADA and Section 504, individuals must have a verifiable disability to access their rights, register with the appropriate disability services program, and must provide documentation of their disability. As discussed in Chapter 7, eligibility for accommodations, and appropriate accommodations, may differ from K–12 to postsecondary settings.

Legislation and PANS and PANDAS

As discussed in previous chapters, individuals with PANS or PANDAS experience a variety of symptoms, including health impairments and sometimes serious mental health issues. In addition, some individuals experience academic challenges, either related to ADHD-like symptoms or frequent absences. Because of the range and variety of symptoms, the majority of students with PANS or PANDAS would most likely qualify for special education services under the Other Health Impairments (OHI) disability category (Rice Doran 2015).

Due to the range of symptoms and complexity of PANS and PANDAS, it is not surprising that it is common for students within the OHI category to have a secondary diagnosis.

Indeed, the second National Longitudinal Transition Study (NLTS-2), a nationally representative study of students from age 16 to early adulthood, revealed that over a third of students with other disability classifications had a secondary classification of OHI (Targett *et al.* 2013). Moreover, high rates of OHI were found in students with emotional or behavioral disabilities (Carter, Austin, and Trainor 2012; Targett *et al.* 2013). These findings are consistent with the symptoms of PANS and PANDAS, such as characteristics of obsessive-compulsive disorder (OCD) and other mental health conditions (Rice Doran 2015). It is important to note that the presence of disability does not guarantee services provided by the previously discussed legislation. In order for a child to receive special education services, the disability must adversely affect the student's access to the general education curriculum. In order to qualify for protection under ADA and Section 504 of the Rehabilitation Act, the disability must create impairments or limitations to one or more major life function.

Assessment

Both Part B and Part C of IDEA (2004) require local education agencies to conduct thorough evaluations to determine eligibility for special education, and to identify the appropriate interventions and services needed, at no cost to the parent. In addition, the law mandates assessments regarding secondary transition. Although assessments for horizontal or other vertical transitions are not specifically addressed in IDEA (2004), they are integral for successful transition planning.

Secondary transition assessment

As stated above, the use of transition assessments is required by IDEA (2004). Specifically, the student's IEP must include a statement of:

1. appropriate measurable postsecondary goals based upon age-appropriate transition assessments related to training, education, employment, and where appropriate independent living skills;

2. the transition services (including courses of study) needed to assist the student in reaching those goals (34 C.F.R.300.320 [b]; 20 U.S.C.1414 [d] [1] [A]).

Transition services must take into account the student's strengths, preferences, and interests based on these assessments. These requirements are particularly important for identifying the transition needs of students with PANS or PANDAS because of the complexity of the condition, as well as the range and variety of symptoms.

Transition assessment should be a *continuous, individualized* process with the purpose of guiding students and their families in identifying meaningful postsecondary goals, and the transition activities and services that will help them prepare for adult roles. Adult roles involve employment, postsecondary education or training programs, independent living, community involvement, and social/personal relationships.

According to Kortering, Braziel, and Sitlington (2010), the assessment process should be thorough and should include information regarding: (a) background information; (b) interests and preferences; (c) aptitudes or abilities; (d) personal style; (e) interpersonal relationships; (f) self-determination skills; (g) academics; and (h) employment-related skills.

Assessment for other transitions

As stated previously, individuals experience a multitude of transitions throughout their life. When thinking about transition in this broader sense, it may be appropriate to use the term transitions assessments, which gather data about multiple and varied life transitions (Clark 2007). Vertical and horizontal transitions assessments should allow students, their families, and service providers to define goals and identify specific support for the individual's transition needs throughout their life span (Clark 2007). Specifically, the assessments should address: (a) the student's goals and expectations for a transition event or period; (b) specific planning areas; (c) preparation needs; and (d) decision-making that would promote successful transition (Clark 2007).

The purpose of all evaluations and assessments in special education is to inform stakeholders regarding a student's strengths and needs, as well as inform the process of creating an Individualized Education Program designed to assist the student in their academic achievement. Although IDEA (2004) mandates transition planning for the movement from the Program for Infants and Toddlers with Disabilities (Part C) to special education (Part B), which occurs at age three or older, and secondary transition, *intentional* planning is beneficial for the various transitions a student experiences throughout their school career (Pola-Money 2005). Assessments should be used to guide this planning for students with disabilities, including those with PANS or PANDAS, during periods of transition. In order to plan for transitions effectively, stakeholders must be aware of the different types of transitions, the inherent demands and challenges involved, and strategies and supports that can assist students as they move between settings. This is particularly true for students with PANDAS/PANS, as collaboration from multiple personnel is often needed and their health status and level of performance is subject to change.

Horizontal transitions

As defined above, *horizontal transitions* involve movement across settings within the same time frame. For example, students move from classroom to classroom and academic to social settings on a daily basis. Students with disabilities may experience additional horizontal transitions. For example, a student may leave his/her general education classroom once a week to work with a physical therapist, leave the classroom daily to receive language arts instruction from a special educator, or move between home and/or hospital settings and school. Although there are many types of horizontal transitions, the movement from a hospital or homebound setting to school is particularly important to consider for students with PANS or PANDAS.

Like Donna, introduced in the beginning of this chapter, many children and young adults with chronic illness are absent from school for an extended period of time, and receive "homebound instruction." If a student is hospitalized for an extended length of time, he or she may receive services provided by the hospital. It is important to note that when students are absent for an extended period of time, the public school system is still responsible for providing educational and related services, whether it be at home or hospital. Moreover, IDEA (2004) allows special education services to be delivered in a range of settings, including a hospital or the child's home (NICHCY 2012). In these cases, the student's IEP team will convene to determine the type, rate, and frequency of services. As with Donna, the team should also identify strategies and supports to assist the student during the transition period.

Frequent or extended absences may cause academic challenges due to gaps in instruction, as well as social and emotional challenges. Absences often disrupt the formation of friendships, reduce the opportunity for support, and result in peer rejection (Shiu 2001). Children with health impairments and chronic illness may also experience cognitive side effects (e.g., attention, memory, or processing impairments) due to the illness itself or medications or other treatment.

Students may also have difficulty focusing on academics due to fatigue, nausea, or other symptoms (hospital to school). In addition to these challenges, children and young adults with PANS or PANDAS may experience emotional or behavioral difficulties, such as inattention and hyperactivity (often associated with ADHD), impulsivity and difficulty controlling anger or outbursts (Clark, Russman, and Orme 1999), or withdrawal and depression (Boekaerts and Roder 1999). Understandably, these symptoms, as well as challenges related to absenteeism, often reduce academic motivation, which increases the possibility of poor academic outcomes (Shaw and McCabe 2008).

Developing and implementing a systematic transition plan can mitigate the negative impacts related to a chronic illness, as well as issues due to frequent or extended absences (Shaw and McCabe 2008; American Academy of Pediatrics 2005). Transition plans should be guided by an assessment of the student's needs, as well as the academic and social demands of the setting to which the student is returning. Clear and consistent communication is essential to effective transition planning and successful transitions. All service providers working with the child should share information regarding the student's needs, strengths, and progress, with each other, the caregivers, and the student. In addition, service providers should have access to IEPs and other relevant documents. Furthermore, students should be involved in all stages of the planning to the greatest extent possible. Flexible attendance or adjusted school days should also be considered (Shaw and McCabe 2008; American Academy of Pediatrics 2005) because children and young adults with a chronic illness often struggle with varying levels of fatigue, pain, stamina, attention, and alertness (Mukherjee, Lightfoot, and Sloper 2000). Students with medical needs often attend school for half a day, or the schedule may rotate, with homebound services on one day, one half day of school the next, and a full day of school on the third day (Clay et al. 2004; Tate 2000). It is important to monitor the student's health and adjustment during the transition period, and make changes as needed. In Donna's case, her counselor will look for signs of fatigue and other symptoms identified by her doctor, and report concerns to the team.

The presence of social support has been identified as particularly important to managing illness and supporting overall adjustment for youth with chronic illnesses (Lightfoot, Wright, and Sloper 1999). Support systems can be formal or informal, and usually include teachers, parents, and close friends (Kyngas 2004). Moreover, students identified support from a peer with a similar illness as being particularly valuable (Kyngas 2004). Consider the case of Donna, in the beginning of this chapter. Because of the importance of social supports, Donna's team decided to pair her with a peer buddy and to have her check in with her counselor twice a day.

Vertical transitions

Again as defined above, *vertical transitions* occur over time and involve age or developmental benchmarks, such as movement from home to preschool, preschool to elementary school, elementary to secondary schools, and secondary to postsecondary settings. Reaching an educational milestone, whether it be the first day of kindergarten or the first day of college, is exciting and presents opportunities for academic and social development. However, these opportunities are accompanied by new demands and challenges, which can create stress and risk for failure. Many students, with and without disabilities, struggle with these transitions, and require supports to help them adjust to their new environment. The legal requirements regarding transitioning from the Infants and Toddlers with Disabilities Program (Part C) to special education (Part B), and secondary transition were discussed earlier in this chapter. This section addresses potential challenges involved in two key vertical transitions, early childhood and secondary, and strategies to mitigate these challenges.

Early childhood transition

The transition from home or preschool to kindergarten is a significant milestone in a child's life, and sets the stage for future educational experiences (Dockett and Perry 2007). Because of the vast differences between pre-kindergarten and kindergarten educational experiences, it is not surprising that research indicates almost half of typically developing children experience some difficulty during the transition to kindergarten (Rimm-Kaufman, Pianta, and Cox 2000).

Commonly reported challenges included difficulty following directions, lack of academic skills, disorganized home environments, and difficulty working independently (Wildenger and McIntyre 2011). When students enter kindergarten, they typically encounter increased academic and social personal demands, as well as a more structured environment and schedule. Given that children without risk factors experience difficulty during the transition to kindergarten, it is not unreasonable to surmise that children with disabilities will also struggle. Children with disabilities, like Elliott, whom we met in the beginning of this chapter, contend with additional challenges related to their specific characteristics and needs.

As previously discussed, IDEA (2004) requires transition planning when children move from the Infants and Toddlers with Disabilities Program (Part C) to special education (Part B). This process typically occurs at age three, but some states do allow children to remain in the Infants and Toddlers program until they enter kindergarten. Because IDEA (2004) only requires formal transition planning when children move from Part C to Part B services and for secondary transition, formal transition planning for movement between preschool or early childhood programs to kindergarten is not required for most children. However, the literature regarding early childhood transition is consistent in its recommendation of transition planning and preparation, which (as it did with Elliott) should begin well before a child enters kindergarten (Schischka, Rawlinson, and Hamilton 2012). Furthermore, as with Elliott's transition, planning should involve identifying current and potential problems, goal setting, and coordination of the transition (e.g., La Paro, Pianta, and Cox 2000; Newman 1996).

Parents and family members of a child with PANS or PANDAS are also impacted by the child's transition to kindergarten, and may experience stress or anxiety themselves (McIntyre *et al.* 2007; Schischka *et al.* 2012). Parents often feel less connected or involved in their child's elementary school experience as compared with preschool experiences (Wildenger and McIntyre 2011; Schischka *et al.* 2012), and desire more information regarding academic expectations in kindergarten, their child's current skills, and their child's kindergarten program (Wildenger and McIntyre 2011; McIntyre *et al.* 2010). Transition planning meetings can be an effective forum for parents to voice their concerns, and for members to share pertinent information. In addition to planning, fostering communication between home, preschool, and kindergarten contexts is also important in supporting kindergarten transition (Wildenger and McIntyre 2011). Bourne (2007) also recommend ongoing positive communication and collaboration between the family, early childhood and elementary school personnel, and all other professionals during the transition process. Therefore, including Elliott's current and future service providers and teachers, as well as his parents, in his transition team meeting is an integral step in promoting a successful transition experience. Closely related to the benefits of communication and collaboration is the role of relationships in successful transitioning. According to Peters (2010), a child's friendships, peer relationships, and relationship with his or her teacher, are integral to the transition process. Moreover, reciprocal and respectful relationships between the adults working with the child are particularly important (Peters 2010).

Transition planning should be informed by current assessment data regarding the strengths and needs of the child, including academic information, social/emotional skills, and medical and/or health conditions. Planning should also consider the academic and social demands of the particular setting. As exemplified in the story of Elliott at this chapter's beginning, because Elliott is moving to a setting with more peers, and perhaps fewer adults, the team will need to identify strategies to assist him in communicating his needs effectively, and interacting with his peers. Since he will not be monitored as closely in kindergarten and throughout elementary school, he may also need to learn how to self-monitor and let his teacher know if he needs to rest or take a break.

The team should also make arrangements for multiple pre-entry visits to the new school so the child can become familiar with the new school environment and classroom routines (Bourne 2007). Children with disabilities may need more time to become familiar with the new routines and environments (Wartmann 2000). Having Elliott's future kindergarten teacher attend the transition planning meeting allows for communication of this information. It may also be helpful to have Elliott's future teacher visit with him at his current setting, where he feels safe, if possible. This would not only allow Elliott to meet this new person in a comfortable environment, it would allow the teacher an opportunity to observe how he functions in a familiar setting. Furthermore, maintaining continuity between the setting the child is leaving and the one he or she is entering promotes successful adaptation to the new environment, and benefits the transition process for the child, the parents, and the teachers (Bourke *et al.* 2002; Newman 1996; Schischka *et al.* 2012).

Secondary transition

Secondary transition is the process of preparing students for life after they leave high school, and addresses the postsecondary domains of education or training, employment, and community and independent living. As in the case of Eric, referenced at the beginning of this chapter, teams often must balance multiple considerations, including academic skills, health, and social skills, as well as myriad others. In response to negative postsecondary outcomes for young adults with disabilities, IDEA (2004) mandated transition programming for youth receiving special education services, beginning no later than the year the student turns 16, in 1990. Although some progress has been made, particularly regarding high school completion and lower dropout rates, students with disabilities continue to experience more negative post-school outcomes than their non-disabled peers (Newman *et al.* 2009). In light of this, service providers and researchers within the field continue to identify and evaluate strategies and supports to assist young adults with disabilities in their attainment of their postsecondary goals.

Poor outcomes and challenges

The transition from high school to postsecondary life is challenging for the majority of young adults, who must make life-changing decisions just as institutional structure decreases and personal responsibility increases (Schulenberg and Zarrett 2006; Shanahan 2000). However, this process is even more challenging for young adults with disabilities, who "face significant barriers to achieving their (postsecondary) goals" (U.S. Department of Education 2002, p.48). Results of the National Longitudinal Transition Study-2 (NLTS-2) revealed that youth with disabilities are less likely to enroll in postsecondary education

(60% vs. 67%) and live independently (45% vs. 59%) (Newman *et al.* 2011). Furthermore, research examining postsecondary outcomes found of the 73 percent of students with disabilities who enrolled in college, only 28 percent completed their programs, compared with 54 percent of their peers without disabilities (Wolanin and Steele 2004).

Moreover, transition into post-school roles for young adults with PANS or PANDAS may be even more complicated due to the challenges related to the variety of symptoms and complexity of the illness, as was the case with Eric. Specifically, many individuals with PANS or PANDAS manifest symptoms related to OCD or other emotional or behavioral disabilities (EBD). Individuals with EBD experience the most negative post-school outcomes as compared with peers with other disabilities and their non-disabled peers (Newman *et al.* 2009; Salzer 2012). For example, NLTS-2 data showed that 42 percent of youth with EBD were employed for pay outside the home, as compared with youth without disabilities (66%) (Newman *et al.* 2009), and only 34 percent of individuals with EBDs enrolled in a postsecondary education program compared with more than 70 percent of students with sensory impairments, 54 percent of students with autism, and 47 percent of students with learning disabilities (Newman *et al.* 2009). Students with EBDs have also consistently completed their programs of study at a lower rate than their nondisabled peers (Best, Still, and Cameron 2008; Newman *et al.* 2009; Salzer 2012). There are multiple reasons for these poor outcomes, including lack of support from colleges and community mental health systems, cognitive skill problems, perceived stigma, lack of opportunities, and the nature of the mental health condition itself (Belch 2011; Blacklock, Benson, and Johnson 2003; Kiuhara and Huefner 2008).

Youth with serious health conditions and needs face particular challenges as they transition to postsecondary roles. For example, they often have to contend with changes in insurance coverage and reduced access to services (Bargeron *et al.* 2015). They may also have to transition away from pediatric healthcare providers, which can create fear (Burdo-Hartman and Patel 2008; Kennedy and Sawyer 2008; McManus *et al.* 2008), and they may have difficulty finding an adult-oriented provider because adult service providers are not familiar with the issues faced by young adults with serious health conditions (Burdo-Hartman and Patel 2008; Blomquist, Graham, and Thomas 2007). Furthermore, youth may not have the knowledge or wherewithal to find and work with a new provider or take responsibility for their own care (Bargeron *et al.* 2015; Peter *et al.* 2009). Young adults with emotional or behavioral disabilities experience similar challenges. Because many pediatricians do not possess knowledge and skills regarding transition, they often have difficulty assisting their patients through this process (Kennedy and Sawyer 2008). Unfortunately, these difficulties negatively impact the health of young adults with serious health conditions, reporting less appropriate use of services and worse health than their peers (Data Resource Center for Child and Adolescent Health 2012).

Transition planning

As previously discussed, IDEA (2004) mandates transition programming begin no later than the first Individualized Education Program in effect after the student turns 16, with many states beginning transition planning at age 14. Transition planning is guided by the ongoing, individualized assessment process, and includes identifying goals addressing postsecondary employment, education, and community and independent living. In order to assist students in reaching their goals, transition services are identified and provided by specified school personnel, as well as the student and family. IDEA (2004) defines *transition services* as a "coordinated set of activities" designed to be within a results-oriented process focused on improving the functional and academic achievement of the young adult in order to enhance postsecondary achievement. Therefore, transition services should include a wide variety of activities to address the specific and singular needs of the young adult with disabilities. These activities should address not only the student's academic and functional challenges, but should also align with the student's employment, educational, and independent living strengths, interests, and goals.

It is not possible to provide an exhaustive list of transition activities, particularly since activities should be selected based on a student's interests, strengths, and needs. Here is a select list of potential transition activities categorized by the postsecondary domains of education, employment, and community and independent living, as well as the key construct of self-determination (which will be discussed later in this chapter):

Education

- Identify high school course offerings related to career goals.
- Successfully complete course related to career goal.
- Explore support services available at postsecondary schools of interest.
- Research entrance requirements for postsecondary schools.
- Identify postsecondary schools that provide training in career field.
- Complete applications for postsecondary education.
- Attend SAT or ACT prep course.
- Take SAT or ACT.
- Apply to postsecondary school.

Employment

- Complete and review an interest inventory (e.g., Career Game).
- Review career and academic assessments to assist in career planning.
- Obtain specific information about qualifications of jobs of interest.
- Identify postsecondary requirements necessary to achieve career goals.
- Observe/job shadow employee at a business site.
- Participate in school-based work experience.
- Obtain and hold summer or after-school job.

Independent and community living

- Take appropriate medication.
- Recognize need to consult physician.
- Schedule doctor/dentist appointments and keep appointments.
- Monitor health needs and progress.
- Identify money and make correct change.
- Use ATM machine.

Self-advocacy and self-determination

- Attend and participate in IEP meeting.
- Identify appropriate action to take if late or absent from school.
- Identify when assistance is needed and know how to obtain it.
- Meet with teachers to discuss accommodation needs.
- Obtain school records to document disability for accommodations for postsecondary options.
- Develop list of personal goals.
- Identify learning strengths and weaknesses.
- Communicate learning strengths and limitations to teacher or employer.
- Describe disability and education history.
- Obtain information on disability-related legislation.

In addition to the above specified elements of the transition plan, the identification of accommodations is integral to promoting postsecondary success. Although the IEP does not follow a student after they graduate from high school, the Americans with Disabilities Act of 1990 and Section 504 of the Vocational Rehabilitation Act of 1973 provide for the use of reasonable accommodations for individuals with disabilities. Therefore, identifying appropriate accommodations, as well as providing students with opportunities to advocate for and obtain the use of said accommodations, can contribute greatly to a young adult's post-school success. Candelaria-Greene (2014) has identified potential accommodations for students with PANS or PANDAS. Of her list, accommodations that may be appropriate for postsecondary settings may include frequent breaks and separate spaces for stress relief or relaxation and flexibility as needed for attendance issues. Other frequently used accommodations for individuals with health impairments include (Berry *et al.* 2010):

- note takers
- recorded class sessions or meetings
- extended exam time
- alternative testing arrangements
- assignments available in electronic format
- environments that minimize fatigue and injury
- an ergonomic workstation with adjustable keyboard trays, monitor risers, glare guards, foot rests, adjustable chairs, and/or anti-fatigue matting
- speech recognition computer input devices, ergonomic keyboards, one-handed keyboards, expanded keyboards, or miniature keyboards.

Strategies for secondary transition

In addition to quality transition planning, there are a variety of strategies service providers can implement to promote secondary transition success, including the development or enhancement of self-determination and self-advocacy, increasing a student's social capital, and the appropriate use of technology. In addition, the Universal Design for Transition (UDT) framework may assist teachers and case managers in supporting young adults in the secondary transition process.

Self-determination and self-advocacy

Self-determination is a theoretical construct that involves personal abilities and attitudes that empower an individual to identify and pursue goals (Powers *et al.* 1996; Wehmeyer 1996). According to Deci and Ryan (1985), self-determination is "the capacity to choose and to have those choices be the determinants of one's actions" (p.38). Self-determined individuals participate in decision-making, identify goals and the requisites for achieving those goals, participate in selecting courses and career planning, and advocate for their desires and needs (Levine and Wagner 2005; Wehmeyer 1996). Both the Individuals with Disabilities Act (IDEA) (PL-101-476, 1990) and the 1992 Amendments to the 1973 Rehabilitation Act (PL 102-569) recognize self-determination as a significant outcome for youth with disabilities (Wehmeyer 1996). Halloran (1993) goes even further, designating self-determination as "the ultimate goal of education" (p.214).

Self-determination is clearly an integral component of successful transitions because it allows young adults to identify and work towards their personal goals. There are numerous activities and ways to promote self-determination in youth. These include having the student lead their IEP meeting, creating their person-centered plan (Targett *et al.* 2013), explicit self-determination instruction (Trainor, Smith, and Kim 2012), or instruction in self-determination and self-advocacy either explicit or embedded into general education curriculum, and encouraging students to identify goals and monitor their own progress. In addition, the use of self-determination assessments such as the AIR or ARC self-determination assessments is beneficial in monitoring the progress of this important skill.

Self-advocacy is closely related to the concept of self-determination. Test *et al.* (2005) defined self-advocacy as knowing one's self and one's rights, leadership, and communication. It also involves the ability to speak on one's own behalf. In college, this is manifested in students knowing their legal rights regarding accommodations, requesting accommodations for which they are eligible from their professors, and following up with professors when they do not receive these supports. Furthermore, students with disabilities who have strong advocacy skills are more likely to succeed in college and other postsecondary settings (Connor 2012). Ensuring students know their legal rights and responsibilities, providing opportunities for students to practice seeking help from their teachers, and identifying and asking for accommodations and other supports will help enhance the self-advocacy skills of young adults with disabilities.

Social capital

Trainor *et al.* (2012) define social capital as networks of interpersonal connections, such as teachers and other school personnel, acquaintances, and family friends. These connections have value because they can be integral to the development of a career path (Trainor *et al.* 2012). For example, social capital can be used to secure internships, interviews, job shadowing experiences, and sometimes even employment (Trainor *et al.* 2012). Unfortunately, individuals with disabilities often have small or limited networks, and thereby limited social capital.

Development of social networks for individuals with PANDAS/ PANS may be particularly challenging due to anxiety, intermittent behavioral challenges, or interrupted schooling due to health concerns. Including the development of social connections as part of transition planning can lead to increased summer employment (Carter *et al.* 2012) as well as potential career development opportunities in the future. Teachers, case managers, and other service providers can enhance young adults' social capital by utilizing their own networks to secure work and school partnerships and connect youth with mentors or possible employers, encourage youth to join groups related to their interests and hobbies, and increase goals for community engagement (Trainor *et al.* 2012).

Technology

Advances in technology have greatly benefited individuals with disabilities over the last several decades. There are many types of assistive technology (AT) that individuals with health impairments can use to gain more independence and efficiency in daily activities, as well as increased participation in postsecondary settings (Wehmeyer *et al.* 2006). Specific types of AT are discussed, also, in Chapters 5, 7, and 8 of this text. In addition, there are myriad technologies created for all people, such as personal digital assistants, smartphones with contact lists, personal calendars, alarms and task reminder applications, digital recordings, and global positioning systems (GPS) (Connor 2012;

Targett *et al.* 2013) which have multiple uses in postsecondary activities. These devices tend to be less expensive than disability-specific AT, and are less likely to be stigmatizing, because of their ubiquitous use.

Universal Design for Transition

Finally, the relatively new concept of Universal Design for Transition (UDT) may provide a useful framework for transition planning. UDT was conceptualized by Thoma, Barthomolew, and Scott (2009) in response to challenges posed by increased academic demands. Because most young adults with disabilities are working towards a general education diploma, and must adhere to the same academic standards as their non-disabled peers, the majority of transition activities and related instruction must be integrated into their general education curriculum, which poses a challenge to special and general educators due to limited time and resources. The intent of UDT is two-fold. First, it provides a structure for special educators in revising instructional delivery and design to meet required academic standards and enhance preparation for transition into postsecondary roles. The second goal of UDT is to assist general educators in integrating functional and life-skills curricula into academic standards, thereby further preparing youth for life after high school.

UDT builds upon Universal Design for Learning (UDL), discussed in Chapter 5, by adding four components which are aligned to evidence-based secondary transition strategies (Test *et al.* 2009). These components are (Thoma *et al.* 2009):

1. *Multiple transition domains.* Instruction and transition planning should address multiple domains, including postsecondary employment, education, recreation/leisure, community, daily life, healthcare services, and transportation.

2. *Multiple transition assessments.* A variety and range of assessments should be utilized to guide planning and instruction. For students with PANDAS/PANS, as described in earlier chapters, use of multiple assessments is particularly important.

3. *Self-determination.* Academic instruction should integrate self-determination skills when appropriate, and transition planning should include activities to enhance this skill.

4. *Multiple resources and perspectives.* Teachers should draw upon the expertise and resources of service providers and other stakeholders during instructional planning, delivery, and assessment. For students with PANDAS/PANS, this may include school counselors, school nurses, and occupational therapists along with students, families, and teachers.

The addition of these elements to instructional planning is intended to improve the transition outcomes for students while improving academic performance and engagement for all students participating in the lessons (Scott *et al.* 2011). Although this is a nascent concept, early research is promising (Scott *et al.* 2011).

It is not possible to address all issues related to early childhood and secondary transition for individuals with disabilities, including PANS and PANDAS, in this limited space. This section has highlighted key concepts, challenges, and strategies presented in the literature related to these key vertical transitions for individuals with disabilities, with respect to the complex symptoms often manifested in PANS and PANDAS. In addition, a brief list of resources for these two transitions is provided below.

Selected resources for early childhood and secondary transitions
Early childhood transition

- National Center for Early Development and Learning (NCEDL): www.fpg.unc.edu/node/4649

- National Early Childhood Transition Center (NECTC): www.hdi.uky.edu/nectc/NECTC/home.aspx

- The SEDL National Center for Family and Community Connections with Schools: www.sedl.org/connections

- Terrific Transitions: Supporting Children's Transition to Kindergarten: http://center.serve.org/tt

- Part C: Development of the Transition Plan: www. parentcenterhub.org/repository/partc-module8

Secondary transition

- The Adolescent Health Transition Project: http://depts. washington.edu/healthtr

- Healthy and Ready to Work (HRTW) National Resource Center: www.nasuad.org/hcbs/article/healthy-ready-work-hrtw-national-resource-center

- Transition Coalition: www.transitioncoalition.org

- National Center on Secondary Education and Transition: www. ncset.org

- I'm Determined Self-Determination: www.imdetermined.org

- Transitions Resources Pinterest Board (created by Kelly McGinty): www.pinterest.com/kmcgin6/transition-resources

- Disabilities, Opportunities, Internetworking, and Technology – Do It: www.washington.edu/doit

Key points to remember and Conclusion

- Children and young adults with PANS or PANDAS experience a variety of horizontal and vertical transitions throughout their academic careers. Horizontal transitions involve movement across settings within the same time frame whereas vertical transitions occur over time and involve age and developmental benchmarks.

- IDEA (2004) mandates transition planning for two types of vertical transition—transitioning from Part C (Infants and Toddlers Program) to Part B (special education) and secondary transition.

- Services providers should create transition plans for horizontal and vertical transitions, even if not mandated by legislation.

- Strong, positive relationships with families and youth are vital to successful transitions.

- Youth with PANS or PANDAS should be involved, and take a leadership role in the transition planning process when possible, for all types of transitions.

- Effective transition planning, guided by a continuous, individualized assessment process, is integral to successful transition into postsecondary roles.

- Strategies such as self-determination and self-advocacy instruction, developing social capital, the use of technology, and utilizing the UDT framework are beneficial to promoting successful secondary transition.

References

ADA (1990) *Americans with Disabilities Act of 1990*, 42 U.S.C.A. §12101 *et seq.*

ADAA (2009) *Americans with Disabilities Amendments Act of 2008.*

American Academy of Pediatrics, Council on Children with Disabilities (2005) 'Care coordination in the medical home: Integrating health and related systems of care for children with special health care needs.' *Pediatrics 116*, 1238–1244.

Bargeron, J., Contri, D., Gibbons, L., Ruch-Ross, H., and Sanabria, K. (2015) 'Transition planning for youth with special health care needs (YSHCN) in Illinois schools.' *Journal of School Nursing 31*, 4, 253–260.

Belch, H. (2011) 'Understanding the experiences of students with psychiatric disabilities: A foundation for creating conditions of support and success.' *New Directions for Student Services 134*, 73–94.

Berry, D., Brandis, J., Francl, C., Logue, M.B., *et al.* (2010) *Other Health Impairment: A Guide for Supporting Children and Youth in Public Schools.* Oklahoma City, OK: Oklahoma State Department of Education Department of Special Education Services.

Best, L., Still, M., and Cameron, G. (2008) 'Supported education: Enabling course completion for people experiencing mental illness.' *Australian Occupational Therapy Journal 55*, 65–68.

Blacklock, B., Benson, B., and Johnson, D. (2003) 'Needs Assessment Project: Exploring Barriers and Opportunities for College Students with Psychiatric Disabilities.' Unpublished manuscript. Minneapolis, MN: University of Minnesota.

Blomquist, K.B., Graham, L.M., and Thomas, J. (2007) 'Looking for Applause: Determining Transition Health Outcomes.' In C.L. Betz and W.M. Nehring (eds) *Promoting Health Care Transitions for Adolescents with Special Health Care Needs and Disabilities.* Baltimore, MD: Paul Brookes.

Boekaerts, M., and Roder, I. (1999) 'Stress, coping, and adjustment in children with a chronic disease: A review of the literature.' *Disability and Rehabilitation 21*, 311–337.

Bourke, R., Bevan-Brown, J., Carroll-Lind, J., Cullen, J., *et al.* (2002) Special Education 2000: Monitoring and Evaluation of the Policy. Final Report to Ministry of Education. Wellington, New Zealand: Ministry of Education.

Bourne, L. (2007) 'A story of transition to school.' *Kairaranga 8*, 1, 31–33.

Burdo-Hartman, W.A., and Patel, D.R. (2008) 'Medical home and transition planning for children and youth with special health care needs.' *Pediatric Clinics of North America 55*, 1287–1297.

Candelaria-Greene, J. (2014) *Considerations Regarding Academic Accommodations/Compensatory Strategies, and Services for Students with PANDAS/PANS.* Available at http://pandasnetwork.org/wp-content/uploads/2014/09/School-Considerations-2014.pdf, accessed on 7 March 2016.

Carter, E.W., Austin, D., and Trainor, A.A. (2012) 'Predictors of post-school employment outcomes for young adults with severe disabilities.' *Journal of Disability Policy Studies 23*, 50–63.

Clark, E., Russman, S., and Orme, S. (1999) 'Traumatic brain injury: Effects on school functioning and intervention strategies.' *School Psychology Review 28*, 242–250.

Clark, G. (2007) *Assessment for Transition Planning* (Second edition). Austin, TX: PRO-ED.

Clay, D.L., Cortina, S., Harper, D.C., Cocco, K.M., and Drotar, D. (2004) 'Schoolteachers' experiences with childhood chronic illness.' *Children's Health Care 33*, 227–239.

Collins, M.E., Bybee, D., and Mowbray, C.T. (1998) 'Effectiveness of supported education for individuals with psychiatric disabilities: Results from an experimental study.' *Community Mental Health Journal 34*, 6, 595–613.

Connor, D. (2012) 'Helping students with disabilities transition to college: 21 tips for students for students with LD and/or ADD/ADHD.' *Teaching Exceptional Children 44*, 5, 16–25.

Data Resource Center for Child and Adolescent Health (2012) *National Survey of Children with Special Health Care Needs.* Available at http://childhealthdata.org/learn/NS-CSHCN, accessed on 10 March 2016.

Deci, E.L., and Ryan, R.M. (1985) *Intrinsic Motivation and Self-Determination in Human Behavior.* New York: Plenum Press.

Dockett, S., and Perry, B. (2007) *Transitions to School: Perceptions, Expectations, Experiences.* Sydney, Australia: University of New South Wales Press.

Frank, A.R., and Sitlington, P.L. (1997) 'Young adults with behavioral disorders—before and after.' *Behavioral Disorders 23*, 156–164.

Halloran, W.D. (1993) 'Transition Services Requirement: Issues, Implications, Challenge.' In R.C. Eaves and P.J. McLaughlin (eds) *Recent Advances in Special Education and Rehabilitation.* Boston: Andover Medical Publishers.

IDEA (2004) *Individuals with Disabilities Education Improvement Act of 2004*, 20 U.S.C. §1400 *et seq.*

Kagan, S. (1992) 'The Strategic Importance of Linkages and the Transition between Early Childhood Programs and Early Elementary School.' In *Sticking Together: Strengthening Linkages and the Transition between Early Childhood Education and Early Elementary School* (Summary of a National Policy Forum). Washington, DC: U.S. Department of Education.

Kennedy, A., and Sawyer, S. (2008) 'Transitioning from pediatric to adult services: Are we getting it right?' *Current Opinions in Pediatrics 20*, 403–309.

Kiuhara, S.A., and Huefner, D.S. (2008) 'Students with psychiatric disabilities in higher education settings: The Americans with Disabilities Act and beyond.' *Journal of Disability Policy Studies 19*, 2, 103–113.

Konrad, M., and Test, D.W. (2004) 'Teaching middle-school students with disabilities to use an IEP template.' *Career Development for Exceptional Individuals 27*, 101–124.

Kortering, L., Braziel, P., and Sitlington, P. (2010) 'Age Appropriate Assessments: A Strategic Intervention to Help Youth with Emotional or Behavioral Disorders to Complete High School.' In D. Cheney (ed.) *Transition of Secondary Students with Emotional or Behavioral Disorders: Current Approaches for Positive Outcomes* (Second edition). Champaign, IL: Research Press.

Kyngas, H. (2004) 'Support network of adolescents with chronic disease: Adolescents' perspective.' *Nursing and Health Sciences 6*, 287–293.

La Paro, K.M., Pianta, R.C., and Cox, M.J. (2000) 'Teachers' reported transition practices for children transitioning into kindergarten and first grade.' *Exceptional Children 67*, 1, 7–20.

Levine, P., and Wagner, M. (2005) 'Transition for Young Adults who Received Special Education Services as Adolescents: A Time of Challenge and Change.' In D.W. Osgood, E.M. Foster, C. Flanagan, and G.R. Ruth (eds) *On Your Own Without a Net: The Transition to Adulthood for Vulnerable Populations.* Chicago: University of Chicago Press.

Lightfoot, J., Wright, S., and Sloper, P. (1999) 'Supporting pupils in mainstream school with an illness or disability: Young people's views.' *Child: Care, Health and Development 25*, 267–283.

McIntyre, L.L., Eckert, T.L., Fiese, B.H., DiGennaro, F.D., and Wildenger, L.K. (2007) 'The transition to kindergarten: Family experiences and involvement.' *Early Childhood Education Journal 35*, 83–88.

McIntyre, L.L., Eckert, T.L., Fiese, B.H., DiGennaro, F.D., and Wildenger, L.K. (2010) 'Family concerns surrounding kindergarten transition: A comparison of students in special and general education.' *Early Childhood Education Journal 38*, 4, 259–263.

McManus, M., Fox, H., O'Connor, K., Chapman, T., and MacKinnon, J. (2008) *Pediatric Perspectives and Practices on Transitioning Adolescents with Special Needs to Adult Health Care* (Fact Sheet No. 6). Washington, DC: The National Alliance to Advance Adolescent Health.

Mukherjee, S., Lightfoot, J., and Sloper, P. (2000) 'The inclusion of pupils with a chronic health condition in mainstream schools: What does it mean for teachers?' *Educational Research 42*, 59–72.

Newman, L. (1996, January) *Building the Bridges: Early Intervention to School.* Paper presented at the sixth First Years of School Conference, Hobart, Australia.

Newman, L., Wagner, M., Cameto, R., and Knokey, A.-M. (2009) *The Post-High School Outcomes of Young Adults with Disabilities up to 4 years After High School: A Report from the National Longitudinal Transition Study-2* (NLTS2) (NCSER 2009-3017). Menlo Park, CA: SRI International. Available at www.nlts2.org/reports/2009_04/nlts2_report_2009_04_complete.pdf, accessed on 10 March 2016.

Newman, L., Wagner, M., Knokey, A.M., Marder, C., *et al.* (2011) *The Post-High School Outcomes of Young Adults with Disabilities up to 8 years After High School: A Report from the National Longitudinal Transition Study-2 (NLTS2)* (NCSER 2011-3005). Menlo Park, CA: SRI International.

NICHCY (2012) *Other Health Impairment.* Disability Fact Sheet #15, National Dissemination Center for Children with Disabilities. Available at www.parentcenterhub.org/wp-content/uploads/repo_items/fs15.pdf, accessed on 10 March 2016.

Peter, N.G., Forke, C.M., Ginsburg, K.R., and Schwarz, D.F. (2009) 'Transition from pediatric to adult care: Internists' perspectives.' *Pediatrics 110*, 1307–1311.

Peters, S. (2010) *Literature Review: Transition from Early Childhood Education to School.* Report to the Ministry of Education. Wellington, New Zealand: Ministry of Education.

Pola-Money, G. (2005) *Transition Issues.* Medical Home Portal. Available at www.medicalhomeportal.org/clinical-practice/transition-issues, accessed on 10 March 2016.

Powers, L.E., Sowers, J., Turner, A., Nesbitt, M., Knowles, A., and Ellison, R. (1996) 'TAKE CHARGE: A Model for Promoting Self-Determination among Adolescents with Challenges.' In L.E. Powers, G.H.S. Singer, and J. Sowers (eds) *On the Road to Autonomy: Promoting Self-competence for Children and Youth with Disabilities.* Baltimore, MD: Paul H. Brookes.

Rehabilitation Act Amendments of 1992 (1992) *Rehabilitation Act of 1992*, PL. 102–569, 29 U.S.C. 701.

Rehabilitation Act of 1973 (2006) *Rehabilitation Act of 1973*, PL 93-112, 29 U.S.C.A. §701 *et seq.*

Rice Doran, P. (2015) 'Sudden behavioral changes in the classroom: What educators need to know about PANDAS and PANS.' *Beyond Behavior 24*, 1, 31–37. Available at www.academia.edu/15102564/Sudden_Behavioral_Changes_in_the_Classroom_What_Educators_Need_to_Know_about_PANDAS_and_PANS, accessed on 2 March 2016.

Rimm-Kaufman, S., Pianta, R., and Cox, M. (2000) 'Teachers' judgments of problems in the transition to kindergarten.' *Early Childhood Research Quarterly 15*, 147–166.

Rous, B. (2004) *The Individuals with Disabilities Education Act and Transition. Transition Alert.* Lexington, KY: National Early Childhood Transition Center.

Salzer, M.S. (2012) 'A comparative study of campus experiences of college students with mental illnesses versus a general college sample.' *Journal of American College Health 60*, 1, 1–7.

Schischka, J., Rawlinson, C., and Hamilton, R. (2012) 'Factors affecting the transition to school for young children with disabilities.' *Australasian Journal of Early Childhood 37*, 4, 15–22.

Schulenberg, J.E., and Zarrett, N.R. (2006) 'Mental Health during Emerging Adulthood: Continuity and Discontinuity in Courses, Causes, and Functions.' In J.J. Arnett and J.L. Tanner (eds) *Emerging Adults in America: Coming of Age in the Twenty-first Century.* Washington, DC: American Psychological Association.

Scott, L., Saddler, S., Thoma, C., Barthomolomew, C., Virginia, N., and Tamura, R. (2011) 'Universal design for transition: A single subject research study on the impact of UDT on student achievement, engagement and interest.' *i-manager's Journal of Educational Psychology 4*, 4, 21–31.

Shanahan, M.J. (2000) 'Pathways to adulthood: Variability and mechanisms in life course perspective.' *Annual Review of Sociology 26*, 667–692.

Shaw, S., and McCabe, P. (2008) 'Hospital-to-school transition for children with chronic illness: Meeting the new challenges of an evolving health care system.' *Psychology in the Schools 45*, 1, 74–88.

Shiu, S. (2001) 'Issues in the education of students with chronic illness.' *International Journal of Disability, Development and Education 48*, 269–281.

Targett, P., Wehman, P., West, M., Dillard, C., and Cifu, G. (2013) 'Promoting transition to adulthood for youth with physical disabilities and health impairments.' *Journal of Vocational Rehabilitation 39*, 229–239.

Tate, J.O. (2000) 'Court decisions and 1997 compliance issues that affect special education programs in rural schools.' *Rural Special Education Quarterly 19*, 3–9.

Test, D.W., Fowler, C.H., Richter, S.M., White, J., *et al.* (2009) 'Evidence-based practices in secondary transition.' *Career Development for Exceptional Individuals 32*, 2, 115–128.

Test, D.W., Fowler, C.H., Wood, W., Brewer, D., and Eddy, S. (2005) 'A conceptual framework of self-advocacy for students with disabilities.' *Remedial and Special Education 26*, 1, 43–54.

Thoma, C.A., Bartholomew, C., and Scott, L.A. (2009) *Universal Design for Transition: A Roadmap for Planning and Instruction*. Baltimore, MD: Paul H. Brookes.

Trainor, A., Smith, S., and Kim, S. (2012) 'Four supportive pillars in career exploration and development for adolescents with LD and EBD.' *Intervention in School and Clinic 48*, 1, 15–21.

U.S. Department of Education, National Center for Education Statistics (2002) *The Condition of Education 2002*. Washington, DC: U.S. Government Printing Office.

Wartmann, S. (2000) 'The transition from kindergarten to school for children with special needs.' *Research Information for Teachers 1*, 11–15.

Wehmeyer, M.L. (1996) 'Self-determination as an Educational Outcome.' In D.J. Sands and M.L. Wehmeyer (eds) *Self-determination across the Life Span: Independence and Choice for People with Disabilities*. Baltimore, MD: Paul H. Brookes.

Wehmeyer, M.L., Palmer, S.B., Smith, S.J., Parent, W., *et al.* (2006) 'Technology use by people with intellectual and developmental disabilities to support employment activities: A single-subject design meta analysis.' *Journal of Vocational Rehabilitation 24*, 2, 81–86.

Wildenger, L., and McIntyre, L. (2011) 'Family concerns and involvement during kindergarten transition.' *Journal of Child Family Studies 20*, 4, 387–396.

Wolanin, T.R., and Steele, P.E. (2004) *New Report: Higher Education Opportunities for Students with Disabilities: A Primer for Policymakers*. Available at http://eric.ed.gov/?id=ED485430, accessed on 10 March 2016.

Reimagining School Paradigms

What PANDAS/PANS Can Teach Us

PATRICIA RICE DORAN, ED.D.

As several teachers and experts have noted in the preceding chapters, PANDAS and PANS challenge schools and educators in unique and unexpected ways. Our system conceptualizes student learning as a consistent process resulting in consistent growth. It is common for students to make academic gains each year; it is within the realm of possibility, if unfortunate, for them to remain more or less at the same level; and rare indeed for them to lose ground and forget skills gained in previous years.

It is a given, in behavior modification protocols, that all behaviors serve a function and that addressing the perceived function will ameliorate an undesired behavior.

We expect that going to school each day is normal and required, a rite of passage in modern industrialized nations, and that the best way to deal with school avoidance or separation anxiety is to minimize it and encourage the student to go anyway.

We create IEPs that, in many states, require us to choose one discrete disability category for a student whose needs may be best described by several or by none.

As a society, even beyond schoolhouse walls, we draw rigid distinctions between mental health and bodily health, expecting that services provided to those who are chronically ill have little to do with services for those with psychiatric or psychological challenges. This bifurcation is reflected everywhere: in hospitals, where psychiatric floors might be far away from infectious disease units; and in health insurance plans, where procedures for accessing mental health benefits are different and often more arduous than procedures for accessing routine medical treatment. It is reflected further in schools or workplaces, where individuals with psychological or psychiatric difficulties often feel their experiences are minimized because their needs are not visible in the way that, say, a pair of crutches or a hearing aid might be.

Likewise, we tend to draw equally rigid distinctions between those who are "sick" and those who are "well," not always mindful that many families with PANDAS and PANS feel stuck in a borderline zone between those categories, fearful of relapse and often balancing health-related precautions with quality of life and normal childhood experience.

Because PANDAS and PANS can upend many of these accepted frameworks and practices, their sudden onset may also challenge educators, whose classrooms are built around carefully constructed, consistent academic and behavioral routines. As discussed in earlier chapters, those routines may border on being irrelevant or untenable for children in acute PANS exacerbations.

Many teachers and parents, in this book and in the authors' collective experience, have been candid about the elements of our educational system that they feel do not work. A few have offered suggestions for educational models that might work better. Physicians, also, have identified flaws in our current models: "[These] children need to be treated as children, not diseases. And we as physicians are trained to treat the disease. There is a certain [idea that] we have to treat and get out, prescription-pad medicine, treating an acute illness. And Western medicine has been very good at treating acute illness, treating trauma. But when it comes to treating chronic illnesses, we're not [as good]" (O'Hara 2016). These sentiments also resonate with current trends in education, repudiating the kind of piecemeal and disjointed thinking that prevents us from seeing and serving the entire child. In recent years, educational experts have endorsed the concept of teaching the "whole child," addressing the child's social, emotional, and even physical needs along with academic ones (ASCD 2012; Liew and McTigue 2010). It seems clear, particularly when considering the potentially devastating impact of illnesses such as PANDAS/ PANS, that a "whole child" approach must be adopted in medicine, in education, and most especially in areas where those fields overlap.

Below, drawn from parents' feedback, expert recommendations offered elsewhere in this book, and the author's own views, some recommendations are offered to address the question: What must schools look like to serve our children with PANDAS/PANS adequately—or, even better, extraordinarily well? An unintentional by-product of considering this question is a roadmap to more accessible, flexible schools for all students: other learners with health needs, students with social challenges, those with emotional or behavioral disabilities, and so on.

1. *Flexible attendance.* As discussed in Chapter 1 and Chapter 6, attendance is often one of the first casualties of a PANDAS/ PANS exacerbation. "School refusal" is usually an inaccurate term to describe this phenomenon, as students often are not consciously "refusing" to attend school but are prevented from attending by complex physical, and sometimes psychiatric, symptoms. Promptly informing families of options for homebound or intermittent home instruction can minimize long-term problems, as students will be most successful when families and school personnel can collaborate early on to develop an appropriate plan. Classroom teachers should also work closely with families and with school counselors to ensure that returning to school is a low-stress and positive experience, with transition supports provided as the student returns, leaves, and returns again. Attendance in class, even for students who are present in school, may be sporadic if students are experiencing pain, fatigue, or urinary frequency; careful and collaborative planning can ensure students are still able to access missed content without being exposed to unnecessary stress.

2. *Technology-assisted instruction.* From electronic copies of notes, to readily available calculators, to the use of Skype, FaceTime, or even robots to help absent children connect with classmates, technology offers extraordinary opportunities to improve access as well as rigor for children with PANDAS/PANS.

Technology might encompass the use of tablets or laptop computers as an alternative for writing; use of text-to-speech or speech-to-text software; online communication between families and teachers; or video conference or video chat for students who are absent that day, to name just a few options. Indeed, students experiencing long-term absence could still complete assignments and even group work quite successfully using technology as an aid.

3. *Multiple means of assessment.* The UDL-based approach discussed in Chapters 5 and 7 is good common sense and makes assessment work better for all learners. For learners with disabilities, that approach is not simply an add-on but an essential. Poor handwriting may make it impossible for a student to demonstrate knowledge using paper and pencil; testing anxiety may mean she is far better able to show mastery on an oral assessment or take-home paper than on a closed-book exam. Using multiple methods of assessment not only fosters student success but, equally important for educators, allows the teacher to collect accurate data and make well-founded decisions about future instruction, as he or she has correct information about what a student actually knows.

4. *Malleable timelines for progress and mastery.* Educators everywhere bemoan the rigid schedules for proficiency which standardized testing imposes on schools, teachers, and students. For students with PANDAS/PANS, in particular, rigid time frames are even worse. A student whose illness flares up in the winter may be above grade level in the winter and three grades behind by May. How can one measure that student's progress accurately? And how can one serve that student's academic and therapeutic needs in a curriculum which presumes the student can keep up with a steady, linear march toward grade-level proficiency by April?

5. *Balance between structure and adaptability.* Structure and routine are essential for learning to take place, as any experienced educator will affirm. When students with PANDAS/PANS experience

symptoms (obsessions, compulsions, overwhelming anxiety, sensory issues, or severe tics), classroom routines are often disrupted. It is essential to balance the importance of routine with an accurate understanding of health-related challenges. Insisting that a student continue the routines that worked when she was healthy may be inappropriate during a PANDAS/PANS exacerbation. Keeping consistency, without crossing the line into rigidity, is helpful for many students with disabilities and especially for those with PANDAS/PANS.

6. *Positive behavior support and environmental management.* Increasingly, our understanding of the brain leads us to accept that many behaviors are not fully voluntary and can be far better controlled through prevention than through response, particularly punishment. The ideal classroom for children with PANDAS/PANS would have a carefully built environment, one with sensory supports, safe spaces, and multiple options for assignments and activities. Building these supports into each day's instruction will minimize disruptive behavior by removing barriers to participation—a key tenet of UDL.

7. *Inclusive practice.* Inclusive practice is, itself, an area worthy of more discussion. Including children with abrupt swings in performance or challenging relationships with peers is, at best, a tricky proposition—but required by both law and best practice. And in the 40 years since IDEA was passed, schools and classrooms have become far more inclusive. But just as the general education classroom may not be the right environment for every child, the public school environment itself may not be the right fit for a child in an acute PANDAS/PANS exacerbation at every time. One qualitative study found that approximately half of PANDAS/PANS parents reported their children leaving public school for homeschool or homebound instruction, either temporarily or permanently (Rice Doran and O'Hanlon 2015). It is for this reason that flexibility regarding attendance, and effective transition planning, are also important.

There are, doubtless, numerous other improvements that would help students with PANDAS/PANS succeed in school. In conversations with families, two words that this writer hears repeatedly are "compassion" and "understanding." Even more than planning skills and ability to differentiate, even more than a detailed understanding of neurobiology, students and their families—particularly during times of adversity and stress—need sympathy and acceptance. This fact, indeed, is true of most families whose children have disabilities, not just those dealing with PANDAS/PANS. And in years to come, our understanding of PANDAS/PANS, and the interrelatedness of our physical and mental well-being, will certainly continue to improve and change. The role of caring and dedicated educators, though, will not change. For that reason, continued professional learning about illnesses such as PANDAS/PANS, and how they impact students and families, is paramount. As long as schools are open and children with PANDAS/PANS attend them, it will always be possible for one educator—one teacher, one therapist, one principal—to change the entire trajectory of a student's experience by extending that compassion and understanding.

References

Association for Supervision and Curriculum Development (ASCD) (2012) *The Whole Child Initiative*. Available at www.ascd.org/whole-child.aspx, accessed on 10 March 2016.

Liew, J., and McTigue, E. M. (2010) 'Educating the Whole Child: The Role of Social and Emotional Development in Achievement and School Success.' In L.E. Kattington (ed.) *Handbook of Curriculum Development*. Hauppauge, NY: Nova Sciences Publishers.

O'Hara, N. (2016) Interview. Quoted in *My Kid is Not Crazy* (Dir. T. Sorel). University of South Florida. Released 2016. See www.mykidisnotcrazy.com, accessed on 10 March 2016.

Rice Doran, P., and O'Hanlon, E. (2015) *Families' Experiences with PANDAS and Related Disorders*. Poster session at Council for Exceptional Children Convention, San Diego, April 2015.

Appendix A

Sample Physician Letter for Student with PANS

(COURTESY MARGO THIENEMANN, M.D.)

SAMPLE–NOT FOR DISTRIBUTION

To those concerned:

I am a physician caring for _____ _____. I am writing this letter at the request of_____ and her parents to convey and describe his/her diagnosis and offer recommendations for accommodations that may help _____ benefit from educational opportunities. _____ has a diagnosis of Pediatric Acute-Onset Neuropsychiatric Syndrome.

PANS is a medical problem usually precipitated by an infection. When it is precipitated by strep, it is called PANDAS (Pediatric Auto-immune Neuropsychiatric Disorder Associated with Streptococcal Infections). It is thought that, in susceptible individuals, following an infection, the body's immune system can react abnormally. This is somewhat like an allergic reaction. The immune reaction can cause both emotional and neurological symptoms. The symptoms can be activated each time the individual with PANS has another infection, which may impact their performance at school. If the infection is identified the symptoms may get better with treatment and time.

The emotional symptoms of PANS can include obsessions, compulsions, separation anxiety, ADHD symptoms, and moodiness. The neurological symptoms can include tics, trouble with handwriting, and frequent urination. Not all symptoms are present in all individuals. Patients with

PANS frequently experience fatigue and amplified sensitivity to sounds, lights, smells, and tastes.

PANS is not contagious. It seems to occur more often in families who have a history of reactions to strep, such as arthritis and rheumatic heart disease.

As flares of PANS symptoms are caused by infections, individuals with PANS must be vigilant to avoid getting sick.

Symptoms of PANS wax and wane. The same student can feel, act, and perform differently on different days and different weeks depending on where they are in the course of the illness. There will be intermittent absences and medical appointments.

I believe that the following accommodations would be helpful for

_____:

(of course, one may add/delete to customize for a particular patient)

- Please notify the family if strep or any other infection is seen in her class or school.

- Please anticipate that _____ is likely to miss some school and may have days where she is not feeling good and unable to either attend school or attend the full day of school.

- Please allow _____ to attend school less than full time. Specifically, until further notice, I recommend that _____ attend school ***.

- If _____ has trouble with handwriting, please allow _____ to use a keyboard and/or dictate assignments and tests to a parent or proctor.

- If _____ has trouble with handwriting, please provide _____ with a note-taker or with class notes.

- When parents communicate that _____ is ill and/or unable to complete in-class work and homework, please accept completed work as sufficient. We also recommend evaluating _____'s grade based on quality, not quantity of work.

- If _____ requests, allow _____ to share this information with his/her classmates. _____ hopes that in doing so, if he/she behaves differently, classmates will have some understanding that he/she has a medical illness.

Our medical team supports and values school attendance and success, and we believe these recommendations will help achieve this goal.

Thank you for your consideration of these issues.

If you have questions or concerns, please contact our office.

SAMPLE–NOT FOR DISTRIBUTION

Appendix B

PANDAS and PANS

Quick Facts for Teachers

What are PANDAS and PANS?

Pediatric Autoimmune Neuropsychiatric Disorders Associated with Strep (PANDAS) and Pediatric Acute-Onset Neuropsychiatric Syndrome (PANS) are neuro-psychiatric disorders triggered by an underlying autoimmune response. Frequently, students may experience symptoms after a "strong stimulant" to the immune system (NIMH n.d.) such as strep infection, flu, or even the common cold. In a student with PANDAS or PANS, the immune system is thought to mistakenly react and cause brain inflammation in the basal ganglia region (NIMH, n.d.; Murphy, Gerardi, and Parker-Athill 2014). This reaction causes neurological, psychological, and cognitive symptoms as a result of basal ganglia inflammation.

PANDAS and PANS may be treated with anti-inflammatory medications (such as ibuprofen), antibiotics to treat or prevent infection, immune-modulating therapies (such as steroids), intravenous immunoglobulin (IVIG), and plasmapheresis (PANDAS Network 2014). Cognitive behavioral therapy and additional medications may also be part of a student's treatment plan if needed.

What symptoms might my students with PANDAS/PANS exhibit?

Students with PANDAS/PANS may exhibit the following symptoms (NIMH n.d.; Swedo, Leckman, and Rose 2012; PANDAS Network 2014; Chang *et al.* 2015):

- sudden onset of symptoms, or abrupt, "episodic," changes in functioning
- restricted eating (this may present as generalized anorexia or aversion to specific foods, textures, etc.)
- obsessive-compulsive symptoms
- motor and vocal tics
- heightened anxiety, including separation anxiety and school-related anxiety
- sensory issues
- increased urinary frequency
- handwriting changes and deterioration in school performance
- impulsivity, inattention, and poor concentration.

This list is not exhaustive, and a student's family and/or care providers may be able to provide further details or additional information about specific symptoms, as every student is different.

What accommodations and supports might be helpful to my students with PANDAS/PANS?

Parents of students with PANDAS/PANS have reported their students benefit from:

- extended time
- writing accommodations (keyboard, laptop, specially designed writing tools, graphic organizers)
- math accommodations (calculator, manipulatives)
- frequent breaks
- "safe spaces" to use in the event of behavioral difficulties or acute symptom flares
- positive behavioral supports and interventions
- sensory supports (including occupational therapy when needed)

- adapted or modified tasks, particularly those requiring motor control or sustained effort
- advance planning for health-related absences, including home and hospital transitions as well as absences related to appointments and treatment.

Again, this list is not exhaustive; see school toolkit resources at www. PANDASNetwork.org for more information and suggested supports. See also Candelaria-Greene (2014) and Tona and Posner (2011).

What else should I know and do about PANDAS/ PANS so I can meet my students' needs?

- Student needs and performance may vary widely from week-to-week and day-to-day.
- Provide positive behavioral supports and actively work to minimize students' stress. Stress can increase anxiety and exacerbate symptoms.
- Have a plan in place for acute symptom exacerbations as well as day-to-day, less intensive supports.
- Report outbreaks of illness to parents/family; students with PANDAS/PANS may experience symptom increases simply from being exposed to an infection.
- Report any abrupt changes in behavior, eating habits, or school performance to parents/families.
- Students with PANDAS/PANS may have frequent absences and benefit from strong and proactive teacher communication.

References

Candelaria-Greene, J. (2014) *Considerations Regarding Academic Accommodations/Compensatory Strategies, and Services for Students with PANDAS/PANS*. Available at http://pandas network.org/wp-content/uploads/2014/09/School-Considerations-2014.pdf.

Chang, K., Frankovich, J., Cooperstock, M., Cunningham, M.W., *et al.* (2015) 'Clinical evaluation of youth with pediatric acute-onset neuropsychiatric syndrome (PANS): Recommendations from the 2013 PANS Consensus Conference.' *Journal of Child and Adolescent Psychopharmacology 25*, 1, 3–13.

Murphy, T.K., Gerardi, D.M., and Parker-Athill, E.C. (2014) 'The PANDAS Controversy: Why (and how) is it still unsettled?' *Current Developmental Disorders Reports 1*, 4, 236–244.

NIMH (n.d.) *Information About PANDAS.* Available at www.nimh.nih.gov/labs-at-nimh/research-areas/clinics-and-labs/pdnb/web.shtml.

PANDAS Network (2014) www.PANDASNetwork.org.

Swedo, S., Leckman, J., and Rose, N. (2012) 'From research subgroup to clinical syndrome: Modifying the PANDAS criteria to describe PANS (Pediatric Acute-onset Neuropsychiatric Syndrome).' *Pediatrics and Therapeutics 2*, 113, 1–8.

Tona, J., and Posner, T. (2011) 'Pediatric Autoimmune Neuropsychiatric Disorders: A new frontier for occupational therapy intervention.' *OT Practice, November 2011*, 14–22.

Where can I find more information?

PANDAS Network, the leading parent advocacy and research organization in the field: www.PANDASNetwork.org.

Subject Index

Author Index